NEW GROWTH FROM OLD

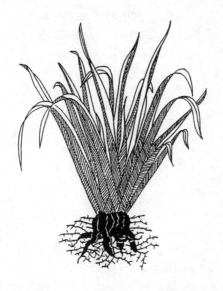

The Whānau in the Modern World

JOAN METGE

illustrated by Toi Te Rito Maihi

Victoria University Press

VICTORIA UNIVERSITY PRESS
Victoria University of Wellington
PO Box 600 Wellington
New Zealand

© Joan Metge 1995

ISBN 0 86473 246 5

First published 1995

Royalties to the Kōtare Trust
for Māori purposes

Printed by GP Print, Wellington

CONTENTS

ILLUSTRATIONS

PHOTOGRAPHS (after p. 160)

The Hamiora Whānau Hui, Kōtare, 1985: The hākari
A wedding procession, Kōtare, 1955
A whānau unveiling hui in the 1980s
The Hamiora Whānau Hui, Kōtare 1985:
    The descendants of Aorangi
Sharing the caring, Muriwhenua, 1970s
Double bonding, Kōtare, 1970s
Whānau summer at the seaside, Kōtare, 1960s

All photographs printed with permission of whānau representatives

FIGURES

ILLUSTRATIONS by TOI TE RITO MAIHI

DEDICATION

ACKNOWLEDGEMENTS

Over the years during which this book has been in preparation, a large number of Māori have contributed to the development of my understanding of the whānau. In the text I describe them as kai-whakaatu, people who have both informed and enlightened me. In deference to their own wishes, I shall not identify them individually by name but, speaking of and to them as a group, I record my warmest aroha and appreciation for the generosity with which they have admitted me to their family circles over the years, included me in their whānau gatherings, talked with me about their experience of whānau, and shared the insights gained from reflecting upon it. Above all, I thank them for the readiness with which they gave me approval to give depth to my text by quoting their words and telling their stories.

I have dedicated this book to nine kuia of this company who have died in recent years. The whakataukī I quote in the dedication applies equally to all my kai-whakaatu, living and dead. Truly this has been a cooperative enterprise.

Nāu i whatu te kākahu, he tāniko tāku.
You wove the body of the cloak, I made the tāniko.

The tāniko border of a kaitaka cloak catches the eye with its bright colours and distinctive pattern; the plain body has a quieter beauty inhering in the regular weaving of extremely fine fibres. Each important and beautiful in its own way, the two parts complement each other, together forming a distinctive whole.

He taonga anō tō te iti, he taonga anō tō te rahi, waiho mā te aroha hei paihere, kia puta ai te painga ki ngā uri whakatupu.

While the research for this book had its genesis in Kōtare in the 1950s, most of it was carried out while I was fifth Captain James Cook Fellow in 1981-83. I am truly grateful to the officers of the Royal Society of New Zealand for the award of this fellowship and for their support during my tenure.

To Rima Eruera, Shane Jones, Keri Kaa, Haimona Snowden and Tawhao Tioke, I am indebted for additions to my treasury of whakataukī, for help in teasing out their implications, and for permission to use those which are particular taonga of their iwi.

While I cannot name names for reasons of confidentiality, I sincerely thank those whānau representatives who supplied photographs of whānau activities and gave me permission to use them.

I thank Toi Te Rito Maihi for her enthusiastic response to my invitation to illustrate whakataukī about the whānau and to allow her painting Waiata o te Harakeke to be used for the cover. Her imaginative illustrations have delighted and inspired me.

I record my warm gratitude to my friends and fellow scholars, Robin Fleming, Keri Kaa, Wiremu and Jossie Kaa, Areta Koopu, Erihapeti Murchie, George Parekowhai, David Ross, Anne Salmond and Jeff Sissons, whose constructively critical comments helped greatly to improve my draft text.

I am also indebted to the editors of Victoria University Press, Fergus Barrowman and Rachel Lawson, for their unfailing support and for their patience in dealing with a text which kept growing.

Joan Metge
Wellington
October 1995

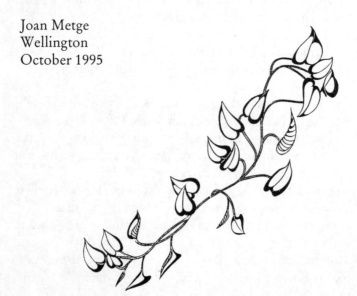

Expression of an Inward Self
with a Linocut

I build something up
Complicated and complex
I hope—
But alas!
Nothing so deep emerges.

Only simple lines
hacked out of a piece
of wornout lino—
that curve and dip to a traditional line
Almost moronic
in their upward
outward bend to the left
to the right
What the hell!

Why should I lie
to myself?
I am what I am
Carved out of a line
of heavy footed deep rooted
simplicity

Wanting to love well
eat well die with the thought of
kumara vine stretched out
reproducing an image—
many images—of itself,
its hopes
drenched in warmth
with roots forever seeking
the sun.

Arapera Hineira Kaa (1955: 18)

FOREWORD

Hutia te rito o te harakeke
kei hea te komako e ko?
Rere ki uta
Rere ki tai.
Ki mai koe ki au,
'He aha te mea nui o te Ao?'
Maku e ki, 'He tangata, he tangata, he tangata.'

Ko nga korero e rarangi ake nei, i roto i tenei pukapuka.
Kei te tino tautokotia e Te Runanga O Te Rarawa.
Ko te Kai Tuhi, Ko Dr Joan Metge.
He whaea tenei kua whitikitia ki roto e te iwi o Te Rarawa.
He whaea rangimarie, aroha, wairua pono
Ko te tino hohonutanga o nga korero
E pa ana ki te whanau.

If the centre shoot of the flax bush were plucked,
Where would the bellbird sing?
You fly inland
You fly to sea.
You ask me,
'What is most important in the world?'
I would say, ''Tis people, 'tis people, 'tis people.'

Dr Joan Metge has been associated with Te Runanga O Te Rarawa for fourteen years and we have come to know her as a friend. She has been associated with the Iwi of Te Rarawa even longer—about forty years.

A careful listener, deep thinker, quiet speaker, and a humble, caring person among us, Joan has been claimed as one of our own. We treat her as part of the wider Whanau and Hapu network of Te Rarawa.

So we were happy that her newest book is about that universal and basic building block of all people everywhere—the Whanau.

Like us Joan knows that, just as te rito o te harakeke is the source for the flax's new growth, the Whanau is the source for society's growth.

It is a universal theme, as is the truth that if the source or the spring is poisoned then so is the mainstream. Conversely if the springs are clean and clear, so is the mainstream.

Knowing Joan and her works, I and Te Rarawa feel this book will go some way toward a cleaner, clearer spring of society within Aotearoa, and a flourishing from the heart of new growth.

No reira e nga Iwi nga hau e wha. Te Manaakitanga o Te Matua Nui i te rangi ki a koutou katoa.

Na

John Campbell
Chairman of Te Runanga O Te Rarawa

Chapter 1

THE FLAX BUSH: FAMILY AND WHĀNAU

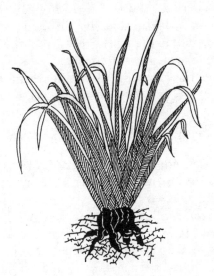

Parapara waerea a ururua,
kia tupu whakaritorito te tupu o te harakeke.[1]

Clear away the overgrowth, so that the flax will put forth
many young shoots.

F lax bushes are a familiar feature of the New Zealand
landscape, growing wild in swamps and wet alluvial soils,
carefully bred and tended in gardens and weavers'
plantations. Each bush is made up of long, swordlike flax blades
growing in fans. The roots of these fans are so entwined that
they cannot be separated except with a sharp spade. Growth takes
place at the centre of each fan, where the new shoot (rito) emerges
between its two predecessors.

When gathering flax, Māori weavers cut only the outer blades
of each fan, leaving the rito and its protectors, so that growth
will continue.

Māori use the flax bush (te pā harakeke)[2] as a favourite
metaphor for the family group they call the whānau. They identify
the rito in each fan as a child (tamaiti), emerging from and
protected by its parents (mātua) on either side. Like fans in the
flax bush, parent-child families in the whānau share common
roots and derive strength and stability from forming part of a
larger whole. Like rito, children are the hope of continuity into
the future. Flax and whānau alike live through cycles of growth,
dying and regeneration. New life grows from the old.

Flax provides the inspiration for many Māori proverbs. The
one at the head of this chapter is a reminder that the whānau, like
the flax bush, grows best when it is cultivated with loving care.

Whānau, family and household

The word whānau comes to modern Māori from their pre-
European ancestors but, as part of a living language, its meanings
are constantly being reworked and extended.

In its basic verbal form, whānau means 'to be born'. According
to Māori experts,[3] its original reference was to a set of siblings
(brothers and sisters) born of the same parents but, like family in
English, it has acquired a range of other meanings distinguished
by context. The most important of these is a large family group
comprising several generations and parent-child families related
by descent from a recent ancestor. The concept of 'the whānau'
in this sense has remained important to the Māori people from
pre-European times to the present, in spite of changes in function.

Early European visitors to Aotearoa New Zealand identified
'the whānau' as 'the basic social unit of Māori society' in the late
18th and early 19th centuries. According to their description, it
was a domestic unit comprising several parent-child families
related by descent and marriage, moving between several living
sites and engaging in a variety of productive activities under the
leadership of a kaumātua (household head).

After New Zealand was established as a nation in 1840, policy-
makers of British origin entrenched the parent-child family of
the British cultural tradition as the approved form of family. For
well over a hundred years, Parliament passed laws which undermined the whānau by outlawing aspects of its practice (relating

to marriage, adoption and the guardianship of children) and otherwise refusing to recognise its existence (Durie-Hall and Metge 1992: 58-59). At the same time the whānau's economic base was undercut by loss of land and the incorporation of the Māori population into a capitalist economy based on individual employment, individual property rights and individual legal responsibility.

Nevertheless, in family life as in other ways, Māori have resisted direct and indirect pressures to assimilate to the dominant pattern. They continue to recognise and promote, under the name of whānau, a family group which has many continuities with the pre-European whānau, notably in the stress laid on descent and the values espoused, but which has undergone significant changes in functions and goals. Membership in descent-based whānau has ceased to be universal and become a matter of choice. Adult Māori choose whether or not to take up membership in whānau of this sort, which of the whānau open to them to support and how active to be in whānau affairs. Their degree of commitment varies at different stages of their life, typically increasing with age.

Since no statistics are collected on the subject, it is not known what proportion of the Māori population are active members of whānau of the traditional, descent-based kind. It is generally assumed to have declined to less than one half, possibly to less than one third, but these are no more than informed guesses. Over the last fifteen years there have been signs of increasing participation in whānau, as part of a renewed emphasis on Māori cultural identity. New kinds of whānau have emerged, modelled on the traditional whānau and its values. Even among those not currently active in whānau, the concept has become a powerful symbol of ngā tikanga Māori (Māori cultural ways).

Whether they belong to a whānau or not, virtually all Māori grow up in and/or establish parent-child families and family households. In 1976, 7.5% of Māori households contained a couple only, 53% contained one parent-child family and 24% contained extended family combinations. The corresponding proportions for non-Māori households were 22%, 47% and 9% respectively. In 1991 the proportion of Māori households containing one parent-child family was 54.5%, the proportion containing a couple without children had risen to 13.5% and the proportion containing extended family combinations had fallen to 16.6%. In spite of these changes, Māori households remain more likely than non-Māori to consist of kin related in families and less likely to consist of a couple, one person or non-family.[4]

Whatever their family situation, Māori are an integral part of the wider New Zealand society, constantly and often intimately involved in social relations with members of other ethnic groups, particularly Pākehā, as spouses, relatives, workmates and friends.[5]

Teasing out the relationships between whānau, family and household in the changing world of the late twentieth century is a complex and difficult task in which many people are currently engaged. This book is a contribution to ongoing processes of description, analysis and planning for the future.

Māori and te iwi Māori

The Māori people (te iwi Māori)[6] have a special status as the indigenous people of Aotearoa New Zealand[7] and signatories with the Crown of the Treaty of Waitangi in 1840. Though their forebears came as immigrants from Eastern Polynesia, they lived and developed a distinctive way of life in Aotearoa for over a thousand years before the arrival of Europeans (Davidson 1984).

While demographers, social scientists and the general public continue to debate the definition of 'a Māori',[8] the Māori determine the issue in their own way. They specify descent from a Māori parent or ancestor as the basic requirement and, provided that is fulfilled, accept as Māori those who identify themselves as Māori. Attempts to impose a narrower definition in terms of linguistic and cultural competence are generally rejected.

Taken collectively,[9] te iwi Māori is characterised by a combination of characteristics: genealogical descent from the pre-European inhabitants of New Zealand, distinctive physical features, distinctive values and ways of organising social life, shared history, and consciousness of kind ('a we feeling'). Those who identify themselves and are identified by others as Māori do not necessarily display all these characteristics in their own person.

Far from being homogenous Māori individuals have a variety of cultural characteristics and live in a number of cultural and socio-economic realities. The relevance of so-called traditional values is not the same for all Māori, nor can it be assumed that all Māori will wish to define their ethnic identity according to classical constructs. At the same time, they may well describe themselves as Māori, rejecting any notion that they are 'less Māori than their peers'. . . . self-identification . . . conveys little in terms of lifestyles, access to resources and participation in distinctly Māori institutions such as whānau and hapū. (M.H. Durie, Black et al. 1994: 3)

Responding to pressure from Māori and social scientists, official agencies have moved over the last ten years to recognise the importance of self-identification in the definition of Māori individuals. On the 1991 Census form, in a departure from previous practice, respondents were asked two questions: 'Which ethnic group do you belong to?' and 'Have you any New Zealand Māori ancestry?'

In response to the first question, a total of 435,619 declared themselves as belonging to the Māori ethnic group, either alone (323,998) or in conjunction with other groups (111,621). The 1991 Census identified this total as 'the New Zealand Māori ethnic group' and 'the total New Zealand Māori population' (Statistics 1992: 15). As such it made up 12.7% of the total New Zealand population.

In answer to the second question, 511,278 acknowledged having Māori ancestry, making up 15% of the total New Zealand population (Statistics 1992: 47). Of those who acknowledged Māori ancestry, 75,659 did *not* identify themselves as Māori.

Non-Māori, Pākehā, European

The population of New Zealand includes members of many ethnic groups besides the New Zealand Māori. While these are recognised by their own names when appropriate, it is sometimes convenient to refer to all of them collectively by a single term, in contrast with the Māori. Several terms are in use but none is universally accepted. I have accordingly developed my own reference system (Metge 1990: 13-15).

New Zealander I use as the most general term, referring to all citizens of the New Zealand state, including Māori.

The term *non-Māori* is neutral in reference, despite its negative form. I use it when discussing statistical constructs (for example, 'the non-Māori population' and 'non-Māori households') and when necessary to avoid ambiguity.

The term *Pākehā* has its origin in the Māori language but is accepted by many non-Māori New Zealanders as the most useful of the terms available. Following Māori usage, I use Pākehā with two meanings. I use it most often to identify those immigrants or descendants of immigrants from Europe (including Great Britain) who have put down roots and feel that they belong in Aotearoa New Zealand. I also stretch it to include all non-Māori in the pairing 'Māori and Pākehā'. Which meaning is intended is usually clear from the context.

Some non-Māori object to being called Pākehā, believing the term to be derogatory. The word's origin is not known for certain; of several alleged explanations, some are insulting, others are not.[10] In contemporary Māori usage the word is simply descriptive. If derogatory overtones are detected, they originate with the user, not the word itself. The frequent pairing of Māori and Pākehā indicates connection as well as contrast.

The term *European* I reserve for visitors and temporary residents from the continent of Europe. I reject its application to New Zealand citizens of European origin because where they or their ancestors originated matters less than their commitment to Aotearoa New Zealand.

The term *Tauiwi* is used by some to refer to non-Māori New Zealanders. In Māori it has the basic meaning of 'stranger' and is used in contrastive opposition to 'tangata whenua' (person of the land).[11] In that it implies that non-Māori do not belong in Aotearoa New Zealand I find it less acceptable than Pākehā.

Ngā Tikanga Māori

While Māori as individuals display a variety of cultural patterns, Māori as a people lay claim to a set of values and ways of organising social life which are distinctively Māori. For fifty years or more Māori have referred to these distinctively Māori ways as Māoritanga, but over the last ten years they have shown an increasing tendency to prefer the phrase *ngā tikanga Māori*.

Tikanga is a noun formed by adding the ending *-anga* to *tika*, an adjective which means *straight*, *just* (fair) and *right* (correct), in opposition to *hē* (wrong, mistaken).

While *tikanga* has a range of meanings in Māori,[12] when used in the phrase *ngā tikanga Māori* it is fairly translated as 'the right Māori ways' and refers to the rules or guidelines for living generally accepted as tika. Ngā tikanga Māori encompass and hold together ways of thinking (whakaaro nui) and ways of doing (mahinga), principles and practice.

Ngā tikanga Māori are by definition tuku iho nō ngā tūpuna (handed down from the ancestors), in most cases from pre-European times, but this does *not* mean that they are static and unchanging. While the principles are deeply entrenched, there is always scope for choice and flexibility in the way they are interpreted, weighted and applied in particular situations. Under the guidance of group leaders, succeeding generations adapt them to the needs and goals of their time.

Foremost among ngā tikanga Māori is the right of the tāngata whenua of a particular locality to formulate their own tikanga vis-à-vis visitors (manuwhiri). Thus, while the principles are the same throughout Māoridom, the detailed content given to particular tikanga can vary between sections of the Māori social order, between iwi, between hapū, and even between whānau.[13]

Ngā tikanga Māori collectively fulfil the function of maintaining 'law and order'. They have been described in English as customary or custom law, where 'law' is a generic term (E. Durie 1994). However, I prefer not to identify them as *laws* but to reserve that word for Acts passed by the national legislature and enforced through the court system. Ngā tikanga Māori fulfil other functions besides maintaining the rule of law, cover the whole range of human behaviour, including moral and spiritual aspects, and are enforced by other means. Māori themselves make a clear distinction between ngā tikanga Māori and ngā ture, the laws enacted by the New Zealand Parliament.

A changing world

The social and economic environment in which whānau and family operate has changed significantly since the middle of the century, especially over the last 25 years.

Māori urban migration, which began before and during World War II, picked up speed until the relation between rural and urban Māori was totally reversed. Whereas in 1945 75% of the Māori population lived in rural areas, the proportion living in urban areas rose to 56% in 1966, to 75% in 1976 and settled around 80% in 1981. By 1991 Māori born and raised in urban areas made up more than half the Māori population. Many were second or third generation urban dwellers. In the 1980s return migration to the country and out-migration overseas both reached significant proportions.[14]

Migration, especially to urban areas, is often associated with diminished knowledge and interest in tikanga Māori on the part of individuals and families. At the same time, movements to revive Māori ways and protest against loss of land and self-determination have mostly had their origin among urban residents conscious of cultural loss.

Changes in attitudes to family limitation and single parenthood have been reflected in the size and composition of families. From a peak of 6.3 children per woman of child-bearing age in 1963, the Māori fertility rate fell rapidly to 3 in 1977 and 2.2 in 1993, marginally higher than the total New Zealand rate. As a result the average number of children in Māori families also fell to almost the non-Māori rate in 1991. Overall figures, however, mask the fact that Māori women begin child-bearing at a relatively early age: in 1991 those between 15 and 19 had fertility rates three times higher than non-Māori women in the same age group. The proportion of Māori children under 15 being raised by one parent increased from 20% in 1981 to 39% in 1991.[15]

Changes in fertility have also modified the age structure of the Māori population. The proportion of children under 15 declined from the extremely high level of 50% of the Māori population in 1966 to 39% in 1986 and 37% in 1991. Nevertheless, youthfulness remains an outstanding characteristic of the

Māori population, with a major concentration in the 15 to 30 age groups.[16]

Economic restructuring and rising rates of unemployment in the 1980s impacted severely on Māori. From 12% in 1984 the Māori rate of unemployment rose to 24% nationally in 1991 (compared with 10.5% for non-Māori); in some regions it was over 60%. Māori rates of youth and long-term unemployment tripled between 1986 and 1992.[17]

Not surprisingly, these changes have been associated with increasing indications of stress on individuals and families. A high proportion of one-parent families are dependent on income support from the State in the form of Domestic Purposes, Unemployment, Sickness and Disability Benefits. Despite increased life expectancy, Māori levels of health remain consistently lower than those of non-Māori, with particular concern focusing on psychiatric illness, hearing impairment in children, cancer and respiratory disease, infectious diseases and children and women's health. The Māori rate of suicide has risen since 1980 to match that of the non-Māori for the 15 to 24 years age group. In the early 1990s deaths from road traffic injuries for Māori males between 15 and 24 are almost twice the rate for non-Māori males; the rate of hospitalisation following assault is seven times higher for Māori women between 15 and 24 than for non-Māori; and half the children admitted to women's refuges with their mothers are Māori. Māori youth are over-represented among persistent absentees from school and those between 14 and 16 years appearing before the courts. Māori made up 42% of all convicted offenders in 1993 and almost half the prisoners received by penal institutions.[18]

The disparities between Māori and non-Māori just outlined are substantially reduced or eliminated when controlled for socioeconomic factors, age and educational qualifications. This does not deny the individual and family tragedies behind such statistics and begs the question of why such a high proportion of Māori are concentrated in the economically disadvantaged strata of New Zealand society.

The incidence of such problems causes deep concern to Māori and Pākehā, official agencies and ordinary citizens alike, and continuing attempts are made to identify causes and remedies.

In addressing problems of family stress among Māori, some commentators focus mainly on individual responsibility and remedies, but many, especially Māori, place them in a wider frame of reference and emphasise the damage inflicted on Māori individually and collectively by colonisation and its concomitants: the policies of assimilation and integration, concentration in the poorer sectors of a capitalist economy and class system, the undermining of the whānau, massive urban migration, and the alienation of many Māori from their cultural roots.[19]

In proposing remedies, those who take this wider view stress the importance of collective as well as individual responsibility and action. From the 1970s Māori leaders, organisations and protest groups have become increasingly active and outspoken in pressing the State to honour the Treaty of Waitangi by dismantling institutional racism in government agencies, recognising the existence and validity of ngā tikanga Māori, and restoring te rangatiratanga Māori, the right of Māori to make and implement decisions affecting them in their own way and according to their own values. Their aims were articulated in national hui, especially the Hui Kaumātua (1979), a series of Wānanga Whakatauira beginning in 1980, the Hui Taumata (1984), the Hui Whakaoranga (1984) and the Hui Whakapūmau (1994).[20]

In all these discussions, Māori have used the word whānau with great frequency, both to describe what they see as a key element of Māori social organisation and to serve as a symbol for Māori values. In particular, Māori planners have highlighted the whānau in the development of particular programmes.

Māori initiatives

In 1977 the philosophy of Tū Tangata was adopted by the Department of Māori Affairs to empower Māori to 'stand tall', by drawing on their own cultural strengths to pursue and achieve their aspirations. Providing advice and seeding grants only, the Department supported a series of consciousness-raising Wānanga, established Kōkiri Centres providing skills training and counselling, and facilitated the launching of Kōhanga Reo and Mātua Whāngai programmes. Central to all these developments was a whānau style of working (Puketapu 1982).

Giving effect to the priority accorded the Māori language in the Hui Kaumātua, the Kōhanga Reo movement was established in 1981 to provide pre-school children with a Māori language environment. The movement's founders chose the term whānau to describe the group of parents, teachers and kaumātua (elders) which run each local kōhanga reo (language nest). This title was chosen to provide such groups with a model of group action which stressed aroha (altruistic love), cooperation, collective responsibility, and consensus decision-making (Government Review Team 1988: 20).

At about the same time, Māori public servants and volunteers concerned about alienated Māori youth developed the Mātua Whāngai programme. This involved the Departments of Māori Affairs, Social Welfare and Justice working with local Mātua Whāngai committees to place Māori children in need of care and protection with families from their own whānau, hapū or iwi (Māori Affairs-Social Welfare-Justice 1986). Despite difficulties (including the phasing out of the Department of Māori Affairs, fluctuations in resourcing, continuing migration and rural and urban differences), the Mātua Whāngai programme continues to operate in many parts of the country.

In 1986 a Ministerial Advisory Committee consisting of six Māori and two Pākehā produced the Report *Puao-Te-Ata-Tu* (*Daybreak*) setting out 'a Māori Perspective for the Department of Social Welfare' (Ministerial Advisory Committee 1986a & b). Based on extensive consultation with Māori communities, this report made recommendations designed to incorporate tikanga Māori into all Social Welfare Department policies for the future and to correct those deficiencies in law and practice which undermined the connection between Māori children and young people and their whānau, hapū and iwi. *Puao-Te-Ata-Tu* was adopted as official policy in 1987. Though its implementation was disrupted by the restructuring of the Department of Social Welfare in 1991, *Puao-Te-Ata-Tu* stands as a landmark in policy-making to which Māori in particular make frequent reference.

Empowered by their experience with Mātua Whāngai and *Puao-Te-Ata-Tu*, Māori made major contributions to the debate about the way in which children and young persons were handled by the Family and Youth Courts and to the final form of the Children, Young Persons, and Their Families Act passed in 1989 (Hassall 1996; Olsen, Maxwell and Morris 1993: 6). For the first time this Act gave legal recognition to the whānau and provided for the convening of Family Group Conferences at which family groups were given a major decision-making role. It also made provision for the legal responsibility for young Māori to be vested in hapū or iwi where necessary (Children, Young Persons, and their Families Act, section 79; Durie-Hall and Metge 1992: 77).

As a result of these developments, New Zealand policy-makers and legislators have widened their definition of family, admitted the word whānau to their official vocabulary and adopted a policy of consultation with Māori when reviewing family laws, while many social workers have learnt significantly to amend their practice when dealing with Māori. In New Zealand society as a whole, the word whānau has become known to and used by a wide range of people. In the mid 1990s Māori commonly use it without translation or explanation when speaking English as well as Māori, the news media use it increasingly without a gloss and most non-Māori are used at least to hearing or reading it. Without question whānau has joined the limited number of Māori words which are part of the New Zealand as distinct from the Māori vocabulary.

In search of understanding

Yet increased familiarity with the word whānau has not been matched with increased understanding of the family type which is its primary referent. There is in fact a great deal of confusion, among Māori as well as Pākehā, as to what its primary referent is. This confusion is compounded by the way Māori use the word with a wide range of meanings and slide between them without clearly signalling the fact.

In ordinary and even in professional interaction, Māori who know the whānau from the inside typically take it for granted and fail to see or address other people's confusions and misunderstandings. The publications associated with the programmes just outlined offer little help. The Mātua Whāngai booklet offers an explanation so complicated that it makes sense only to those who already understand the subject (see below pp 58-60). *Puao-Te-Ata-Tu* gives a brief description of the whānau as part of 'the traditional Māori system of pre-European times', notes that 'this social system was not set in cement' but does not discuss the nature or consequences of subsequent changes (Ministerial Advisory Committee 1986b: 7). The Children, Young Persons, and Their Families Act 1989 offers a very broad definition of 'family group' but none at all of whānau.

Of the published sources available, those by Māori writers in the form of fiction or autobiography are particularly illuminating.[21] Creative rather than analytic, these works typically assume understanding of Māori social organisation and values, leaving much to be read between the lines. They are concerned with particular cases: it is not their purpose to identify or describe common patterns and roles, let alone to explain them. They do, however, provide a rich source of illustration of such patterns to those who recognise them.

Ethnographic accounts of contemporary family life by Māori are tantalisingly rich but limited in number and scope. Makereti drew on her own experience in Te Arawa for her book *The Old-Time Maori* (1938) but used it mainly to reconstruct the 'olden days' before the coming of the Pākehā. Pat Hohepa (1964) and Maharaia Winiata (1967) discussed contemporary family forms as part of general studies of their own home communities, both of which were rural and traditional, maintaining a way of life handed down from the ancestors.

Pioneering research on Māori child-raising by Ernest and Pearl Beaglehole (1946) was followed in the 1960s and 1970s by a series of research studies by James Ritchie, Jane Ritchie and the Rakau Studies team. These were primarily concerned with relations within the parent-child family, interpreted within a psychological framework.

My own interest in Māori families in general and the whānau in particular dates from my first fieldwork research, studying the Māori migration from rural to urban areas in the 1950s. As a Pākehā anthropologist I could take nothing for granted but had to learn, slowly and painfully, to understand and appreciate a way of family life very different from my own. In my first published work, *A New Maori Migration*, I reported in detail on the large family groups which I found operating in the rural community of Kōtare in the Far North and in the city of Auckland (Metge 1964: 61-67 and 164-79), concentrating on relations above the domestic level. In the general text *The Maoris of New Zealand* (1967 and revised edition 1976), I discussed both large family groups and parent-child families, but placed the discussion of the former in a chapter entitled 'Descent and Descent Groups' and the latter in a chapter on 'Marriage and Family'.

Over the following years I became increasingly convinced that this separation was a mistake and that relations in the Māori parent-child family were best treated and understood in association with those of the larger group. As Captain James Cook Fellow between 1981 and 1983, I began what developed into ongoing research into the part played by relatives other than parents in child-rearing and the principles and practice of Māori adoption. In the later 1980s and the 1990s, as increasing attention came to be paid to the whānau as word and concept, I acknowledged its widening range of reference and re-examined the family group which is its primary referent in an article entitled 'Te Rito o te Harakeke' (Metge 1990).

New growth from old

The present book brings together my research and thinking on the whānau over a period of forty years. This has involved observation and participation in whānau life in Kōtare, Auckland and Wellington and extensive discussions with Māori who were willing to talk about their own experience and the insights gained by reflecting upon it. They have been kai-whakaatu, people who have imparted (literally 'made to come out') both information and understanding.

In my choice of title and frequently in the text, I stress that the whānau is subject to constant change, some of it intrinsic and repeated, some of it the irreversible result of reaction and adaptation to changes in the social, economic and political context. This presents a major problem for anyone attempting to study Māori family life, for the range of variation is very wide both over time and in different places and iwi. In this book I aim not to chart the full variation but rather to open up the subject for debate and further research.

In Part I, after outlining past anthropological work on the subject, I survey the range of meanings Māori currently give to the word whānau and then build a generalised model or picture of the primary referent within this range, a model broad enough to encompass the major variations which have developed over the last forty years in urban as well as rural areas. In reasonable confidence that this model has general validity in the early 1990s, I use the present tense. In Part II, I emphasise the dynamism of the whānau by examining the development of one of the Kōtare whānau between 1955 and 1985. In Parts III and IV, I explore two particular aspects of child-rearing in the whānau (sharing the caring and adoption) and in Part V whānau methods of dealing with problems. In Parts II to IV, whenever I wish to emphasise that the evidence brought forward relates specifically to past decades and/or that its applicability in the present is uncertain, I use the past tense.

Ngā kai-whakaatu

Searching my research records, I have identified 88 Māori who discussed their experience of whānau with me over the last 16 years, contributing to the growth of my understanding and directly and indirectly to the text of this book.

These kai-whakaatu were chosen or chose themselves because they had firsthand experience of whānau as children and adults and were interested in reflecting on that experience and contributing to a study we hoped would enhance understanding of the whānau and tikanga Māori generally. Most I knew from previous research or through professional or social contact but others I met as a result of a planned attempt to extend the range of contributors. They are mostly people who identify strongly as Māori, are fluent speakers of the Māori language, have a deep knowledge of tikanga Māori rooted in firsthand experience, and maintain close ties with their own whānau, hapū and iwi, whether living in their iwi territory or not. To protect their privacy, I have used pseudonyms when referring to them and their places of origin and when quoting their words.

With 75 of these kai-whakaatu I recorded discussions which could be described as interviews, in that they were arranged beforehand, took place in relative privacy, sometimes in my home and sometimes in theirs, and were recorded at the time either on tape or in my field notebook as they chose. These were supplemented with less formal discussions with these and other kai-whakaatu in the course of ordinary social interaction or at hui where recording was inappropriate. In such cases I recorded the purport of the exchange as soon as possible afterwards.

Both interviews and less formal discussions were open-ended. I nominated the topic, explained my interest in it and asked questions from time to time, but left it mainly to my[22] kai-whakaatu to decide what ground to cover and at what depth. As I expected from prior experience, they discussed the whānau by recounting their own experience. Limiting my questions to the bare essentials, I found that my kai-whakaatu not only covered those left unasked but also produced insights I had not anticipated. Wherever I made use of the results in this book, whether by retelling or direct quotation, I referred the draft text to the speaker to check and obtained their permission for publication. This process often stimulated additional comment, so that the research process continued right up to the time that the text went to press.

While most interviews involved myself and just one kai-whakaatu, a significant number involved other people. In 13 cases I spoke with husband and wife together, in two cases with two sisters, in three cases with two work colleagues, and once with six. Discussion continued through several interviews with 40 of the kai-whakaatu. Interviews usually lasted one to two hours but sometimes took the best part of a day. Often, as is Māori practice, we discussed other, related subjects along with the whānau, especially whakamā and Māori methods of learning and teaching. While some of that material is included here, much of it has been published already or will appear later.

At the time of interview my kai-whakaatu ranged in age from 25 to 70. Nearly half (41) were living in rural areas and small towns within their own iwi territory, 23 in Kōtare, the community I know most intimately. The rest were living in urban areas outside their iwi territory. Half (44) gave their primary allegiance to one of the iwi of Muriwhenua (the Far North), 10 to the other iwi of Tai Tokerau (Northland) and 12 to the iwi of Tai Rāwhiti (the East Coast between Gisborne and Hicks Bay). Of the remaining 22, nine identified with iwi stemming from Mataatua, five with Tainui iwi, three with Taranaki iwi, two each with Ngāti Kahungunu and Ngāi Tahu, and one with Te Arawa. Combining concentration on Tai Tokerau with representation from a wide variety of other iwi helped establish the many features of the whānau which are common to all.

Accounts of personal experience, whether of the recent or more distant past, are subjective rather than objective represent-ations, filtered through the lens of the tellers' own perceptions. While recognising this, I have no difficulty justifying my extensive use of such accounts. My kai-whakaatu were strongly motivated to tell the truth as they saw it, warts and all. Their maturity enabled them to reflect on their experience wisely and to discern patterns more effectively from a distance than when they were immersed in it. Recorded independently, their accounts sup-ported, reinforced and amplified each other, whether contributing to the general pattern or providing examples of divergence from it.

With very few exceptions, the kai-whakaatu who have contributed to this book have had a positive experience of whānau life and enjoyed talking about it. At the same time, because the whānau they know contain a variety of personalities and circumstances and are linked with others through marriage, they are well aware that others have had unhappy experiences, that whānau do not always function well and that some may even be dysfunctional.

Conclusion

This book is intended, in the first place, to provide basic inform-ation for the many Pākehā who interact with Māori as spouses, friends, work colleagues and service providers and to help them achieve understanding of a family type very different from their own. In spite of urban migration and pressures to lose touch with their cultural origins, Māori still belong to whānau in significant numbers and value their membership enough to make it imperative for non-Māori to seek such understanding.

As for the many Māori who have never had direct experience of whānau membership or are currently separated from it, it is dangerous to assume that they have been totally assimilated to Pākehā family patterns and can be dealt with without reference to the whānau or tikanga Māori. The kind of upbringing experienced by my kai-whakaatu and those like them has had a crucial effect on their parenting practice, whether they follow or repudiate it, and its influence extends through succeeding generations. Māori who have little conscious knowledge of Māori concepts and tikanga have often subconsciously absorbed a great deal from parents, relatives and friends who are culturally Māori. Reproducing a deeply entrenched pattern of behaviour without bringing it to consciousness can have unanticipated and undesirable consequences, especially when surrounding circumstances have changed and parts of the pattern have been lost. Over the last twenty years, Māori have established numerous non-kin associations which they call whānau and have modelled on the whānau of primary reference.

This book is therefore offered, secondly, as a contribution to the debate about the causes of current problems among Māori families, especially what is often stigmatised as parental neglect, and to the development of policies and strategies for handling them more effectively.

Chapter 2

VIEWS FROM ANTHROPOLOGY

Kia ū ki tou kāwai tupuna, kia mātauria ai, i ahu mai koe i hea, e anga ana koe ko hea.[1]

Trace out your ancestral stem, so that it may be known where you come from and in which direction you are going.

The word kāwai is at once the branching stem of plants of a creeping habit, like the kumara, and the branching line of descent for which the kumara vine is a favourite metaphor. This saying advises speakers to identify their forebears, so that listeners can 'place' them. In this chapter it is interpreted as applying to intellectual as well as biological forebears.

Anthropologists have been seeking to define the whānau and understand its workings for over 70 years. Anthropological writings on the subject are important for several reasons. As well as a general definition or model of 'the whānau' they record descriptions of particular whānau in particular communities at

particular times. They include contributions from Māori
anthropologists who themselves grew up in whānau and knew
them from the inside. And they have influenced as well as been
influenced by Māori definitions and understanding.

Modelling the 'classic' whānau

As early as the 1920s three New Zealand anthropologists built
up a picture of the whānau as they believed it to have operated in
Māori society before it was affected by contact with Europeans.
This model was constructed by reference to early European
records, the writers' experience of Māori communities which
cherished traditional ways, and information supplied by Māori
informants.

Differing in background and training, the three anthropologists checked and complemented each other's work. Elsdon
Best worked among the Tūhoe of the Urewera region from 1895
to 1910 and visited other iwi while employed as ethnologist at
the Dominion Museum for 20 years. A licensed interpreter and
fluent speaker of Māori, he had access to knowledgeable Māori
scholars as informants but was handicapped in the application of
anthropological terms and ideas by lack of formal training (Craig
1964). Raymond Firth turned from economics to train as a social
anthropologist in London in the mid 1920s. His doctoral thesis
on the economics of the Māori, published in 1929, was based on
extensive use of library resources (including Best's works) and
illuminated by several fieldtrips to remote Māori communities
(including Tūhoe). The sections on social organisation were
reprinted largely unchanged in the revised edition of 1959 (Firth
1929, 1959, 1957: 58fn). Te Rangi Hiroa (Peter Buck) had a dual
heritage, Irish on his father's side, Ngāti Mutunga and Ngāti Tama
of Taranaki on his mother's, and was at home in both cultures.
He served as Medical Officer for Māori Health, Member of
Parliament for Northern Māori and doctor to the Māori Battalion
during World War I until his interest in anthropology took him
to Yale University, a doctorate in anthropology and the position
of Director of the Bishop Museum in Hawaii (Condliffe 1971).
He published a major work on Māori culture in 1949.

After pointing out that whānau meant both 'offspring' (the

children of common parents) and 'a family group', Best devoted a few brief but influential paragraphs to defining and describing the latter in *The Maori* (1924: 340). His description was challenged on some points but confirmed in general by Firth in *Economics of the New Zealand Maori* (1959: 110-24) and Te Rangi Hiroa in *The Coming of the Maori* (1949: 333-37). The three anthropologists agreed on identifying 'the whānau' in the late eighteenth century as:

- a family group usually comprising three generations: an older man and his wife, some or all of their descendants and in-married spouses, or some variant (such as several brothers with their wives and families) representing a stage in a domestic cycle;
- a domestic group occupying a common set of buildings (sleeping house or houses, cookhouse and storage stages) standing alone or occupying a defined subdivision of a village;
- a social and economic unit responsible for the management of daily domestic life, production and consumption;
- the lowest tier in a three-tiered system of socio-political groups defined by descent from common ancestors traced through links of both sexes, the middle tier consisting of hapū and the highest of iwi.

As Firth summed up:

> In matters of organisation each whanau was fairly self-reliant, the direction being taken by the head man of the group in consultation with other responsible people. As a rule it managed its own affairs without interference, except in such cases as came within the sphere of village or tribal policy. (1959: 111)

This model of the whānau is often referred to as 'the traditional Māori family', but I prefer to use the term 'classic', to emphasise its location in the late 18th and early 19th century, before contact with Europeans effected major socio-economic changes in Māori

society. The word traditional is thus left free to be used to describe
patterns of family life which have been handed down from generation to generation to the present day (see below, pp 49-59).

Describing this classic whānau as 'the basic social unit of Māori
society . . . the smallest unit with a degree of self-determination',
Best asserted that both the individual and what he called the 'true
family' (the parent-child family) were 'lost' in the whānau, their
interests totally subordinated to those of the group (1924: 341).
Firth, however, marshalled evidence that the parent-child family
had some separate functions and greater significance within the
whānau than Best allowed. He pointed (in particular) to the sexual
exclusiveness and economic interdependence of husband and
wife, and to the fact that parents and children occasionally worked
as a unit for economic ends, camping in the forest or by the sea
(1959: 116-24). Best's observation that the whānau as a whole
had greater rights over children than their parents did was
supported by Hiroa with examples of the part played by grandparents in the education of his own contemporaries (Hiroa 1949:
358-60).

To illustrate his general definition, Best described a whānau
known to him, presumably among the Tūhoe in the 1890s. This
whānau was (he reported):

> composed of two brothers, a sister, and their children,
> grandchildren, and great grandchildren, in all ninety-two
> persons. The parents of the first-named generation, the true
> forebears of the group, are dead, their living children being
> now from seventy to eighty years of age . . . this group . . .
> is composed of four generations, and is about ready to
> become a clan. (1924: 343-44)

Checked against his own definition, this group had several
unusual features. It consisted entirely of persons sharing the same
descent, no mention being made of husbands or wives; the most
senior generation consisted of three siblings, without one being
identified as head or leader; and it was exceptionally large. While
the lack of detail on residential and economic patterns makes it
difficult to determine the group's exact nature, the example is
important because it highlights two problems: the status of

husbands and wives in the whānau and what happened to a whānau as its numbers increased, especially in relation to hapū.

Best, Firth and Hiroa all failed to pick up the conceptual ambiguity between defining the whānau as a family and domestic group including in-married spouses and identifying it as the lowest tier in a hierarchy of groups defined on the basis of descent. Since they did not see the problem, none of them suggested that the word whānau was defined differently in these different contexts.

Recognising that whānau increased in numbers generation by generation, Best, Firth and Hiroa all suggested that whānau became or grew into hapū (Best 1924: 340, Firth 1959: 111-12, Hiroa 1949: 333-35). This formulation recognised the importance of change over time but overlooked the complexity of the process and the difference in the functions carried out by whānau and hapū. The number of members added in each generation increased unevenly and could even decrease because of disease, famine and war. When members of a whānau fell out or increased past an optimum size, some moved out to set up separate households, creating several new whānau in place of the old. Whether or not these new whānau combined to establish themselves as a hapū depended on their having not merely the numbers but also effective leadership, adequate resources and the fighting capacity to defend their independence.

Given the state of anthropology at the time, the model of Māori social structure developed by Best, Firth and Hiroa was a remarkable achievement but it was limited in its provision of detail and its handling of variation, process and change. Over the years it has attracted and benefited from critical refinement and amplification. Meanwhile a popular and simplified version has been widely accepted and re-presented by Māori and non-Māori as the basis of the Māori social order not only in the pre- and immediate post-contact period but throughout the 19th and 20th centuries. The phrase 'whānau-hapū-iwi' is often used as a shorthand reference for this structure but Māori experts prefer the reverse formulation 'iwi-hapū-whānau', because it respects the metaphor implicit in the terms used, iwi (people, tribe) being logically prior to hapū (pregnancy), and hapū logically prior to whānau (birth).[2]

In the 1950s and 1960s, as Professor of Social Anthropology at the London School of Economics, Firth revisited the study of the classic Māori social structure during an academic debate about the status of descent group systems which were neither patrilineal nor matrilineal. Two articles he wrote in this connection (Firth 1956, 1963) did much to clarify the terminology and the issues in general and in relation to the hapū. In these articles he adopted the term 'ambilineal' to describe both the Māori method of tracing descent through links of either sex and the resulting type of descent group, and reserved 'ambilateral' for the method of affiliation to such groups through either or both parents. Stressing the potential for choice in ambilineal systems, he highlighted the importance of residence with the group and participation in group activities as criteria for establishing group membership. Although he concentrated on the hapū with its political functions, leaving aside the domestic whānau, these articles are relevant to discussion of the whānau because they advanced understanding of the principles and processes at work in the Māori social order as a whole.

Describing the whānau in the 1950s and 1960s

While this debate was going on at the highest levels in academia, I was struggling with firsthand material on contemporary Māori kinship groups below hapū level obtained as a graduate student during fieldwork in Auckland and the rural community of Kōtare in the Far North in 1953-55 and 1958-59. The fruits of this struggle were presented in my doctoral thesis in 1957 and in a revised form in *A New Maori Migration* in 1964.

Three other anthropologists, all Māori, wrote studies of Māori rural communities within a few years of mine. In each case the community was their own and the whānau was discussed as part of a wider study.

Maharaia Winiata, a member of Ngāi Terangi in the western Bay of Plenty, completed his PhD thesis at the University of Edinburgh in 1952; an edited version was published posthumously in 1967 as *The Changing Role of the Leader in Maori Society*. As background to his exploration of Māori leadership, Winiata briefly discussed household composition, the internal organisation of the whānau and interaction between whānau heads in Huria near Tauranga in the 1940s and 1950s (1967: 107-9, 115-19). Tantalisingly brief, these passages provide clues rather than evidence on the composition, objectives and processual flexibility of whānau at that time.

Pat Hohepa, a member of Ngāpuhi from southern Hokianga, presented the results of a field study in Paerau in Northland in an MA thesis for the University of Auckland (1961) and in book form as *A Maori Community in Northland* in 1964. He devoted five pages to a discussion of what the people of Paerau called whāmere (a transliteration of family) and spent a chapter exploring how whāmere organised activities on the marae and during the annual cleaning of the cemetery (1964: 65-69, 70-91).[3]

Hugh Kawharu, a member of Ngāti Whātua from the Auckland region with degrees from both Oxford and Cambridge Universities, wrote about a community of tāngata whenua located in Auckland city in his book *Orakei: A Ngati Whatua Community*, published in 1975. In a chapter on aspects of social organisation, he devoted three pages to a discussion of 'The Extended Bilateral Family' and briefly examined descent as the basis for local group organisation and the composition of households (1975: 50-52).

Winiata, Hohepa, Kawharu and I all dealt with small groups of relatives which were described by the people themselves as *families* when speaking English and as *whāmere, whānau* and sometimes *hapū* when speaking Māori. Despite differences in presentation and terminology in our published works, it was obvious that the groups described were essentially the same. They were ancestor-oriented, defined by the people with reference to a kaumātua, living or recently dead, on the basis of descent traced through both male and female links. They were identified by their kaumātua's name and associated with a particular stretch of inherited land. Their members were distributed among several different households, mostly located in the community of the kaumātua's ancestors. Group members managed their day-to-day affairs on a household basis but acted together as a group to sponsor life crisis hui and to care for whānau property. In-married spouses participated fully in the daily life of households and contributed to group activities as workers at hui but were usually excluded from key leadership positions. Because group activities were discontinuous and occasional, individuals could and did give allegiance and support to more than one whānau or whāmere.

Kawharu and I noted that, in addition to their membership in ancestor-oriented whānau, individual Māori also recognised kinship ties traced from themselves to a large circle of whanaunga (relatives), delimiting what anthropologists call an ego-oriented personal kin universe. This comprised relatives connected in different ways and belonging to several different whānau. The word *whanaunga* means relative in the widest sense, whether the connection is by descent, marriage or adoption. It derives, not from *whānau*, but from *whanau*, which means 'to incline or bend down' (H.W. Williams 1971: 487). These ego-oriented kin universes ceased to exist with the death of the individuals to whom they were oriented.

The groups described by Winiata, Hohepa, Kawharu and myself differed from the whānau described by Best, Firth and Hiroa for the late 18th century in significant ways. They were generally larger; they comprised more than one household; they did not function as production units; and their members cooperated not on a daily basis but from time to time and on special occasions. In these respects they were more like the 18th-century hapū than the 18th-century whānau.

The reasons for the changes that had taken place are easily identified. The whānau of the 1950s and 1960s were integrated into a centralised market economy. Members had to work individually for money incomes, had limited opportunities for cooperative activity, and often had to leave their home communities in search of work. They were also affected by current ideas and laws regarding family life and housing, including the appropriate number of occupants in a household.

To emphasise that the Kōtare groups differed in these ways from the classic whānau, I decided not to use the label whānau in describing them. In *A New Maori Migration* (1964) I used the people's own alternative label of family, placing it in single quotation marks ('family') to distinguish it from the parent-child family. Later, in *The Maoris of New Zealand* (1967 and the revised edition 1976), I amended this to 'large-family'. At the same time, finding that Kōtare 'family' members insisted that descent was the basic criterion of 'family' membership, I identified the Kōtare 'families' as a type of descent group and placed my discussion of them under the heading 'Descent-Groups' (1964: 55-71; 1967: 119-34; 1976: 136-38), separated from the sections on ego-oriented kinship and family life.

Yet I knew from observation that participation (or non-participation) in group activities was also a relevant factor in the recognition of who were or were not 'family' members. Descendants of the 'family' ancestor who lived elsewhere and/or did not periodically contribute labour or money were not included among the members listed for me and those who suddenly turned up and tried to claim membership privileges were challenged to demonstrate their commitment. In-married spouses living in Kōtare played an active part as workers at 'family' hui, and when doing so were included 'under the umbrella' (as they put it) of the 'family' name. In the absence of kaumātua qualified by descent they were sometimes invited to act as speech-makers at hui.

To accommodate my perception that both descent and participation were important, I made use of Firth's complementary concepts of social structure and social organisation (Firth 1954):

> While the 'family' could be defined in structural terms as a bilateral descent-group of shallow depth which segmented every one or two generations, in terms of organisation and action it consisted of all those descendants of its progenitor present in the community at any given time, together with their accompanying or widowed spouses and foster children, in so far as any chose to take part. (Metge 1964: 63-64)

I further underlined the ambiguous position of spouses and children adopted from outside the 'family' by coining the term 'attached members' (1964: 63), a deliberate contradiction in terms.

Winiata had no hesitation in using the term whānau for groupings he saw as intermediate between household and hapū and in English identified them as extended families. Hohepa used only whāmere, the term used by the people of Paerau, side-stepping the choice of an English one. Kawharu decided against using whānau on the grounds that 'it may be used to refer to five levels and types of kin associations'. Instead he identified the Orakei-based groups by an anthropological label, 'the bilateral extended family', but placed his discussion of them under the heading 'Descent Category Focus', on the grounds that the rationale and incentive for cooperation in these groups was provided by 'descent unqualified by residence' (Kawharu 1975: 50, 72).

The works of Winiata, Hohepa and Kawharu dealt with tāngata whenua ('people of the land') living in communities where they had inherited ancestral land. In *A New Maori Migration* I was also concerned with emigrants from rural areas living in the city in the territory of other tribes. Many of those I talked to maintained close ties with 'families' based in the country, continuing to contribute to their clubs and marae and taking the dead home for burial. Others, however, were active members of kin groups with a strong corporate life centred in the city itself. These I classified into two main types (1964: 166-70, 174-79). The first consisted of a senior, living couple, their unmarried children, and their married children and sometimes grandchildren together with their families, all focused on the home of the senior couple as base. This I called the 'extended-family' type. Groups of the second type identified themselves to outsiders as 'one big family' but proved on investigation to comprise people related in a variety of ways, including affinal and indirect linkages. They were drawn together on a relatively short-term basis by mutual need and mutually rewarding cooperation, but were liable to disband suddenly. For groups of this kind I coined the term 'kin-cluster'. I saw both types as transformations of the rural 'family' with many similarities but some significant differences, notably the lack of an ancestral land base and, in the case of the kin-cluster, the lack of a unifying core of descendants.

Winiata, Hohepa, Kawharu and I were all wrestling with the problem of the relative importance of descent, local residence and participation, in the formation and operation of groups below hapū level. All of us used the term family, while making it clear that we were using it to refer to a unit larger than the parent-child family, but Kawharu and I felt it important to stress the significance of descent in the formation of these groups by placing discussion of them under headings containing the word descent.

Whānau and hapū

While aware that whānau were contained within hapū, Winiata, Hohepa, Kawharu and I did not explore the relationship between them in any depth.

In *A New Maori Migration* I reported that the Kōtare 'families' said that they 'belonged' to named hapū but were hazy about the details of their connection. The hapū concerned did not function as corporate groups and were only names mentioned at hui. (Wider experience showed that Kōtare was unusual in this respect.) At a certain stage in their development, Kōtare 'families' broke up into new groups of the same kind. While these regarded themselves as having links and obligations to each other, the relationship remained essentially informal and they did not describe themselves as a hapū or take on a hapū name. The list of Kōtare hapū had not changed since the nineteenth century.

Kawharu noted that the bilateral extended families of Orakei periodically segmented without giving rise to hapū.

At the head of a family is the (great) grandfather. The family draws its inspiration from him and when he dies it splits into its component segments, each under its own head, without ever necessarily re-forming again. (1976: 2)

New hapū had come into being in Orakei within the last 200 years, but for reasons other than family expansion.

Winiata made no mention of the segmentation of whānau or the formation of hapū as such but he provided an illuminating account of how kaumātua from Huria whānau widened their support base to become leaders of hapū and iwi (1967: 111-12).

Hohepa concentrated entirely on the whāmere of Paerau as they were at the time of study. It is not clear whether his failure to discuss the relation of whāmere to hapū was due to preoccupation with whāmere or because hapū were unimportant in Paerau.

What little evidence the four of us produced did not support the proposition that whānau 'grew into' hapū.

Developing understandings

Trained in British functionalism, a theoretical approach which emphasised functional relationships in the present and undervalued historical depth, Winiata, Hohepa, Kawharu and I concentrated our energies on describing the whānau in its contemporary form in our different communities. We accepted the model of the classic whānau as background without examining it critically and without attempting to chart the process of change over the intervening years.

From the late 1960s on, anthropologists and historians have taken an increasingly critical approach to the study of the Māori social and economic order both before and after contact with Europeans. The result has been a growing emphasis on variation (between iwi and regions), change and development, and a growing appreciation of the complexity of the patterns and processes involved. Publication, however, has been slow and mostly focused at the level of hapū and iwi. Preparing the revised edition of *The Maoris of New Zealand* (1976), I decided against revising my discussion of the whānau because it would have required a major reorganisation of the text; I have regretted the lost opportunity ever since. Five articles published in the last 20 years have helped directly and indirectly to advance understanding of the whānau.

Though he was primarily concerned with hapū, Steven Webster included the whānau/'family' in his discussion of 'Cognatic Descent Groups and the Contemporary Maori: A Preliminary Reassessment' (1975). Difficult even for specialists, this densely argued article explored the relation between the ideology of descent, which enables hapū to persist through time, and the practical processes of restriction and recruitment, which enable them to function as groups. In this article Webster made a crucial distinction between the hapū as descent category and the hapū as descent group. The hapū descent category was defined ('closed') by descent alone and thus comprised all the descendants of the hapū ancestor, regardless of where they were living or whether they kept in touch. The hapū descent group was defined by descent plus participation in group activities and comprised only those members of the descent category who lived and worked together (1975: 137). Webster pointed out that Māori use of the terms whānau and hapū was flexible and rhetorical, the precise reference being 'contextually determined' and 'perfectly clear to members of the same community' (1975: 124). Unfortunately he did not highlight this insight or provide examples and it went largely unnoticed.

In 'The Traditional Maori Family' (1978), Margaret Orbell re-appraised the writings of early European observers and drew on Māori oral literature to present a revised study of the classic whānau of the late 18th century. Identifying 'the family' as Best's whānau-household, she reported that most of those mentioned in the records contained between 15 and 30 persons and comprised a 'male head', his wife or wives, some of his married sons and daughters, perhaps slaves and poor relatives, and perhaps some grandchildren. The number of generations present was limited to two or at most three by high mortality and low life expectancy. Emphasising that the whānau was structured on the basis of rank and sex, with elder siblings taking precedence over younger and males over females, Orbell provided fascinating detail on brothers' control over their sisters' marriages, the special relationship that existed between mother's brother and sister's son (for whom the term irāmutu should be reserved), the belief that parents held their children in trust for the group, limitations on parents' ability to control and teach their children, and the assumption of these responsibilites by 'uncles and aunts'. In an important endnote Orbell criticised the standard translation of hapū as sub-tribe, pointing out that there were at least two levels of hapū: small hapū which sometimes acted separately and sometimes together, and large composite hapū which formed separate war alliances and sometimes fought among themselves.

In 1990 I reviewed both anthropological and Māori approaches to the concept of whānau in 'Te Rito o Te Harakeke: Conceptions of the Whaanau'. In this article I highlighted the fact that Māori gave the word whānau not one but many meanings, made a first attempt to chart the range, and explored the relation between the whānau as descent category, descent group and extended family through the medium of a case study.

This article was followed that same year by 'The Māori *hapū*:

A Generative Model', in which Eric Schwimmer explored the formation of new hapū. Instead of whānau simply growing into hapū, Schwimmer demonstrated that hapū formation was a highly complex process which involved the fission and fusion of existing hapū and periodic restructuring of their genealogical basis in response to historical challenges.

In '*Tipuna*—Ancestors: Aspects of Cognatic Descent' (1991), Anne Salmond used references drawn from myths, proverbs and Māori writings to illuminate the reports of early European observers on Māori groups of all kinds. Working from this broad base, she stressed the 'tremendous flexibility' characteristic of Māori social life and attributed it to the interaction of four principles, which she identified as:

> the unity of all phenomenal life through genealogical connection; the complementarity of male and female; the principle of primogeniture; all of which can be overcome by a fourth principle of competitive striving expressed in a language of war. (1991: 337)

These principles provided the general philosophical underpinning for the pre-contact social order as a whole and were worked out in practice at groups at every level, including the whānau. Salmond also pointed out that the labels hapū and whānau were often used imprecisely, being applied on occasion to groups larger and smaller than those which they usually identified, that relations between whānau and hapū were affected by many factors besides descent, and that the lives of individuals involved a constant negotiation between an array of genealogical possibilities and the necessity of practical choice, especially at the life crises of birth, marriage and death (1991: 343).

Finally, in 1992 I cooperated with Māori lawyer Donna Durie-Hall to write the article, 'Kua Tutū Te Puehu, Kia Mau: Māori Aspirations and Family Law'. This summarised Māori family forms and associated values as background to evaluating New Zealand family law from a Māori perspective.

Anthropological terms and their use

In writing about Māori social organisation, anthropologists draw
upon an extensive vocabulary of technical terms, developed for
the tasks of describing and comparing phenomena in many
different cultures. Many of these terms are derived from words
in common use in English. In re-working them for their special
task, anthropologists try, but do not always succeed, to make
them as neutral and free from cultural assumptions as possible.
When using these terms, it should be remembered that they are
tools developed to help in the search for understanding, not
representations of essential truth.

One of the most useful distinctions made by anthropologists
and other social scientists is that between 'category' and 'group'.
To explain this distinction I cannot do better than quote Roger
Keesing:

> A *cultural category* is a set of entities in the world—people,
> things, events, supernaturals—that are classed as similar
> for some purposes, because they have in common one or
> more culturally relevant attributes . . . (categories) exist
> only in human minds . . . they are sets we *draw mental
> lines around* in particular contexts.
>
> A *social group*, on the other hand, consists of actual
> warm-blooded human beings who recurrently interact in
> an interconnected set of roles—that is, positions or
> capacities. Thus groups can be distinguished from forms
> of aggregation, such as crowds or gatherings, whose
> interaction is temporary and limited. (Keesing 1976: 231)

In the Māori context these terms enable us to distinguish between
a *descent category*, which is made up of *all* the descendants of
Ancestor X, thought about in the abstract without reference to
any social interaction between them, and a *descent group*, which
is made up of those descendants of Ancestor X who interact
recurrently in terms of interconnected roles.

Social scientists also distinguish between *corporate groups*
which have an ongoing life, short-term *gatherings* and *action-
groups* of people who come together to perform a particular task

and then disband (Keesing 1976: 231-32).

The anthropological terms *descent, descendant, descent line, descent category* and *descent group* are needed in any discussion of Māori social organisation because of the emphasis Māori place on ancestry as a basis for kinship connection and group formation. Built into these technical terms is a spatial metaphor which places the ancestor 'up' 'at the top' and traces the connection to his or her descendants 'down' through the generations. Like many metaphors which are used frequently, this one has ceased to be appreciated as such: it has become a dead metaphor.

Māori use the same spatial metaphor when they refer to a speaker 'bringing the line down' from an ancestor (tupuna) to his/her descendants (uri), thinking of the ancestor as having higher mana. However, they also use several other metaphors, which draw on other spatial relations. Whakapapa, the word most often used when tracing connections between ancestors and descendants, literally means 'to place in layers'. Māori experts say that tracing whakapapa involves placing succeeding genera-tions one above the other on the ancestor as foundation, thus moving from 'down' to 'up'. For most Māori however this too is a dead metaphor, and they have no qualms about tracing a whakapapa *down*. Māori have a particular fondness for the image of the kumara vine, whose branches (kāwai) extend horizontally, putting down suckers at intervals, and for that of the tree, in which the ancestor is identified as the pūtake (roots and base), the descent lines and groups stemming from the ancestor as branches (kaupeka) and small families and individuals as twigs (rārā) reaching up to the light.

Carrying over the English word *family* for use as a technical term presents a different problem: it has a wide range of meanings, some of which are so different from each other that they are virtual opposites. The *Concise Oxford Dictionary* gives ten meanings for family. Of the six which refer to human beings, the first stresses kinship connection by both descent and marriage: 'a set of parents and children, or of relations, whether living together or not'. The second stresses common residence: 'the members of a household, especially parents and their children'. The third stresses common parentage: 'a person's children'. The fourth and fifth stress common descent: 'all the descendants of a common ancestor' and 'a race or group of peoples from a common stock'. The sixth applies the term metaphorically: 'a brotherhood of persons or nations united by political or religious ties'. Asked which of these meanings comes first to mind, English speakers of Anglo-Celtic background usually point to the parent-child family (R Williams 1983: 131-34).[4]

In developing *family* as a technical term, anthropologists affected by contemporary usage created the terms *nuclear family* to refer to the unit of parents and children and *extended family* to refer to a collection of interconnected and/or overlapping nuclear families, usually envisaged as a second order grouping where the component nuclear families act separately for some purposes and together for others.[5] Thus, in spite of the fact that the word family can refer to a category or group composed entirely of persons descended from a common ancestor, in anthropological usage both the nuclear family and the extended family involve connection by marriage as well as descent.

Given this background, it is no wonder that readers were confused when anthropologists writing about the whānau in the 1960s and 1970s identified it as a type of family but discussed it under headings stressing descent. Doing so was a contradiction in terms. Yet that contradiction itself signalled anthropologists' perception that the whānau was at once a descent group and something other than a descent group. The problem was one of presentation rather than understanding.

The word *traditional* is another which causes difficulty. It has often been used to identify Māori society and culture 'as they were', so that it has become in many minds a synonym for 'pre-European'. Applied in a 20th-century context, it is often taken to mean 'the same as in pre-European times', ignoring change. These usages are ambiguous and misleading. The *Concise Oxford Dictionary* defines *tradition* as 'a custom, opinion or belief handed down to posterity, especially orally or by practice' and *traditional* as 'of, based on or obtained by tradition' (1990: 1293). Numerous anthropological studies have shown that transmission orally or by practice favours flexible adaptation, modification, innovation and incorporation of new cultural elements. In New Zealand the archaeological record and comparison of accounts of the doings of the ancestors provide convincing evidence of extensive changes in technology and in social and economic organisation between first settlement and the coming of Europeans (Davidson 1984), and the same processes have been at work in post-European times. As long as this is recognised, the word traditional is the best translation I know to render the Māori phrase 'tuku iho nō ngā tūpuna' (handed down from the ancestors), and I shall use it with that meaning.

Conclusion

In their research and writing anthropologists have concentrated on studying one particular kind of whānau, a group defined on the one hand by descent and on the other by common goals and activities. During the 1970s we became increasingly aware that Māori give the word other meanings, shifting between them according to context and adding new applications as they see fit. Despite this proliferation of meaning, however, the group on which anthropologists have concentrated remains the primary referent to which the word is applied.

Anthropological studies of 'the whānau' in this primary sense (as of hapū and iwi) have focused on two periods: that of early contact in the late 18th and early 19th century, and the second half of the 20th century. Comparison of the anthropological models constructed for these two periods reveals similarities and differences, continuity and change. While much remains to be done to trace the course of these transformations and the processes at work, establishing the contrast alone has been a valuable contribution, providing a much needed counter-balance to the popular tendency to see the whānau as timeless and unchanging.

The process of transformation continues to the present day. In particular, new variations arise as migrants settle and put down roots outside their ancestral communities. The time has come to develop a definition of the whānau which both differentiates it from the groups which use it as a model and recognises variations on the basic theme.

Chapter 3

THE MANY MEANINGS
OF WHĀNAU

Ko te toka i Akiha,
he toka whitianga rā;
Ko te toka i Māpuna, koia tāu e titiro ai, ko te ripo kau.[1]

The rock at Akiha is a rock
the sun shines on;
the rock at Māpuna, all you can
see is the eddy.

Rocks covered by the sea make good fishing grounds, but if you do not recognise the signs of their presence they are dangerous. The same can be said of hidden meanings. As Māori have increasingly asserted their pride in their cultural heritage in recent years, the word whānau has come back into common use. In the 1960s it was not among the words I heard

Māori use without translation when speaking English and even in Māori it was sometimes replaced by a transliteration of family. Since about 1985 Māori have been using it frequently in both Māori and English and it appears increasingly in the speech of Pākehā and in print, often without translation. When glossed at all, whānau is typically rendered as 'family group' or 'extended family', terms which to most Pākehā indicate a collection of parent-child families. As a result misunderstandings abound, not only between Māori and Pākehā but also between Māori of different generations and with different degrees of Māori knowledge.

To avoid confusion and improve understanding, it is important to recognise that Māori people apply the word whānau to an increasingly wide variety of categories and groups.

Meanings inherited from the ancestors

Five contemporary usages are continuous with those of pre-European Māori society, though adapted where necessary to cope with change. These traditional usages are restricted in application to relatives (whanaunga) connected by descent and sometimes by marriage.

Fluent Māori speakers use whānau, firstly, for a *set of siblings*, brothers and sisters born to the same parents but excluding the latter. Best reported hearing this usage early this century, probably among the Tūhoe (1924: 343). Māori experts identify this as the original meaning of the noun, arising from its verbal form, which means 'to be born'.[2] This usage is rarely heard these days. When it does occur, it is often misinterpreted by listeners expecting one of the more common meanings.

Whānau is used by Māori, secondly, to refer to all the descendants of a relatively recent named ancestor traced through both male and female links, regardless of where they are living or whether they know or interact with each other. In Māori they are 'te uri a Mea', where 'te' may be singular or collective, uri means 'offspring, descendants' and 'Mea' is 'So-and-So'. In anthropological terminology, this is a *cognatic descent category* of limited depth. The sole criterion of inclusion is descent.

Māori use whānau, thirdly, to refer to those descendants of a relatively recent ancestor who act and interact together on an ongoing basis and identify themselves as a group by symbols such as the ancestor's name. In Māori they are equally 'te uri a Mea'. In anthropological terminology, they constitute a *cognatic descent group* of limited depth. The criteria for membership are descent plus active participation in group activities. Such groups exist independently of individuals, who often move in and out of active participation. Where in classical times members of a whānau of this kind lived and worked together as one household for much of the year, nowadays they are commonly distributed among several households.

Māori use whānau, fourthly, to refer to a group consisting of a descent group core with the addition of members' spouses and children adopted[3] from outside, a collection of individuals and parent-child families who act and interact together on an ongoing basis under a common name. This is the group which Māori identify as 'te pā harakeke', the flax bush. In anthropological terminology, this is an *extended family*. The criteria for membership are descent or connection by marriage or adoption, and active participation in group activities. In all respects except composition it is identical to the whānau descent group.

Māori sometimes apply the term whānau, fifthly, to descent groups of much greater genealogical depth, namely to hapū and iwi. In some cases this is on the grounds that they contain the word whānau in their name, for example, Te Whānau-a-Āpanui. The use of the 'a' instead of the 'o' form of the possessive in this name indicates that the original reference was to the offspring of Āpanui as a sibling set. This has been forgotten by all but the iwi experts and the meaning of the phrase is stretched to refer to a collectivity made up of the descendants of the siblings in question. Occasionally also Māori speakers use the word whānau to describe a hapū or iwi, especially when addressing an assembly of their members. Such a usage is a metaphorical extension of the fourth usage above, used rhetorically to remind hapū and iwi members of their responsibilities and appropriate behaviour towards each other.

The second, third and fourth of these usages were widespread among Māori in the 1950s and 1960s in both rural and urban areas and they have continued in importance into the 1990s. There are, however, differences of opinion about which is most important. These differences will be explored more fully in the next chapter.

Developing new meanings

In the course of this century, the word whānau has acquired a host of new meanings, some a matter of extension or convenience, some metaphorical, some creative new applications.

A sixth usage of whānau refers to the small family consisting of *one or two parents and their children.* There does not seem to have been a specific term in classic Māori for the parent-child family separate from the extended family household. Under the entry 'family', Biggs' *Complete English-Maori Dictionary* lists the terms hapori, ngare, puninga and pūtoi as well as whāmere and whānau, but reference to native speakers of Māori and to Williams' *Dictionary of the Maori Language* makes it clear that these four terms referred to categories of persons connected by common ancestry, not to parent-child families. I once heard a Māori lecturer identify the parent-child family as a hunuku but I have been unable to obtain confirmation of such a usage. Williams' *Dictionary of the Maori Language* glosses hunuku as 'family encumbrances'! Over the last century, as social, economic and religious changes resulted in increasing emphasis on the parent-child family, Māori began to refer to it either as whāmere, a transliteration of family, or as whānau. Over the last ten years, with the increasing success of the Māori language campaign, whānau has ousted whāmere as the preferred term for the parent-child family. Whānau is the only word given under family in Ngata's *English-Maori Dictionary*, but the example given could apply to either the parent-child family or the extended family (Ngata 1993: 146).

Today, in the 1990s, whānau is frequently used, seventhly, for a group which is not based clearly on descent but is made up of kin related in a variety of ways, who act and interact for common ends, identify themselves by a common name and model themselves on the whānau as extended family. I once described this sort of group as a *kin-cluster* (Metge 1964: 166, 169-70). Such groups are typically located away from the communities where their members are tāngata whenua, usually in a city. They are formed for reasons of convenience; without the binding power of descent they fall apart more easily, more often and more completely than extended families (see p 42).

On occasion the whānau can only be described, eighthly, as an *elastic band*. Māori who would normally apply the word to a group of limited size stretch it elastically when it suits them to do so. At the ordination of a Māori kaumātua to the priesthood of the Anglican church in the 1960s, the cathedral was packed by kinsfolk who had travelled long distances to be there. The presiding bishop, a Pākehā, invited members of the new priest's whānau to take communion with him. According to a niece, 'the whole of Ngāti Pōrou and Whānau-a-Āpanui went up'. When the bishop exclaimed: 'They can't all be whānau!' a Māori priest explained: 'If you are a forty-second cousin, you are whānau.' He might have added: 'on occasions like this!' Several years ago I heard a speaker on radio talkback say: 'Whānau? It's not only blood kin, it's ethnic, it means all Māori. The moment I walk into a group of Māori women I am part of their whānau.'

Fluent speakers of Māori feel that it is appropriate to use the word whānau, ninthly, to greet or refer to an *assembly of people of like mind and interests gathered for a common purpose*. This is another metaphorical extension, adopted to express or elicit feelings of solidarity on particular occasions. In Anglican church services, worship leaders address the congregation with the phrase 'E te whānau!', where formerly they would have said 'Brothers and sisters!' When I spoke about the many meanings of whānau at the 1994 conference of the New Zealand Association of Social Anthropologists, Matiu Waimea (attending at my invitation) said to me afterwards was: 'If I had addressed the meeting, I would have said, kia ora tātou, e te whānau. It was a group of people gathered together in good faith for a common purpose.'

Increasingly whānau is being used, tenthly, for an ad hoc *action-group* mobilised on behalf of a particular person to support him or her in a testing situation: a job interview, a public speaking engagement, taking up a new appointment, appearing for trial before a court or disciplinary committee. Sometimes those in attendance all belong to a single whānau descent group or extended family, often they are a mixture of members from at

least two, and increasingly they include non-kin, Māori and
Pākehā friends and colleagues. Māori language experts approve
this metaphorical extension to non-kin provided that those
involved are genuine friends and supporters but they can be
scathing if they suspect that numbers have been inflated to make
an impression.

Finally, there has been an amazingly rapid expansion in the
metaphorical use of whānau to refer to groupings of people who
are *not* connected by kinship, let alone descent. Radically new
usages are continually emerging. I can distinguish another five
applications: by the time this book is published there may well
be more.

In 1974 representatives of the Department of Education and
the Ministry of Works and Development jointly developed a new
form of secondary school organisation, looked for a name and
chose 'the whanau system' (sic).[4] Under this system a 'whanau'
is a group of teachers and up to 250 students from Forms 3 to 7
who occupy a largely self-contained and flexible block of class
and common rooms for a large part of their school life. Some
schools have only one or two 'whanau' within the normal
structure; others are organised entirely on the 'whanau' principle.
The idea has now been adopted in primary schools also. Each
school develops the concept in its own particular way, but
generally the emphasis is on what is described as 'a family
atmosphere', involving mixed age and ability groups, shared
teaching, close, personalised interaction between staff and
students, flexibility, choice, self-directed and cooperative
learning, and integrated studies. An increasing number of
'whanau' of this kind are bilingual, using Māori as well as English
for learning and teaching. A few use other second languages.
Adoption of the Māori word, originally an afterthought, has had
a powerful influence on the way these school 'whanau' have
developed by stressing whānau values such as aroha, mutual
support, cooperation and unity.

Very early in its history the Kōhanga Reo movement adopted
the term whānau for the collectivity of children and adults
associated with a particular kōhanga reo. In rural areas the
members of a kōhanga reo whānau are mostly kinsfolk to each
other, but they are usually drawn from several whānau linked in

one or two hapū, and they welcome local residents from outside the hapū as members. In urban areas kōhanga reo whānau typically comprise non-kin from a variety of backgrounds, including Pākehā.

> However, the kohanga reo whānau resembles the traditional whānau closely in that it involves a wide age range, from the very young to the elderly, and persons playing a variety of roles . . . Finally, and most importantly, the kohanga reo whānau is committed to the values on which the whānau is based and its methods of operation.
> (Government Review Team 1988: 20)

As children from kōhanga reo have moved into primary schools, the word whānau has come to be used for classes participating in bilingual and Māori language immersion programmes, and sometimes for their classroom bases. These differ from the secondary school 'whanau' in aspects of organisation and teaching method, notably the use of Māori as the language of instruction.

The word whānau is frequently used in the identifying titles chosen by groups associated with non-traditional marae established in urban areas, at schools and tertiary institutions, and in government departments. Such groups typically include members of many different iwi and some Pākehā. Instead of using the name of an ancestor as their reference point, they commonly qualify the title Whānau with the name of the marae or of the meeting house: for example, Te Whānau o Te Herenga Waka at Victoria University of Wellington and Te Whānau o Tū Tahi Tonu at the Auckland College of Education. However, when the Wellington College of Education was looking for a Māori title to complement its English one, Te Whānau o Ako Pai was chosen after lengthy discussion to refer not to the group which looks after the College's meeting house Te Ako Pai but to the whole College, as a considered symbolic statement about the way staff and students wished to see themselves.[5]

Sports teams and other clubs also often describe themselves as a whānau. The aerobic champions of New Zealand for 1987 attributed their achievement in part to the fact that they 'encouraged a sense of whānau for camaraderie and support'

(*Dominion*, Wellington, 1 May 1987). The five-member team consisted of Māori from four different tribes and a Rarotongan.

Most of these non-traditional meanings refer to groups with an ongoing life separate from that of individuals, who can and do move in and out of membership. By describing their group as a whānau, members signal to themselves and the world at large that they have modelled it on the whānau extended family. They use the word whānau as symbol and charter, a constant reminder of the whānau values to which they aspire.

Three meanings (the eighth, ninth and tenth) differ from the rest in referring not to groups but to temporary collections of people assembled ad hoc, for a particular purpose, and subsequently disbanding. In the case of the 'elastic band', those involved are relatives, though from beyond the whānau's usual limits. In the other cases, they often include or are entirely composed of non-relatives.

Shifting between meanings

Not only do Māori use the word whānau with this wide variety of meanings, but they frequently shift between different meanings, often in a single sentence, just as English speakers do with family. This causes no problems when both parties are aware of what is happening, as in conversations between kaumātua of similar age and experience. But if one party is unable to follow these shifts in meaning he or she is likely to become confused, jump to the wrong conclusion and respond inappropriately, with potentially disastrous results.

Ample evidence of this tendency to shift between meanings and of the confusion which results is afforded by the policy statement entitled *Maatua Whangai* (sic),[6] which leaves anyone not accustomed to Māori discourse completely baffled (Māori Affairs-Social Welfare-Justice 1986).

The Mātua Whāngai programme was developed jointly by three government departments with the aim of diverting young Māori from social welfare and penal institutions to the care of their own iwi. The first step in this process takes place at the iwi level with the establishment of Mātua Whāngai working groups (rōpu), both on the tribe's home territory ('Tribal Rōpu') and among tribal emigrants in other, mainly urban areas ('Taura Here Rōpu'). These rōpu build up registers of families affiliated to particular iwi, act as liaison between families and government departments concerning the placement of children and young persons, monitor the quality of care given, and provide moral and financial support to the care-givers.

In the booklet *Maatua Whangai* the whānau is defined as 'the family, the size of which varies from grandparents, parents and children to an entire tribe' (p 10); in other words, the word whānau is applied to a three-generation family, to the tribe as a whole, and to groups between these two extremes. This and comparable applications of whānau to 'the entire tribe' should, I suggest, be interpreted as a metaphorical extension, emphasising that tribal members are kinsfolk whose behaviour to each other should be modelled on that of members of the same whānau. Both the distinction and the connection between whānau, hapū and iwi are clarified in the next sentences: 'The whānau for the purposes of this report is the basic unit of care . . . The hapū is a group of whānau. The iwi are groups of hapū that converge back to an eponymous ancestor . . . The basic unit of care can be one of any or many nuclear families.'

On the next page, the whānau is described as 'made up of maternal and paternal grandparents and their brothers and sisters—father and mother, their brothers and sisters on both sides and all their offspring (children)'. Charting the relatives so named shows that they can be traced back to eight ancestors, the parents of the four grandparents. In technical terms, the relatives so listed belong not to one descent category but to eight overlapping ones. They are not a descent group, not an extended family, but (in anthropological terms) a kindred, that is, a collection of kinsfolk centred on the children of 'father and mother'.

Elsewhere in the text (on pp 6 and 10), whānau occurs linked with hapū and iwi by hyphens: whānau-hapū-iwi (in that order).[7] This combination is used as a shorthand term for 'Māori social organisation', which is seen as consisting of the linkage of these three types of social group in a single framework. This is clear from the contexts in which the combination occurs and from the Māori statement on p 6: 'Ko te Kaupapa Maatua Whāngai kua

tuhia nei, kei te whakahoki i tera tauira, otira, ma te whānau, ma
te hapū, ma te iwi hei whakahaere ano i ona tikanga ake.' ('The
Mātua Whāngai Programme set out here constitutes a return to
the pattern of former times, enabling the whānau, the hapū and
the iwi once again to manage its affairs in accordance with its
own practices and values.') The word tribe is sometimes used in
the same way, so that references to 'the tribe' or 'the iwi' may
indicate either the tribe as a particular kind of group, different
from the whānau, or the total Māori social order, including the
whānau. The ambiguous term 'Tribal Whānau Development'
(p 4) can be taken to refer both to the tribe's responsibility to
assist whānau to develop and to the development of tribal
organisation on the model (that is, embodying the values) of the
whānau.

Conclusion

Māori people use the word whānau with a wide variety of
meanings. Four of these—sibling set, cognatic descent category,
cognatic descent group and extended family—have their roots
in the pre-European Māori social order, but the two last-named
have undergone significant changes in function in response to
changing circumstances. There are also many derived and new
meanings, developed to meet the challenges of new social
situations. In particular there has been an explosive increase in
the metaphorical use of the word for groups which are not based
on descent or kinship connection but which aspire to the quality
of group life associated with the whānau in people's minds.

New usages should not be dismissed as wrong: the people
who use a language have every right to develop it in ways that
suit their purposes and meet their needs. In practice however
some usages prove to be more, some less, useful than others.
Above all, it is vitally important that those who hear the word
whānau used or wish to use it themselves take the time to check
out which of its many meanings is intended and which is
appropriate in the particular context.

Chapter 4

THE WHĀNAU WHICH COMES FIRST TO MIND

He kūaka mārangaranga,
kotahi te manu i tau ki te tāhuna,
tau atu, tau atu, tau atu ē.¹

Godwits take off to flock in the air, one bird lands on the
sandbank, then another, and another, and another.

E ach year flocks of godwits fly thousands of miles from
Siberia to summer in New Zealand. If startled while
feeding in the estuaries of Northland, they take off and
fly as a flock; then the braver individuals peel off and return to
earth one by one, followed by the rest, until the flock is feeding

together again. Like a flock of godwits, members of the same whānau alternate between acting individually and as a group.

Having established that the word whānau has not one but many meanings, we can now ask which of these many meanings is the *primary* referent for contemporary Māori, that is, the meaning which springs to mind first when they hear or read the word, the meaning most likely to be intended when they use the word without qualification. The root meaning (a sibling set excluding parents) no longer fills that role; indeed it is known to relatively few.

When asked to define *the* whānau, the concept which came to mind *first* on hearing the word, the kai-whakaatu I questioned typically responded with a list of relatives of their own by name or relationship. At first hearing this often seemed to be a descent category, the descendants of a fairly recent ancestor, but further enquiry usually revealed that those named kept in touch, supported each other in major and minor crises, regularly worked together for common purposes, and identified themselves collectively by the name of a common ancestor. In short, they constituted a *corporate group* as defined on p 47.

Whānau membership

What sort of a corporate group this was, however, was not clear, because the respondents held differing views about the inclusion or exclusion of relatives not descended from the ancestor chosen as reference point.

Some respondents, mostly older ones, restricted whānau membership to descendants of the chosen ancestor, excluding their husbands and wives and any adopted children who did not share that descent. Asked whom she regarded as belonging to her whānau, Atakura Waru replied:

> I would say the descendants of my great-grandparent ... I would include my children and grandchildren but not my husband. I will never be a member of his whānau. I don't have a sense of responsibility to transmit things to him either. My responsibility is to protect and transmit to my children because they are part of the rope of [my] people.

Defining whānau membership in this way identifies the whānau as a cognatic descent group of limited depth. It means that one person is clearly marked out as foundation ancestor.

Some respondents, mostly younger ones, extended the limits of whānau membership to include husbands, wives and adopted children in addition to the descendants of the chosen ancestor. Defining whānau membership in this way identifies the whānau as an extended family. It means that two people, a husband and wife, are marked out as foundation ancestors.

Respondents of all ages alternated equivocally between the two positions, unwilling or unable to make a clear-cut choice. A kaumātua in his sixties whose parents are dead, Nika Pirikawa, first limited his whānau to 'just the close family, my own children, my brothers and sisters, my brothers' and sisters' children', a definition which emphasised descent, then changed his mind and redefined it as 'my children, their husbands and wives and children, my brothers and sisters and their husbands and wives and children', this time including the spouses. (Failing to include his own wife was, I am sure, an oversight.)

The difficulty created by this divergence of opinion about who belongs to the whānau is more apparent than real. It melts away once it is recognised that a whānau descent group and a whānau extended family defined with reference to a common ancestor overlap to a very large extent in membership and share identical functions and goals. The whānau extended family consists of the members of the whānau descent group plus in-married spouses and those adopted children who are not descended from the foundation ancestor through a birth parent. The whānau descent group consists of those members of the extended family who trace descent from the foundation ancestor through both male and female links. Members of a descent group and extended family which overlap in this way work together as one group under the one ancestral name and the same leaders.

Given that the whānau descent group is contained within the whānau extended family, is it really necessary to distinguish them in this way? Why not accept extended family as the primary meaning of whānau? I believe that making this conceptual distinction *is* necessary, because Māori make it, especially those knowledgeable in tikanga Māori. Under certain circumstances

and for certain purposes they identify one person as foundation
ancestor, recognise only his or her descendants as 'real' or 'full'
members of the whānau and restrict (or try to restrict) key roles
as front persons for the whānau to these descendants, explicitly
excluding the spouses and adopted children who do not share
that descent.

To appreciate fully that form of the whānau which Māori
recognise as primary, I find it necessary to hold these two
meanings in tension, not giving absolute priority to one or the
other but recognising that each assumes priority for different
purposes. The whānau can be likened to a holographic postcard,
which achieves a three dimensional effect by incorporating several
overlapping images. While the subject is essentially a unity,
different aspects come to the fore when it is viewed from different
angles. In the case of the whānau, descent is emphasised, and the
meaning of whānau as descent group comes to the fore, when
the focus is on group property deriving from ancestors, the choice
of public representatives and relations with hapū and iwi. General
family relations are emphasised, and the whānau as extended
family comes to the fore, when the focus is on mutual support,
child-raising and the organising of hui. When the whānau is
viewed from one perspective, the descent group is of primary
importance and the extended family is seen as an extension of it.
When it is viewed from another perspective, the extended family
appears to be primary and the descent group a core contained
within it.

Given this overlap between the whānau descent group and
the whānau extended family, the whānau in its most important,
primary meaning is most usefully thought of as one group rather
than two and identified by the Māori term rather than an English
one. If an English translation is considered necessary, extended
family is to be preferred as the wider referent, but it is far from
satisfactory, since it fails to indicate the importance of descent
in whānau organisation. In the following chapters I shall
mostly use 'the whānau' untranslated to refer to the two kinds
of groups united in one and 'whānau descent group' and 'whānau
extended family' to make it clear when the emphasis is on one or
the other.

Group symbols

The members of a whānau express their group consciousness by the use of collective symbols. The most obvious of these is a name, usually the name of the foundation ancestor combined with the words whānau or family: Te Whānau ō Wiremu, Te Whānau Wiremu, the Wiremu Whānau, the Wiremu Family, the Wiremus. Where the ancestor identified as foundation is male, as is mostly the case, the name is either his surname or his personal name adopted as a surname by later generations. Because descent and affiliation to whānau can be traced through women as well as men, many members of the whānau do not themselves bear the whānau name as surname: not infrequently those who do are outnumbered by those who do not. Where a whānau is attached to a particular land base and community through a female tupuna, members sometimes choose her name as whānau symbol, sometimes her husband's.

The name derived from the foundation ancestor is much more than a useful identifying tag: it has symbolic power. As Atakura Waru pointed out:

> In my home context they never refer to me as a Waru, they say I am married to a Waru. They gave me my grandfather's name, so that they would have full control over me and my upbringing.

Where a female ancestor was married to an outsider, use of his name marks out a whānau as different in the community. This may serve as a reminder of powerful connections elsewhere but more often is associated with the marginalisation of its members in the community.

As a further defining symbol many whānau add the name of the place they regard as their main base. Until well into the 1970s it was taken for granted that this would be in an ancestral community, but today, as a result of migration (between rural areas as well as to urban areas), many whānau are firmly based in other places. Thus the Wiremu whānau based in Puriri, where its ancestor was a landholder, emphasises its connection with that district to differentiate itself from the Wiremu whānau of Totara

50 kilometres away, which stems from a Wiremu who took up residence in his wife's community, and from the Wiremu whānau formed by emigrants from Puriri based in Auckland.

Whānau which have a whānau marae may use that as a symbol of their identity. For other whānau the home of the senior couple often assumes similar functions as main gathering place and symbolic tūrangawaewae (land base).[2]

The functions of the whānau

In its primary meaning, the word *whānau* identifies a working group, a group that *works*, literally and figuratively, a group that has functions.

Whānau members typically live distributed among several households. These may be close to each other but some at least are likely to be scattered at a distance and even located in different districts, both rural and urban. These households manage their own day-to-day affairs but also maintain a flow of communication and support between them. Whānau members also combine to work together as a group on an 'occasional' basis, in both senses of the word: from time to time and on special occasions.

The functions which whānau carry out in this way are of five main kinds.

Firstly, there is the support and succour of individual members and parent-child families. Such help is usually provided quietly and informally by one or more members acting in response to perceived need or direct request and according to their ability to do so. It includes: lending or more often giving money, from small sums to large; passing on used clothing and equipment; providing and sharing transport; making land available for gardens; sharing harvests of fruit, crops and seafood or a shrewd buy at the markets; providing labour and skills (carpentry, sewing, painting, motor maintenance) for nothing or at a cut rate; and providing accommodation and meals for short terms and long, for children with or without parents, for holidays and in times of need. Those who are well off give more in money, while those whose incomes are low contribute in other ways, especially labour. Repayment is made on a generalised basis, not precisely targeted, and often in a different form. It may be made to the original giver's dependents rather than to him or herself, and is commonly delayed, for weeks, months or even years, until an appropriate occasion. Economic support is both an expression and a concomitant of moral support.

The first study to focus specifically on this aspect of whānau functioning, *Tā Te Whānau Ohangā: The Economics of the Whānau* by Julia Taiapa, was completed in 1994. The evidence it contains accords with and amplifies my own experience, as summarised in the previous paragraph. In particular, Taiapa concludes that households whose members are active in whānau are not independent economic units: resources flow between household and whānau, with both positive and negative effects on household economics.

> For those Māori families involved in active whānau, it can be expected that an unspecified and unpredictable amount of the total income may go out of the household for whānau purposes, often taking precedence over basic subsistence needs. . . . Loans, gifts of money and goods can make a major difference to standard of living in low income households, just as the giving of money for whānau purposes can drain the finances of those who have money to give. (Taiapa 1994: 53)

Taiapa also notes that tension between household and whānau needs can affect relations between spouses (Taiapa 1994: 39, 49).

Giving within the whānau is defended by thoughtful whānau members as a form of investment or insurance. As Taiapa points out, the returns are social rather than economic. Givers cannot count on receiving repayment exactly when needed or in the form desired (Taiapa 1994: 51). Most, however, consider that any short-term financial embarrassment suffered as a result is outweighed by other considerations, especially moral support and their own sense of satisfaction. Taiapa sums up informants' views on giving to whānau in these words:

> Just as parents expressed giving to children as part of the nature of being a parent, so giving to whānau is part of the

nature of belonging to whānau. Being able to give was
important and highly valued. It gave the giver pleasure . . .
It was not a matter of being paid back. (Taiapa 1994: 40)

Closely associated with this first function is the second, the
care and upbringing of the children of group members, who are
regarded as the responsibility, not of their parents only, but of
the whānau as a whole. This aspect of whānau action is dealt
with in detail in Chapters 8 to 10.

Thirdly, there is the care and management of group property.
In some cases, this includes an ancestral land base with one or
more of the buildings necessary for use as a marae (meeting-house,
dining hall, kitchen) and/or a family home. Sometimes this land
base has the status of a Māori reserve granted by the Māori Land
Court but often it is held on ordinary Māori freehold title in the
names of several deceased and older whānau members. Some of
the existing whānau marae were founded in the 1920s and 1930s
at the time of the great revival of marae building led by Sir Apirana
Ngata. Others were built in the 1950s and 1960s, despite
Government policy which granted marae reserve status and
building subsidies only to hapū. Urban migration resulted in
many whānau marae falling into disrepair, but as urban Māori
revive an interest in or actually return to their ancestral communities, these are being resurrected by descendants of the original
builders.

Whether or not they have a marae, many whānau have portable
taonga which they regard as belonging to the descent group
collectively. These comprise articles of recognisably Māori
provenance, such as bone and greenstone ornaments, weapons,
tokotoko (walking sticks used by orators), woven flax cloaks,
whakapapa books and photographs, often dating from the
nineteenth century. Mostly these taonga are held by senior
members of the whānau; sometimes they are placed in a museum
or bank vault on terms which enable them to be retrieved when
needed for special occasions like tangihanga and inter-tribal
gatherings. Whatever the position at law, those who hold them
or hold the right to uplift them from their place of safe-keeping
are regarded as kai-tiaki (custodians). It is their responsibility
not only to see to the present safety of such taonga but to provide

for it in the future by choosing a successor from within the whānau. Usually taonga held by men are passed on to their sons, and those held by women to their daughters, but if the kai-tiaki consider their own offspring unsuitable, they may survey the whole whānau for a successor.

Also reckoned as a taonga belonging to the whānau is mātauranga Māori (Māori knowledge), whether it takes the form of general knowledge, specialist skills such as carving, weaving, whai-kōrero (speech-making) and waiata (song-poems), or knowledge of the ancestors, lands, taonga and stories of the whānau itself. As with other taonga, holders of such knowledge are expected to pass it on to younger whānau members. This is not an easy task, when whānau members come together only occasionally and young people's interests lie in other directions. In recent years however, with an increase in appreciation of tikanga Māori in society in general, many kaumātua have been delighted to be sought out as mentors by younger relatives.

Some of this knowledge is stored in 'whakapapa books', which often contain stories and waiata as well as whakapapa. Such books are never complete in themselves. The Māori experts who compiled them omitted some details because they were highly tapu and rarely noted the source, date and place of the material they recorded, holding such details in their heads. This makes it imperative that access to whakapapa books is amplified by instruction and guidance from their custodians.

Whānau knowledge is most often and most effectively trans-mitted through personal contact and in the form of stories (kōrero). Kaumātua recall that, when they were young, whānau members commonly gathered at the home of the senior couple on Sunday afternoons and sat around yarning, on the grass, on the verandah and in the kitchen. Often there was one particularly gifted storyteller round whom the children clustered. Many also heard stories from older relatives (grandparents, aunts and uncles) who lived with them. While the frequency of such sessions is greatly reduced in the 1990s, a good deal of reminiscing still takes place when families get together in homes or at the marae. Whānau reunions usually include special sessions of instruction in whakapapa and whānau history. Perhaps the best place to hear whānau stories is in the kitchen at the marae where the workers talk while preparing and cleaning up after meals.

The stories told in these ways and places are not weighty stories about distant ancestors, but more personal stories about whānau members of past and present generations and kōrero pakiwaitara (light-hearted, entertaining stories). Many feature the whānau's land base and the taniwha and kai-tiaki (guardian animals) living there and are intended to teach the young in particular about the nature of their environment and the dangers lurking there. These stories are recognised as whānau property as surely as tangible objects. Whānau members who want to share them with a wider audience through books and tapes are expected to seek approval from other whānau members first. Failure to do so causes conflict and division in the whānau.

The fourth function of the whānau is the organisation of hui (large-scale gatherings usually attended by guests) to mark important events in the life of whānau members or of the whānau as a whole. While each iwi has its own rules governing the conduct of hui, these vary in detail rather than basic principle (Metge 1976: 246-64; Salmond 1975; Tauroa 1986: 111-14).

The most important of these hui is the tangihanga, the formal gathering to mourn for someone who has died. Normally the whānau bears the responsibility of organising and underwriting tangihanga for its members, providing the appropriate welcome, accommodation and food for all who come to mourn with them over a two to three day period. (If the deceased was a major public figure, however, the hapū takes over.) Members of the whānau pani (the bereaved immediate family of the deceased) are relieved of the burden of organisation by relatives less closely related: the women sit alongside the coffin receiving the mourners, while the men spend some time there but also carry out specific physical tasks such as digging the grave. The reception of visitors, the karanga (calling on to the marae) and whai-kōrero (speech-making) on behalf of the whānau are carried out by whānau members outside the whānau pani and such visitors as they invite to join them.

The whānau also organises hui to celebrate weddings, twenty-first birthdays, the unveiling of memorial gravestones and exceptional achievements such as winning a scholarship and being named on honours lists.

Then there are the whānau hui designed to celebrate and strengthen whānau solidarity. Whānau members gather, with invited friends and relatives, to celebrate significant stages in the building or renovation of their marae, from the ritual marking out of the foundations to the lifting of the last tapu at a formal opening. Reunions, large and small, are attended mainly by whānau members. In Kōtare in the 1950s and 1960s, most local whānau moved out to the isolated west coast for the summer holidays, setting up large tent camps, ordering stores in bulk but living mainly on seafoods collected and shared cooperatively. Nowadays, when the descendants of the former campers mostly live in the city, many return yearly at Christmas and New Year, to camp on the coast or to stay with relatives in tents, caravans and double garages built for the purpose. At these annual get-togethers, whānau members hold annual general meetings of whānau clubs and increasingly provide teaching sessions on Māori language, tikanga and whakapapa. From time to time, whānau with common origins combine to stage a really large reunion to which they invite all the descendants of the chosen ancestor, including those who are Pākehā. In such cases the whānau members still living in the ancestral community do most of the organising, but others engage in fundraising to assist them. (A detailed account of a reunion is in Chapter 7.)

As with informal support, contributing to whānau hui can be a major drain on the budgets of the whānau's constituent households, sometimes leading to tension between spouses with different loyalties, but the costs are generally considered to be outweighed by the intangible rewards. In her report on the economics of the whānau, Taiapa concludes:

> Participation in whānau events such as tangi offers spiritual, personal and cultural enrichment which most of the respondents claimed to value far above the money they put in. . . . Participation in marae activity and whānau life confers meaning and value on a Māori quite independently of their job and earning level. . . . The overall impression left by the group discussion of whānau activities was one of enjoyment, commitment and energy. Whatever the cost in money terms, life and enthusiasm flowed through

speakers' descriptions of events, processes and people. This
enthusiasm suggests that whānau can be an important
source of self esteem, and make their members' lives rich
and meaningful. The money invested is returned in a
different form. (1994: 51-52)

A whānau which is functioning effectively also carries out a
fifth function: dealing with its own internal problems and
conflicts. How this is done will be explored in Chapter 13.

Organisation

In carrying out these functions, whānau organise themselves with
varying degrees of formality. Some have no continuing framework but call special meetings to make decisions and lay plans as
and when the need arises. Some form kōmiti (clubs) or kōtahi-
tanga (unions), formal associations which hold more or less
regular meetings, keep formal minutes recording discussion and
decisions, and use receipt books and a bank account in the
management of group money.

'Front' roles as kai-kōrero (speech-makers), kai-karanga
(callers) and kai-whakahaere (directors of proceedings) at hui and
as chairpersons of whānau kōmiti are filled by the most senior
descendants of the whānau ancestor fitted for the task. Behind
the scenes at hui, those with the greatest expertise and experience
take charge of particular aspects of the work to be done: the
ordering of stores, the hangi making, preparing the meeting-
house, the preparation and cooking of food, the setting of tables
and serving of guests, keeping accounts and so on. Other members
work under their direction according to personal preference,
ability or the need for workers.

Popular perception that the whānau is dominated by a single
kaumātua and that this kaumātua is invariably male does not
accord either with the Māori ideal or usual practice. (The word
kaumātua applies to both sexes. Males of that status are koroua,
women are kuia.) In most whānau men and women of kaumātua
status work in partnership, recognising each others' abilities and
special areas of expertise as complementary. The eldest sibling
(mātāmua—in some iwi the eldest male sibling) of the most senior

generation has a special status in the whānau: he (or she) is te kai-pupuri i te mana, 'the one who holds the mana' on behalf of the group. While in one sense this status cannot be taken away, in another it depends on his actions being approved by the group. If too dictatorial, he (or she) is likely to be resented, resisted and if necessary limited to a ceremonial figurehead. The most effective mātāmua sits back, listens to the debate, and sums up the consensus decision at the end. In many whānau, several kaumātua, siblings or first cousins to each other, form a collective leadership, with the mātāmua acting as coordinator and public spokesperson.

Within this collective leadership the kuia make a special contribution. They supply the leading kai-karanga, whose role is the essential complement to that of kai-kōrero: they issue the invitation without which visitors cannot enter the marae and in doing so set the tone for the subsequent exchange of greetings. In some iwi selected kuia may engage in speech-making during hui in the presence of visitors, usually after the welcome ceremony is over and inside the meeting-house. When visitors are not present, the kuia take a very active part in discussion and decision-making, not infrequently dominating them by force of personality, Māori knowledge and practical good sense.

Often a koroua and a kuia work as particular partners. Most often they are brother and sister, sometimes husband and wife. In the former case the partnership is an equal one, in the latter the in-married spouse plays a supporting role to the one who belongs by descent.

The success of whānau operations also requires cooperation between the generations. While the kaumātua fill ceremonial roles out front, the middle-aged cope with the more physically demanding work behind the scenes as work supervisors at hui, as leaders of the haka team, as secretaries and treasurers of whānau clubs. Young people and children usually carry out the less skilled tasks under supervision, working their way up to positions of responsibility over the years. Forward-looking kaumātua may choose to push those who are fluent in Māori into responsibilities beyond their years, encouraging them to practice as speech-makers and callers at whānau hui. This has its pitfalls, since it can encourage whakahīhī (conceit) in the favoured and resentment in those who feel overlooked.

Inevitably, given the differences between the generations in experience, knowledge and interests, tensions surface from time to time, especially between kaumātua who hold to conservative ways and young people with wide experience of the modern world, whether acquired in academia or from the popular culture of the streets. Yet while the kaumātua have more mana, they are also linked by descent and by special ties of affection to their grandchildren. In the whānau more than in hapū or iwi, kaumātua and rangatahi, old and young, have strong reasons for working towards accommodation. Observing traditional tikanga, wise kaumātua recognise twin responsibilities to support their grand-children in their personal development and to feed them with knowledge of tikanga Māori; as young people become aware of their identity as Māori they realise that it has its roots in the whānau and what their elders have to teach.

The whānau, time and change

Change is an integral part of life for every whānau. Its member-ship is constantly changing as existing members are lost to death or competing claims on their loyalty and as new ones are acquired by birth, adoption and marriage. Individually, members grow older and develop in various ways, marrying, migrating, acquiring new skills and ideas, losing mobility and physical capability with age, moving periodically into new roles.

Characteristically, the whānau itself passes through a cycle of growth, segmentation and regeneration. As the members of a whānau increase in number and in genealogical distance from the foundation ancestor, internal tensions and divisions become more marked. Sections of the whānau strain towards independ-ence, contributing less and less to joint activities. Sooner or later they break up into separate groups.

Newly independent whānau may drift apart until they lose touch completely, but usually they remember their former connection, turn to each other first for help in trouble and some-times hold joint reunions. Often they continue to identify them-selves as 'a whānau', but in this context the word refers to a descent category rather than a descent group.

In addition, whānau have, over the last 200 years, gone through a series of irreversible, historical changes. The most traumatic were associated with incorporation into a capitalist market economy and urban migration, but conversion to Christianity, participation in wars at home and overseas and technological advances in transport and mass media have also had important effects.

For many reasons, the extent and pace of change has increased over the last 25 to 30 years. Urban migration accelerated in the 1960s as a result of a shift in emphasis from small- to large-scale farming operations and the Government's policy of relocation. By 1981 60% of the Māori population was living in the main urban centres and 21% in secondary and minor ones; in the 1990s the total Māori urban population is stabilised at 82%. As a result, only a small minority of Māori now live in their ancestral communities. The large majority are living elsewhere, often outside the territory of their own iwi and inside that of another, dispersed among members of other iwi, Pākehā and other ethnic groups. Though no statistics are available, it is obvious that the Māori urban population includes a large and rising proportion of Māori who have been brought up in the city, often in families which have been established there for two or three generations. Māori rural communities have suffered generations of emigration, some more than others, losing both their more troublesome and their more able members.[3]

From the early 1970s the number of one parent families increased steeply to 40% of all Māori families with dependent children in 1991. During the 1980s the level of unemployment rose to 27% of Māori men aged 15 or more in 1992 and 23% of Māori women. Although rural areas were seriously affected, there was a significant increase in return migration from urban to rural areas, mostly from Auckland to Northland. [4]

The period as a whole was marked by a significant rise in Māori consciousness of identity, expressed in an efflorescence in traditional and contemporary Māori arts and Māori initiatives in education, health, welfare and justice.

These changes have had the effect of greatly increasing the diversity of whānau in form and operation, while reducing the differences between those of urban and rural areas. They have placed most whānau under stress. Some have become dysfunctional and some have fallen apart without regenerating, but others have risen magnificently to the challenge, developing new and effective ways of overcoming the problems facing them.

Whānau in the wider context

Whānau are rarely isolated, stand-alone groups. Typically they are connected with others by ties of descent from the common ancestors, intermarriage and long association.

As we have just seen, some whānau have particularly close ties with each other because they began life as branches of a single group.

According to the accepted Māori model of Māori social organisation, every whānau should be able to place itself as belonging to at least one hapū and one iwi, the connection being thought of as a descent line linking the ancestors of iwi, hapū and whānau.[5] Whether a whānau is based in its ancestor's home community or away from it, being able to establish connection with one or more hapū and iwi has advantages. It grounds whānau members in the Māori world and enables them to apply for assistance from marae committees, Mātua Whāngai rōpu, and Tribal Trust Boards. Many whānau rely on their kaumātua to keep records of their hapū antecedents and ancestry, especially when they are based in or in touch with an ancestral community. Some urban-based whānau, concentrating on their present location and problems, have lost touch with their hapū and iwi. The network of Māori kinship connections is so extensive that they can usually find someone to supply the information when they want it.

Māori active in whānau mostly take spouses from outside their own whānau. While few whānau observe or even know about the traditional tapu on marrying kin closer than third cousin, young people usually find outsiders more attractive than kin as partners. Where both spouses belong to functioning whānau, their union brings the two whānau into close association, especially when it is marked by a formal wedding ceremony and hui, which they share in staging. Children born of the union tie the two whānau more closely still, since they have tūpuna in each and potentially at least belong to both.

It is one of the distinctive features of Māori social organisation that descent from ancestors (and ascent from descendants back to ancestors) is traced through links of both sexes. This has two important consequences. First, individuals have many descent lines and can claim membership, if they wish, in more than one descent group at each level of social organisation, that is, in more than one whānau, more than one hapū, and more than one iwi. However, descent alone is not enough to close the membership of these three types of groups. For *full* as distinct from nominal or potential membership, those who are eligible on grounds of descent have to back up their claims with active participation in group affairs (take ahi kā), especially as regards whānau and hapū.

Secondly, whānau are both optional and non-exclusive. Every whānau includes members who belong to the whānau of their other, in-married parent or that of their spouse. Many Māori juggle loyalty and commitments to two or three whānau, sometimes favouring one, sometimes trying to keep an even balance, sometimes switching priorities with changing circumstances.

Conclusion

In this chapter I have drawn on my own experience and discussions with Māori to abstract and summarise the distinctive features of the whānau of primary reference, that is, the features that make it different from other kinds of family. In previous writings, I have described this process as constructing a model, a simplified picture of the main features of the phenom-enon under study. This concentrates on what is general, common and relevant and leaves the idiosyncratic out of account. To use another metaphor, it paints a picture of a class of objects, places or peoples, with the aim of representing the quintessential characteristics of the class, not of particular members of it. In Māori, it is an ahuatanga, a likeness, a reproduction of the general form of the original while remaining separate from it.

One of the problems with constructed models is the difficulty of building in a sense of time. That is why the metaphor of te pā harakeke is so important: it is a constant reminder that the whānau is continually in the process of growth and change.

The model of the whānau presented here is a revision of my

own earlier writings on the subject. I resolve the problem of whether the whānau is a descent group or extended family by insisting that it is both, one or the other being emphasised in particular contexts. I identify a descent group core, group consciousness and repeated corporate action as the defining features of the whānau. Discarding the idea of an ancestral land base as essential, I now recognise extended families living away from such a base as whānau in the primary sense as long as they have a descent group core, though I continue to exclude kin clusters, which lack one. Where formerly I identified rural whānau as the primary whānau and regarded urban whānau as a departure from it, I now prefer to place rural and urban whānau with a descent group core on an equal footing, regarding them as variations on a common theme.

Real life whānau do not and should not be expected to conform too closely to the constructed model. Each has its own character, its own degree of integration and effectiveness, created and recreated out of the interaction between the personalities of its members and the circumstances of time and place. Members' right to work out their own identity and tikanga must always be respected.

Chapter 5

WHĀNAU VALUES

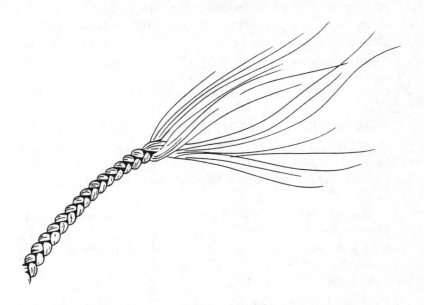

He kōpū puta tahi, he taura whiri tātou;
whiringa a nuku, whiringa a rangi, te whatīa e.[1]

Issue of one womb, we are a rope woven of many strands;
woven on earth, woven in heaven, it will not break.

Māori used flax fibre to make many kinds of rope. After scraping, the fibre was twisted into strands by rolling on the thigh and then up to eight strands were plaited into ropes, both square and round. The heaviest were used for mooring canoes. Likening the whānau to a rope woven in this way stresses the strength that comes from being bound together by shared descent, shared values and shared goals.

The whānau which comes first to mind is associated with a set of values (whakaaro nui) which whānau members ideally use to govern their relations with each other and with outsiders. These values are an integral part of the Māori value system as a whole,[2]

79

but they have particular meaning in the whānau context.

When people who are *not* linked by descent choose the word whānau to describe themselves, they make a symbolic statement indicating that they have modelled themselves upon the whānau which comes first to mind and adopted its values as their own. When kinship connections are attenuated or absent, common aims and values become doubly important as a means of binding people together.

Aroha

The value which Māori invariably name first in connection with the whānau is *aroha*. This word is usually translated into English as *love*. Like all important concepts, however, both aroha and love have several meanings. Some of these meanings they share, but not all.

In English love has three main aspects: affection, especially between family members (storge in Greek), sexual or erotic love (eros), and altruistic love (agape in Greek, caritas in Latin). In classical Māori, aroha was used primarily for love for those known as kinsfolk, including the gods; it was *not* used for sexual love. After the adoption of Christianity, Māori extended the meaning of aroha to include altruistic love, as shown by God towards humankind. In contemporary practice, aroha is increasingly used by speakers whose first language is English to refer to sexual love.

In addition, aroha has several meanings for which English uses other words. It frequently means to long or yearn for someone: traditional waiata aroha are songs of lament for unfulfilled or lost love, including love for kin and for land. Aroha is the appropriate word for expressing sympathy for the bereaved, compassion and pity for those in sickness or trouble, approval of or pride in someone, and gratitude for kindness and gifts received.

When defining aroha for a general audience, contemporary Māori speakers and writers commonly focus on the most comprehensive of its many meanings, stressing its connection with the divine, the generosity of spirit which puts others before self, and its refusal to impose limits or conditions. Rangimarie Rose Pere defines aroha as:

unconditional love that is derived from the presence and breath of The Creator. . . . a pillar of life from Io Matua (the Godhead, the Divine Parent). . . . Evil and negative forces cannot flourish where absolute aroha reigns. . . . Aroha is truly a divine love because it knows no bounds, and is infinite. (Pere 1991: 6)[3]

While Māori generally endorse this idealistic definition of aroha, they continue to use the word with all its other meanings. In particular, they associate aroha closely with kinship ties, and especially with love for members of the same whānau, hapū and iwi. The Māori version of 'Charity begins at home' is 'Aroha begins with whanaunga'.

In the context of the whānau, aroha refers in the first place to the warm affection which whānau members are expected to feel for each other. Such feelings are usually based on a history of close association in work and play, especially in childhood, but so firmly is aroha attached to the idea of kinship that Māori report experiencing an upsurge of such feelings on meeting kin for the first time. Te Rangi Hiroa remembered:

When I was told that an aged visitor whom I had never seen before was a *tipuna* to me, my heart warmed towards him. I placed him in the same category as my other *tipuna* who resided in the same village and had lavished affection upon me. He was a member of the family. (Hiroa 1958: 342)

Even more important than affectionate feelings, however, are the caring acts expected to be performed towards kinsfolk, especially in times of sickness, need or other trouble. Rangimarie Rose Pere insists that 'aroha is only meaningful when actioned' (Pere 1990: 6). The forms that this caring takes will be explored later in this chapter.

Whanaungatanga

Closely associated with aroha but usually distinguished as a value in its own right is *whanaungatanga*, kinship in its widest sense.

This abstract noun is formed by adding the ending -tanga to whanaunga, the most widely used word for relative. Whanaunga is a generic term, applied to kin of both sexes related by marriage and adoption as well as descent.[4] Whanaungatanga is ego-centred kinship: traced outwards from each individual, it includes not only the members of his or her whānau but a large number of other relatives as well.

The value of whanaungatanga reinforces the commitment members of a whānau have to each other but also reminds them of their responsibilities to all their other relatives. The imperative to extend aroha to *all* whanaunga ensures that every whānau is embedded in a web of cross-cutting kinship ties. Its members are enjoined to look outwards as well as inwards.

Taha wairua, taha tinana

The third value of importance is respect for the spiritual dimension (te taha wairua) which complements and completes the physical dimension (te taha tinana) in the world in which humans live (Metge 1976: 54-58). As Donald Owens put it:

> Whiringa a nuku, whiringa a rangi. Woven together on earth, woven together in heaven. There is an interweaving of the two dimensions. Worldly things have spiritual origins. Things begun on earth must be completed in heaven.

While some Māori repudiate entirely the sacred beliefs of their pre-European ancestors, most value the teachings handed down to them by their ancestors as symbolic ways of understanding the world and have no difficulty reconciling and integrating them with Christian teaching (Marsden 1975). Despite variations in belief and practice, Māori generally accept three basic propositions: the existence of spiritual beings, including one supreme God; the existence of a spiritual realm which intersects with the world in which humans live; and the existence of a spiritual dimension to life in this world. In the poetic language of Māori speech-making, this world is Te Ao-Tū-Roa (the World Standing Long), a world of space, time and mortality, where everything comes to an end. In Te Ao-Tū-Roa, physical substance (tinana) is given life and empowered by the indwelling of mauri (life principle) and mana (spiritual power), which originate in the spiritual realm.[5] Human beings also have a wairua (spirit) which is given by God at birth and returns to God at death, and a hinengaro, a capacity for thinking combined with feeling.

Māori generally agree on the desirability of seeking divine blessing and assistance in daily life, in crises and whenever they are gathered together, whether or not they do so themselves. Those brought up in the same household with elderly relatives recall their chanting karakia (prayers) at dawn and on retiring at night. Whānau meetings are normally opened and closed with prayer and when whānau members stay overnight in one place formal prayers are said or sung night and morning.

Seeking guidance about family relationships, Māori often refer both to the Bible and to the sacred stories about the beginning of the world handed down from their ancestors (Alpers 1964: 15-70). Though set in the distant past, such stories are directly relevant to the present, because they express, in a poetic and symbolically encoded form, what the tellers hold to be timeless truths about the nature of the world and human society. As well as explaining why things are the way they are, creation stories provide and justify patterns of behaviour for the present and future.

In the stories of the marriage of Ranginui (Great Sky) and Papatuanuku (Wide Earth), their separation by the sons they had neglected, those sons' quarrels, marriages and descendants, and the many exploits of Māui-Pōtiki, relationships that are familiar in both senses of the word are used to hammer home the message that all living beings are intimately related and responsible for each other, because they share common origins. The creation stories provide a charter for a caring relationship with the resources of land and sea, for the valuation of women as the source of humankind and guardians of its continuity, and for the honouring of obligations to whānau members. At the same time they demonstrate the disastrous consequences of selfish marital partnerships, parental neglect, rebellion against parents, conflict between siblings, and incest.[6]

Fusing classical Māori beliefs with Christian belief in the

Communion of Saints, Māori believe that their ancestors (tūpuna) live on in the spiritual realm and continue to take an interest in their descendants. They are believed to pass on their own special talents to chosen descendants, to provide protection and support in spiritual crises, and to punish those who offend them or do wrong. Possession or cursing by offended ancestors is one of the explanations which experts in tikanga Māori check out when investigating disturbed behaviour in a whānau member.

Classical Māori beliefs included belief in a link between particular human descent-lines and particular animal species. Māori who grew up in traditional Māori communities were taught that their hapū and whānau are linked in a special way with one or more non-human species, not with the whole species but with an unusual, readily recognisable member of it, such as a white ruru (morepork owl) or an eel with tattoo-like markings (Schwimmer 1963). This animal acts as a guardian (kai-tiaki) to members of the whānau or hapū to which it is attached, warning against danger and death, and punishing those whose actions threaten the group, whether insiders or outsiders.

Emphasising te taha wairua does not mean lack of respect for te taha tinana. Physical activity (mahi) is praised for improving the quality of life of both individuals and groups, for example in the much quoted proverb 'Tama tū, tama ora; tama noho, tama mate' (Up-and-doing is full of life; Lying-around is sickly) (Brougham, Reed, Karetu 1987: 107). Other proverbs recommend looking for spouses who are proven workers.[7] Whether it is waged or unwaged, work which sustains the bodily well-being of others is *not* put down as menial but honoured as the finest expression of aroha. When their whānau stages a hui, the most respected rangatira set a good example by taking their turn at tasks like peeling vegetables, washing dishes and cleaning toilets. In farewell speeches at the end of hui, visitors single out the ringa wera (literally, the hot hands) for special tributes.

Te taha tinana and te taha wairua are related as a complementary pair. Instead of negating they complete and enrich each other. What is valued most is the connection and appropriate balance between them, as is expressed in the proverb 'Te amorangi ki mua, te hāpai ō ki muri' (the tohunga in front, the food-carriers behind) (H.W. Williams 1971: 8). Originally this referred to the ordering of a war-party on the move. Nowadays it is used to stress the importance, in daily life and at hui, of carrying out the appropriate ritual observances *and* backing them up with the provision of food and other services. To omit or do either badly is to court criticism and failure.

Tapu and noa

Subsumed under the contrast between te taha tinana and te taha wairua is another complementary pair, the concepts of tapu and noa (Metge 1976: 58-60, 232-35).

Tapu is a state of being deriving from close contact with beings or forces from the spiritual realm, especially the indwelling of mana. Like most important Māori concepts, it cannot be translated into English by a single word. The common translation of tapu as sacred does well enough in most situations but becomes inadequate when the causes of tapu are malign or polluting. The best short definition is 'set apart under ritual restriction'. Noa, the other half of the pair, is a state of being which is removed from close contact with spiritual beings or forces and hence free from ritual restriction. Few people or things are intrinsically or permanently either tapu or noa; most become one or the other according to context.

Tapu often attracts public attention and respect but is closely associated with danger, anxiety and restrictions on freedom of action. Noa attracts little or no public respect and attention but allows relaxation and freedom of action, within the limits of tikanga. As with te taha tinana and te taha wairua, tapu and noa go together, and cannot exist without each other.

In the 1950s and 1960s and possibly later in the more remote areas, Māori applied the principles of tapu and noa in the domestic as well as the public sphere. In particular, parts of the human body (especially the head and genital area) were regarded as tapu and thus to be protected from inappropriate touching; particular spaces and utensils were reserved for the use of particular family members, especially those with most mana and tapu; and interpersonal relations were hedged with restrictions. Today in the 1990s, these observances have mostly been abandoned in favour of greater personal freedom of action. Important controls may have been lost in the process, because these observances helped to maintain social distance and respect between persons living at close quarters, especially those of opposite sex.

Ora

The fourth value, *ora*, is life of a special quality, *energised* life (Metge 1976: 60-62).

Like aroha, ora has a rich and complex set of meanings which cannot be rendered adequately in English by one or even several words. An adjective which can also be used as a noun, ora signifies *alive* as opposed to dead, *healthy* as opposed to sick, *safe-and-sound* as opposed to injured and in danger. But the kind of life signified by ora is not confined to the physical dimension. It is life of body, mind and spirit, life in all its fullness. The greeting 'Kia ora!' is much richer than is generally appreciated. The founders of the Māori Women's Welfare League had this richness of meaning in mind when they gave the fledgling organisation the Māori title of Te Rōpu Wāhine Māori Toko I Te Ora.

Since the early 1980s the word ora has frequently been used in connection with Māori health initiatives, usually in compounds such as hauora (spirit or breath of life), rapuora or whaiora (seeking health) and tipuora (growing/developing health) (Durie 1994: 69-79). Those responsible for these initiatives do not reduce the meaning of ora to bodily health but, taking a holistic approach, insist on widening the meaning of health to take in the mental, spiritual and familial dimensions of human experience. In particular, they stress the link between the wellbeing of the individual and his or her group, from whānau to iwi Māori. Ora is also *wholeness* of life.

The meaning of ora is thrown into relief by the two concepts commonly linked with it as opposites: mate, which can mean sick, dying or dead, and aituā, which has the wider meaning of misfortune.

Tika, tikanga, pono

As a value *tika* refers primarily to what is right in the double sense of correct and appropriate, morally, spiritually and socially.

Built into it are the other two meanings of the adjective tika: straight and direct, just and fair. The opposite of tika is *hē*, to be mistaken or wrong.

The addition of a noun ending to tika gives *tikanga*, a word which identifies 'the right way', a rule or custom embodying particular values—accepted understandings of what is tika (see p 21, above). Tikanga vary from specific to general and are related in complex and cross-cuttings ways. In any given situation, a variety of tikanga are applicable, some reinforcing, some contradicting each other. For example, the tikanga that hosts make all the decisions about protocol on their own home ground can conflict with the tikanga which enjoins them to 'manaaki ki te manuwhiri' (show respect and kindness to visitors). I note a growing tendency for Maori with a limited range of experience to privilege certain tikanga above others at all times: for example, to insist on carrying out their group's ritual of welcome in full, regardless of inclement weather or visitors' discomfort. In my experience, kaumātua of earlier generations (especially those I observed in the 1950s and 1960s) paid close attention to context. In any given situation, they reviewed both past precedents and present needs and on that basis decided which tikanga were most relevant. Often different tikanga were emphasised in different circumstances. If they gave preference to any one tikanga, it was 'arohanui ki te tangata' (demonstrate loving concern for people).

Closely related to tika is the concept of *pono*, which means to be true, that is, genuine (not hypocritical) and loyal in relations with others. Whānau members are expected to be open and above board with each other, not to dissemble or lie to each other. Pono is a quality especially required of those who occupy positions of leadership in the whānau. To be effective whānau action must be built on mutual trust.

Mana

The sixth value of great importance in the whānau is *mana*. When trying to explain mana to non-Māori, Māori often render it into English as *prestige* or *reputation*. These are secondary meanings. The primary reference of mana is 'spiritual power and authority'

(Marsden 1975: 193), 'divine power made manifest in the world of human experience' (Metge 1986: 62-79). Mana is basically unitary but a variety of qualifiers can be added to indicate differences in source or field of application.

Both individuals and groups 'have mana', that is, their own special share or store of mana. This is a combination of mana acquired by inheritance from ancestors (mana tupuna), by direct contact with the supernatural (mana atua) and as a result of human achievement (mana tangata). This store of mana is not fixed but is affected for better or worse by the holder's behaviour, by the actions of others and by the vicissitudes of life. Individuals also have the particular kind of mana associated with their sex: mana tāne and mana wahine.

Mana tupuna

Within the whānau, mana tupuna is handed on down the descent line, from parent to child in each generation. Sharing in the inheritance of mana tupuna in this way binds together the descendants of the founding ancestor and sets them apart from their in-married spouses. Members of the whānau look not only to their parents but beyond them to their ancestors, with respect and gratitude, as the source of their being and of most if not all their capabilities. They regard themselves, and are regarded by others, not as merely individuals but as living representatives of those who have died. Some have been given the names of ancestors; these are addressed by appropriate kinship terms (Tupu, Koro, Kui) and treated as if they are the embodiments of their namesakes. Older relatives are sensitive to evidence that ancestors with particular gifts (exercised as kai-karanga, kai-kōrero, weavers, carvers, warriors and so on) have passed them on to chosen successors, usually a grandchild or great-grand-child.

Even while it binds co-descendants together, the inheritance of mana tupuna also creates distinctions among them. In each sibling set the largest share goes to the mātāmua (the firstborn, in some iwi the firstborn male), qualifying him or her as leader within the set and eventually in the whānau as a whole. Other siblings receive diminishing amounts in order of birth, modified in some iwi by their sex. In several iwi, the youngest (pōtiki) also receives a special increment of mana.[8] In childhood older siblings exercise authority over the younger ones, often by passing on orders received from parents.

> In ordinary circumstances, when siblings reach adulthood, orders and commands are largely replaced by wishes and requests. Discussion plays a large part in any proceedings, but with greater attention paid to the ideas and requests of the most senior sibling present. Thus an elder's opinion will have greater weight in the public forums; junior siblings are customarily expected to remain either silent or circumspect when a senior sibling is present and can speak for all. (Hohepa 1964: 59)

As Arahi Mahuru explained:

> Ko te tuakana te kai-pupiri i te mana, ko te teina te kai-whakatinana. The tuakana [senior sibling] is the one who holds the mana of the whānau, the teina [junior sibling] is the one who gives it substance, that is, the doer. The teina must always respect his tuakana; whatever he does, he must seek his permission before or his approval afterwards if it is to have mana.

However, inherited mana is only *potential* power until it is realised in action. Lacking the desire or personality for leadership, the eldest sibling may hand that role on to a better qualified sibling. Though he is the youngest among his siblings, Arahi Mahuru does the formal speechmaking for the family, because his eldest brother himself transferrred that role to him. Younger siblings who are particularly gifted or energetic may increase their inherited mana by personal achievement, attract supporters and either oust their elder sibling or establish a separate whānau. Many leaders famous in Māori history were not the eldest in their sibling set.[9]

The whānau as a whole has its own mana. This comprises a core of mana tupuna but is also increased or decreased by the behaviour of individual members and by the way the whānau fulfils its functions as a group. The mana of the whānau as a whole is more than the sum of the mana of its members. Whānau members have a shared responsibility to work to build up the mana of the group and to restore it when damaged. As Rangimarie Rose Pere points out:

> While members of a whānau may quarrel and bicker among themselves, uniting together to keep their mana intact in dealings with people outside their kinship group is of paramount importance. Members of a whānau are often prepared to make personal sacrifices to uphold the mana of their group. (Pere 1982: 33-34)

Though they do not inherit mana tupuna from the whānau ancestors, in-married spouses contribute to the mana of the whānau as workers and therefore have a share in it.

Whakapapa

A corollary of mana tupuna is the value placed on whakapapa (genealogical knowledge). As Cleve Barlow says:

> It is through genealogy that kinship and economic ties are cemented and that the mana or power of a chief is inherited. Whakapapa is one of the most prized forms of knowledge and great efforts are made to preserve it. All the people in a community are expected to know who their immediate ancestors are, and to pass this information on to their children so that they too may develop pride and a sense of belonging through understanding the roots of their heritage. (Barlow 1991: 174)

In addition, in the words of Bishop Manu Bennett, 'one of the functions of whakapapa is to funnel the relation between past, present and future and tie it together'.

Orally or written into books, whakapapa can be set out in several ways. The simplest form is a single line of descent traced from a particular ancestor to a particular descendant, naming a single link in each generation. More complex forms add the names of the siblings and/or spouses of the link in each generation. The most complex form includes the spouses and offspring of all the siblings in each sibling set, constituting a complete family tree. Users choose the whakapapa that is relevant to a particular occasion or create one by a careful choice of links.

Access to genealogical knowledge is important to a functioning whānau for several reasons. Birth order and generational level significantly affect the choice of kinship terms and patterns of behaviour between whānau members and provide a basis for deciding issues of precedence and leadership. Whakapapa enable whānau members to establish linkages with each other, with their hapū and iwi, and with a wide range of whanaunga. Whakapapa give whānau members the knowledge needed to manage relations with other groups, especially at hui, and with strangers. As Kiwa Paki recalled:

> Our parents always said, 'You are going to go and live somewhere else. You need to know your whakapapa, so you don't end up marrying your own cousin.' If you know your whakapapa, you can go to most places and you will find your own people or you will be able to make the links more easily.

Although they stress the importance of whakapapa, older whānau members do not as a rule teach the whānau's children and young people about ancestors further back than their grandparents. On the contrary, they often discourage enquiry. Such knowledge is tapu: refraining from teaching the young too much too soon protects them against unwitting blunders. The custodians of whakapapa should test young enquirers for ability and commitment, select the most promising and mature, and teach them in installments appropriate to their stage of development.

Mana tāne, mana wahine

The kai-whakaatu with whom I have discussed relations between the sexes all stress the complementarity of male and female in marriage, family and whānau, as te tikanga tuku iho nō ngā tūpuna. Males and females have their own special mana, *mana tāne* and *mana wahine*, which adds an extra dimension to mana derived from other sources, entitles them to respect and equips them for specific roles. In essence and when carrying out these roles, males and females go together and complete each other as partners.

There is some variation in the way the partners are valued, some iwi insisting that they are different but equal, others according men a dominant position, especially as regards access to public leadership. In her article '*Tipuna*—Ancestors', Anne Salmond suggests that the doctrine of male dominance arose out of competitive striving in war and was reinforced in the 19th century by the attitudes and practices of the colonial settlers, especially the assignment of the domestic domain to women and their exclusion from property-holding and political decision-making (Salmond 1991: 340, 345). The contradiction between male-female equality and male dominance was and is worked out differently in different areas and generations (Salmond 1991: 340). Writing on 'The role and status of Māori women', Arapera Blank commented on the contrast in attitudes prevailing in the communities where her father's and mother's parents lived. In one community most of the men assumed their superiority and ordered their wives around, while in the other 'women were acknowledged as indispensable for quality daily living and respected for their opinions' (Blank 1980: 35-37).[10] Since its inception in 1951, the Māori Women's Welfare League has taken the lead in re-establishing the equal value of women, women's roles and mana wahine.[11]

Clear-cut differentiation of roles on the basis of sex applies only in limited areas of social life, principally those connected with child-bearing and with formal ceremonial on the marae. In many others no distinction is made, as with most aspects of servicing the marae kitchen and dining-hall during hui. That sex is not a necessary component in many kinship and leadership roles is indicated by the fact that their names (for example, tūpuna, kaumātua, rangatira, and in some iwi mātua) apply to both sexes, requiring the addition of tāne or wahine or the use of an altern-ative term to indicate sex.

Where household management is concerned, there is no one ideal pattern in the assignment of tasks. Many Māori households operate by making a distinction between women's work, comprising mostly tasks inside the house, and men's work, which is mostly out-of-doors, but there are probably as many in which men share to varying degrees in child-care and general domestic tasks and/or women work outside, especially when they live on farms.

In the East Coast community where Moana Paiaka grew up in the 1950s, females were expected to wait on males in some households but not in others.

> In our family, we were all treated as equals. All my brothers were taught how to cook, to wash, to iron, to sew. It was never assumed that the sisters would do these jobs for their brothers. Our mother believed everyone should have a survival kit of domestic skills.

In her study of intra-family income and resource allocation, Julia Taiapa found some gender differences in access to and control over money in Māori couples but there were several alternative patterns and Māori men did not seem to associate controlling the family money with status as bread-winner and head of the family as Pākehā men did. She suggested that this was because they had an alternative source of self-esteem, through whānau participation (Taiapa 1994: 54-55).

My first instruction on the complementarity of men and women came from kaumātua Raniera Kingi (Ngāti Whakaue of Te Arawa waka) in 1959. In Te Arawa, he explained, speech-making on the marae was restricted not only to men but to men selected as qualified to represent their whānau by descent and speech-making skills; the women of each whānau made their contribution by weaving the cloak the whānau speaker wore, singing waiata with him and supplying food and labour in the kitchens, sharing the last two tasks with the other men of the whānau. The women (he said) fulfilled these obligations willingly and with pride, to build up the status of their whānau in relation to others: 'they like to hear the family voice heard.' According to Raniera, the limitation on women speaking applied only to speeches made during formalities on the marae when visitors were present: it did *not* apply to the private proceedings of Tribal

Committees or committees handling marae economics. Far from being denied access to the whakapapa and traditional knowledge needed by speakers, women played an active part in its transmission.

> The women know more than the men in many cases. They were often better students and feel strongly about the need to pass on the knowledge. Often they learnt it young and coach their menfolk.[12]

Raniera recalled that when his uncle asked his wife to weave him two cloaks to wear as a speechmaker, he took over all domestic tasks including the preparation of meals for eight weeks, so that she could devote herself to this tapu task.

Kai-whakaatu trained in the whare wānanga insist that women should be respected and honoured both for their intrinsic mana as women and as the whare tangata (the house which shelters the human foetus), the source of continuing life and growth for whānau, and hence for hapū and iwi. As Arahi Mahuru explained, when he was growing up in a remote Northland community, the males of the household scrupulously avoided using the same articles of personal care as the females, because of 'the mana and tapu of the woman'.

> We were taught to live in total wehi, total respect for that female mana. Not only at times when things may have been normalised or noa, but at all times. There is always a kind of tapu that requires your respect. Even though the mana of the male was quite powerful, the mana of the female was equal, if not more powerful, in a lot of instances.

According to Epa Huritau, the whare tangata is also the whare tapu (the sacred house). Women's status as the whare tangata entitles them to respect and protection, whether or not they are currently hapū (pregnant). They should receive support and care both from their husbands and from their male relatives, especially their tungāne (brothers and cousins of the same generation). Because of the importance of descent to Māori, tungāne have both rights and responsiblities in relation to their tuāhine (sisters and female cousins). These include acting as escorts and screening suitors while the latter remain unmarried, providing whatever foods they crave during pregnancy and taking steps to stop husbands from abusing them. Far from condoning domestic violence or the sexual abuse of women, my kai-whakaatu describe such acts as kinonga (bad deeds) and hara (violations of tapu, therefore sins). They expect such behaviour to be punished by misfortune of supernatural origin and by the victim's whānau. Appalled by current levels of domestic violence and incest, Arahi Mahuru attributed them to failure to pass on the teachings of the whare wānanga properly.

Respect for women is underpinned by reference to the sacred stories of the making of the world (Alpers 1964: 15-130). Though a casual hearing or reading of these gives the impression that males are the central characters, the doers of deeds, deeper study reveals that females also play key roles, often as custodians of knowledge who advise, direct and protect the males. Women are identified metaphorically with Papatuanuku, the primal mother, sharing her status and functions as bearer, nurturer and protector of succeeding generations. When Tāne set about making Hine-Ahu-One, the first human being, Papatuanuku gave him invaluable advice, part of her own physical substance and the ira wahine (female principle), which was as necessary and important as Tāne's contribution. Hine-Ahu-One's daughter Hine-Tītama, who became Hine-Nui-Te-Pō, combined loving concern with fearsome power. When she discovered that her husband Tāne was also her father, she fled to the Underworld where she established the Realm of the Dead; generations later she killed Māui along with his hopes of winning immortality for humankind. While some interpreters hold her responsible for the origin and continuing power of death, others lay the blame on Tāne for knowingly committing incest and on Māui for attempting to violate and kill his own tupuna (Reed 1963: 43-49; Grace and Kahukiwa 1984).

Assertions of male dominance in the Māori social order are often supported by the statement that 'men are tapu and women are noa'. Those who repeat this saying as if it settled the matter assume that tapu has only positive value, while noa has no or negative value. This is an over-simplification of complex ideas.[13]

As any visitor to a marae knows, the value attached to tapu is tempered, where human beings are concerned, by the anxiety and danger which also attaches to it, while noa *does* have value, the value of freedom from restrictions, which leaves people in that state free to relax and enjoy themselves and available to act as an antidote to tapu (Metge 1976: 60). Neither men nor women are all or always tapu, all or always noa. In the right context women as well as men can be tapu and engage in tapu activities, men as well as women can be noa and engage in noa activities. For example, women are tapu when performing the karanga, weaving cloaks and mourning the dead, while men share in the noa activity of preparing and cooking food, at the marae if not in the home.

In discussing the status of women in Māori society, attention is often focused on the role of kai-kōrero (formal speech-maker), which most but not all iwi reserve to men. Largely because of its high visibility and the time allotted to it, this role is often assumed to be the most important on the marae, eclipsing all the women's roles. This is to judge by outward appearance. Though it lasts a comparatively short time, the karanga calling visitors on to the marae is of crucial importance to the encounter between groups. In it the kai-karanga set the tone for subsequent proceedings and transmit information both to their own speakers and to the visitors. Women not actively engaged in speech-making are freed to listen, learn and analyse. Many male speechmakers rely on the women of their whānau for advice before and during speeches and in the choosing of appropriate waiata. Women perform highly valued ritual roles as mourners at tangihanga and as lifters of tapu.[14] Women are in charge of some and sometimes of all the activities behind the scenes at hui, complementing what happens 'out the front' in a different and equally valued way.

Experts from the iwi which restrict formal speech-making to men explain this tikanga in ways which recognise mana wahine, the mana women have as women. One explanation (advanced in particular by Tūhoe) focuses on the nature of the marae-a-nuku (the open marae in front of the meeting-house where the formal welcome ceremony takes place). Known as the courtyard of Tū-matauenga (the god of war in the language of symbolism), it is an arena where fighting orators attack each other, with words and mana. Women are excluded from this fighting to avoid injury to them or to their unborn children.[15] Another explanation (advanced by kaumātua of Muriwhenua) is that the exclusion protects men from the powerful mana which flows from women. As Arahi Mahuru explained:

> Mana wahine, it can be the power of atawhai (loving care) or the power to do harm, you have the two elements. You never know which way it will go where tapu is involved, so you take measures to reduce the risk, not to invite trouble.

In every case the restriction applies only to formal speech-making during the welcome ceremony and is balanced by the exclusion of men from the karanga.

Whatever the reasons given, keeping women out of the potentially combative speech-making in the welcome ceremony has the effect of freeing them for other duties, as kai-karanga and peace-makers. Inside the meeting-house, in the realm of Rongo-mā-tāne (god of cultivated foodstuffs and hence of peace), it is usually women who act to defuse conflict with words, music and humour.

The value of male-female complementarity is expressed in several traditional proverbs.[16] One known to all iwi runs:

> He puta taua ki te tāne, he whānau tamariki ki te wahine.
> (As going out with a war party is to men, so giving birth to children is to women.)

In 18th-century Māori society the sex-specific tasks identified in this proverb both required courage in the face of danger and were equally necessary for the continued life and mana of the community. Te Whānau-ā-Āpanui (in the eastern Bay of Plenty) have a proverb which runs:

> Te mate ki te tāne, he whare pākaru; te mate ki te wahine, he takere haea.
> (Death comes to a man, a house is destroyed; death comes to a woman, a canoe hull is split.)[17]

This proverb identifies each sex with taonga of the highest value to coastal iwi, men with the meeting-house, location and symbol of community decision-making, women with the means of transport, which is also the symbol of their own function as childbearers.

Whether in raising children, caring for visitors, organising hui or singing waiata, the most effective action in the whānau involves women and men working together, sharing the same tasks or carrying out complementary ones, as koroua and kuia, brother(s) and sister(s), husband and wife.

The relation between aroha and mana

Often aroha and mana seem to oppose and even contradict each other. At times, as one of my kai-whakaatu remarked, 'when mana comes in the door, aroha flies out the window'. However, careful consideration suggests that they constitute a complementary pair. Properly handled, aroha and mana balance and complete each other. Where mana is responsible for differences of status among whānau members, with the potential for jealousy and competition, aroha motivates them to work together for the good of all. Where aroha moves whānau members to care both for each other and for outsiders, mana empowers them to carry the task through effectively.

Aroha and mana have two important features in common. They are passed on (tuku iho) from the same ancestors and they both emphasise the importance of solidarity and mutual interdependence between whānau members.

Mahi-a-ngākau

Māori also recognise, as values in their own right, ways of acting towards each other and to outsiders which are motivated by both aroha and mana. These are described in Māori as *kawenga* (burdens, hence responsibilities), *herenga* (bindings, that is, obligations) and *mahi-a-ngākau*, an ambiguous phrase which can mean 'work done *from* the heart' and 'work laid *upon* the heart'. In his *English-Maori Dictionary*, H.M. Ngata chooses it to translate the word *duty*.

First, there is the duty to *support* each other in good times and bad. The Māori words most often used are awhina (help, assist) and tautoko (prop up, support). In the context of the whānau these are synonyms. They both indicate the provision of practical support in the form of labour, goods and money, and moral support expressed by physical presence in times of crisis and words of approval or defence.

Secondly, there is the duty to *care for* each other, expressed in the words ahu (tend, foster), atawhai (show kindness to, foster), awhi (embrace; foster, cherish), manaaki (show respect or kindness to), taurima (treat with care, tend) and whāngai (feed, nourish, bring up). All these words imply meeting not only the physical needs of others but also their need to be nurtured mentally and spiritually. Three of them, atawhai, taurima and whāngai, are given an additional, special meaning in different tribal areas to signify the bringing up of a child by other than its birth parents. In contemporary Māori, manaaki is commonly the word used to refer to hospitality extended to visitors on the marae and in private homes and in translating the wish 'God bless you!' This duty to care for each other includes the responsibility laid upon older generations to teach the young right ways and to hand on knowledge that belongs to and will benefit the whānau as a whole.

Thirdly, there is the duty to *protect* each other against physical and spiritual attack, expressed in the words tiaki (guard, keep), whakamarumaru (shelter) and whakangungu (defend, protect). This involves both countering attacks and insults launched by others and avoiding upsetting or insulting outsiders, breaching tapu or breaking the law, actions which reflect adversely and invite retribution on the offender's group as well as the offender.

Fourthly, there is the duty to *work together* (mahi tahi) for the common good, turning up to meetings and ritual occasions, arriving for hui in plenty of time to help with the preparations, sharing and not dodging the drudgery behind the scenes in the kitchen, toilets and dining-room, contributing one's special skills and material wealth wherever they are needed.

These are general duties, applying to whānau members in general. To them must be added two which are more specifically focused: the duty to value and cherish those of the most senior

generation, the tūpuna and kaumātua of the whānau, and the duty
to value and cherish those of the youngest, the tamariki and
mokopuna. In all cases, the terms are inclusive, referring to
indirect as well as direct descent relationships. Both tūpuna and
mokopuna are classified as taonga.

Utu

Underlying aroha and mana and the ways of acting associated
with them is the important value of *utu*, which is best characterised as the principle of reciprocity. The word utu is often translated into English as revenge but this is a gross distortion of its
significance. Utu is the principle that anything received should
be requited with an appropriate return. When Māori society was
governed entirely by tikanga Māori, utu was the driving force
which governed both warfare, in which injury, death and damage
attracted comparable evils (kinonga) in return, and gift exchange,
in which the giving of goods (foodstuffs, raw materials, artefacts),
services and spouses attracted comparable good gifts (taonga) in
return. In the late 20th century, when intergroup warfare is
proscribed by law and gift exchange has been replaced by the
market economy as a means of economic distribution, the
principle of utu nevertheless remains a powerful ideal governing
relations in the Māori social and political world, between
individuals, whānau, hapū and iwi.

   The operation of utu involves several important rules. First,
the return should never match what has been received exactly
but should ideally include an increment in value, placing the
recipient under obligation to make a further return. Secondly,
the return should not be made immediately (though a small
acknowledgement is in order) but should be delayed until an
appropriate occasion, months, years and even a generation later.
Thirdly, the return should preferably be different from what has
been received in at least some respects: one kind of goods may
be reciprocated by another kind, goods by services, services by a
spouse. By making it difficult to calculate value, a difference in
kind reduces the possibility of exact repayment which would
bring the relationship to a premature end. Fourthly, the return
does not have to be made directly to the giver but may be made

to the group to which he or she belongs or to his or her descendants. In these ways, the principle of utu ensures an ongoing relationship between individuals and groups. It has the function of binding people together by the criss-crossing (tuitui) of reciprocal gifts and obligations.[18]

Where the whānau is concerned, the principle of utu is essential to the management of internal relations. Recipients of affection, approval, support, care, protection and respect from other whānau members are under obligation to reciprocate in kind and to do so generously, without counting the cost. The returns they make are not closely targeted to those from whom benefits have been received but are widely distributed, to the givers' close kin and descendants, to those in need, and to whānau members as a group. The return of significant and costly gifts is delayed until a specific need or comparable occasion arises and the recipient-turned-giver is in a position to meet the cost.

Whānau members also have an obligation to make a return for the mana they have inherited and for the leadership, guidance and example provided by the older members of the whānau. The appropriate return in this case has several aspects. It requires the young to act respectfully, according to what the whānau holds to be the right ways, so that the mana of the whānau and of its tūpuna is increased; to avoid actions which attract adverse notice and criticism and thus diminish the mana of the whānau and its leaders; and, when mature enough, to provide guidance and an example to the next generation.

Where relations between whānau members are not good, where there is dislike, jealousy or abuse of any kind, allowing the injured to take utu by inflicting injury in return would further disrupt the unity of the whānau. Ideally the whānau (or, in serious cases, the hapū) should deal with the problem, either authorising its wisest members to act as mediators (takawaenga) or seeking resolution and healing in a formal group discussion (kōrero or huihuinga—see Chapter 13). These strategies usually halt the exchange of injuries by requiring the transfer of compensation between the parties or from the parties to the whānau itself. A good gift cancels out a bad deed.

Kotahitanga

Another value of great importance is that of kotahitanga—
oneness or unity. To achieve this whānau members must be
prepared to invest time and energy in getting to know each other,
to work through differences in lengthy discussions aimed at
achieving consensus, to keep whānau matters confidential from
outsiders and to stand loyally by each other in disputes with
outsiders.[19]

Kotahitanga also means accepting responsibility for each
other's actions, acting to prevent or control damage and if need
be helping to make reparation to outsiders in order to restore
the whānau's mana.

Relations with outsiders

The principles of aroha, mana, utu and kotahitanga are all
involved in governing the whānau's relations with outsiders,
especially with other whānau. Whānau members recognise a
collective responsibility to reciprocate the help received from
other groups, whether in the form of attendance, speeches and
koha given at hui or more personal support in time of trouble,
and thus to uphold and preferably increase the whanau's mana.
At the same time they recognise a collective responsibility to their
own group to secure compensation for insult or injury by others
for the same reason. According to Rangimarie Rose Pere:

> The same fervour applies if the whānau feels that they have
> been insulted or attacked by people from outside their
> kinship group. They will take steps either to confront the
> offenders and their kinship group or to use other more
> subtle forms of meting out a just and appropriate settle-
> ment. (Pere 1982: 33-34)

Finally, whānau members recognise a collective responsibility
to provide compensation for any loss or injury inflicted on
outsiders by one or more of their number, in order to prevent or
heal a breach of the relationship and to restore the mana of the
whānau.

Negative values

As might be expected, the personality traits and behaviour which are most disliked and attract the heaviest sanctions in the whānau are those which threaten its positive values.

High on the list is any tendency to be self-centred and selfish, behaviour described by the words kaiapa, kaiapo and mahuki, which in Māori are full synonyms. H.M. Ngata illustrates the entry 'self-centred' as follows: '*He was so self-centred that he could not see the needs of his own family.* Na te kaha ō tona kaiapa, kore rawa a ia i mātau ki ngā hiahia a tōna ake whānau.' Significantly, selfishness in Māori thinking has overtones of greed: according to Williams' *Dictionary of the Maori Language*, kaiapa also means covetous and mahuki also means stingy and greedy. In the whānau acquisitiveness or reluctance to share are major faults.

Disapproval is directed, secondly, against those who think too highly of themselves, a condition described most often as whakahīhī (vain, conceited, arrogant), but also by the synonyms whakatoatoa (boasting, self-confident) and whakapehapeha (vain, conceited, boastful). All three words combine the causative prefix whaka-, which implies reflexivity, with the doubling of a word, a procedure which gives it a derogatory twist. These three words highlight what Māori consider the wrong sort of pride, pride which focuses on the self separate from the group and involves looking down on others. The fault here is not in holding a high opinion of one's status and achievements but in asserting that opinion on an individualistic basis, without waiting for the endorsement of the group or group leaders. The whakahīhī forget that mana cannot be arrogated to oneself but is always delegated, by God and by people (Marsden 1975: 193-96; Metge 1986: 63-64, 70). As Keri Waipapa said: 'Ki te tangata kē kia whakanui.' (It is for other people to say you are important.) She went on to quote the proverb: 'E kore te kūmara e pānui i tōna reka.' (The kumara does not proclaim its own sweetness.)[20]

Those who show signs of whakahīhī are quickly cut down to size by other whānau members, for they threaten whānau harmony and reflect badly on the group. Charges of being whakahīhī may be levelled unfairly, especially at those who are

specially gifted or marked out for leadership. Such accusations
may arise from jealousy or they may be a deliberate test of a
leader's calibre and motives. As one of my earliest mentors
explained: 'Clouds gather round the highest peaks.'[21] A good
leader should be self-confident enough to hold to his or her course
in spite of discouragement and wise enough not to engage in self-
justification, which so easily slips into boasting.

Jealousy is another attribute which is frowned upon in the
whānau, that is, being envious or resentful of another person or
of another person's possessions or advantages. The Māori words
used in this context differ from tribe to tribe but usually involve
variations incorporating wene and hae. Most of these variations
have adjectival and/or noun forms which refer to feelings of
jealousy and verb forms which refer to the expression of such
feelings in action. Thus wene as a noun means dislike, envy,
hatred, and as a verb, to grumble or find fault with. Harawene as
an adjective means jealous, as a verb to grumble at. Hae itself
occurs only as a verb, which means literally to slit, lacerate, tear
or cut, and thus to cherish envy, jealousy or ill feeling. Tarahae
as a noun means envy, and as a verb to quarrel or bicker. Pūhaehae
as an adjective means envious, as a noun envy or ill will, and in
the verbal form kōhaehae, to envy or covet. Two other words
give even more graphic expression to the venting of jealousy:
ngau tuarā and muhari, both meaning to back-bite. Jealousy sows
dissension and mistrust in the whānau. It is feared because it is
both common and divisive.

Because cooperation and sociability are at a premium in
whānau life, any tendency to hold a grudge is also frowned upon
as disruptive. Described by the words whakamau and mauāhara,
such behaviour is particularly mistrusted in potential leaders.
Those who indulge in it are likely to find themselves passed over
when appointments are being made.

Since achievement of whānau aims depends on members
working hard and working together, the lazy (māngere) are
resented. They are likely to be rebuked with the proverb 'I hea
koe i te tangihanga o te riroriro?' (Where were you when the
grey warbler sang, at planting time?) (Brougham, Reed, Karetu
1987: 58). Surveying the following generations for successors to
train, kaumātua look not only for signs of ability and interest

but to see how well the candidates work out of the public eye, in the home, on food-gathering expeditions, in the kitchen during hui. They know that those who work hard in those settings are likely to be responsible in other ways as well.

Conclusion

The positive values explored in this chapter are ideals: whakaaro nui means literally 'great thoughts'. Striving to live up to them, real-life whānau and their members succeed or fail to varying degrees. Individuals who inherit more mana than others can use it with humility to manaaki those less well endowed or they can throw their weight about. There are those who embody aroha in action and those who use the concept as a lever to get others to do what they want. The fact that whānau often fall short of their ideals increases rather than diminishes the importance of the latter as guides to behaviour.

Adherence to positive values and avoidance of negative ones are reinforced by a variety of motivations: by the desire to be accepted and admired by other Māori, by fear of gossip or public rebuke, and by spoken and unspoken threats to withdraw support, especially when most needed, in the sorrow of bereavement.

Whānau values are related in complex ways, both competing with and reinforcing each other. In particular situations, choices may have to be made and accommodations reached. As Epa Huritau said:

> The Māori value system has the flexibility built into it to accommodate variation. . . . If we know the principle, we can make adjustments.

When managed wisely, the values of the whānau work together to increase its solidarity and its ability to achieve its aims. Yet even as it unites, mana in particular generates tensions which play a part in its eventual segmentation.

Chapter 6

STRUCTURAL TENSIONS
IN THE WHĀNAU

*Arohaina ō tamawāhine, hei tangi i a koe; arohaina ō
tamatāne, hei tanu i a koe.*[1]

*Demonstrate your love for your kinswomen so that they will
weep for you when you die; demonstrate your love for your
kinsmen so that they will bury you.*

Like families of all kinds, real-life whānau experience
internal tensions and conflicts as part of the normal course
of events. Some of these are unpredictable, arising out of
particular circumstances: personal likes and dislikes, social and
economic pressures, living under crowded conditions or too far
apart for intimacy. But others are, as it were, inbuilt, arising out
of the structure and functioning of the whānau itself. In particular,
emphasis on the importance of descent and inherited mana tupuna
creates lines of tension and potential division within the whānau:
between senior and junior members of each sibling set and
generation, between the descendants of the whānau ancestor and
in-married spouses, and between husband and wife.

The proverb at the head of this chapter emphasises that the
most enduring bonds are those based on descent, provided that
they are carefully cultivated. By implication, it warns against
expecting the love of a spouse to outlast death.

Tensions in the sibling set

The belief that the greatest share of mana tupuna goes to the
firstborn in each sibling set marks them out for positions of
leadership, firstly in their sibling set and, when that sibling set
becomes the most senior generation, in the whānau. In particular
the most senior male is seen as the right and proper person to

106

become representative spokesperson (kai-kōrero) for the whānau when he reaches kaumātua status. Most iwi observe a rule forbidding younger brothers to make formal speeches on the marae when an older brother is present; some forbid it as long as he is alive, whether present or not. Tension develops when able younger brothers feel frustrated at being unable to exercise leadership and oratorical abilities, especially if the eldest brother is ineffective or arrogant or if his failings reflect adversely on the mana of the whānau. If the firstborn is female, she may dispute the leadership with her brother but is more likely to support him in public and argue with or direct him in private. Whānau are particularly fortunate when the eldest brother and sister in each sibling set are able to work as a team.

Tension between siblings can be resolved if they are willing to put the good of the whānau before personal ambition. Not infrequently, the eldest brother voluntarily resigns his public role in favour of a sibling who is better equipped to fill it with credit (see p 89, above). In other cases younger siblings acknowledge their eldest brother in public as titular head but exert influence behind the scenes in personal and whānau discussions to achieve their goals. If an accommodation cannot be reached, the younger siblings usually transfer their allegiance to one of the other whānau open to them.

Tensions between descendants and non-descendants

Emphasis on descent also creates a division between those who are descended from the whānau ancestor and those who are not. As we have seen, there are some Māori, especially from the older generations, who define the whānau entirely in terms of descent (see pp 62-63, above). Even those who give the whānau the wider definition of extended family place in-married spouses and adopted children not descended from the whānau ancestor in a special category.

This division between descendants and non-descendants is reflected in classic Māori kinship terminology. Where English identifies affines by adding the suffix 'in-law' to the terms for the blood relatives mother and father, son and daughter and brother and sister, classical Māori provides a totally different set

of terms: hungawai (or hungarei) for parents-in-law (contrasting
with mātua and whaea), hunaonga for son-in-law and daughter-
in-law (contrasting with tama and tamāhine), taokete, autāne and
auwahine for siblings-in-law (contrasting with tuakana, teina,
tungāne and tuahine).

Within the whānau there is a strong feeling, sometimes spelled
out as a tikanga, that leadership positions such as kai-kōrero,
kai-karanga, officers and members of the executive of the whānau
komiti should be reserved to descendants of the whānau ancestor.
This is strongest in rural areas and where there is group property
to be administered, such as a marae, heirloom taonga, whakapapa
books and knowledge of whānau holdings such as fishing
locations. On the other hand, these restrictions can be waived
under appropriate circumstances, as when the whānau lacks a
kaumātua with the ability and experience for leadership or if an
in-married spouse or adopted child has extraordinary capabilities
or a distinguished whakapapa.

In-married spouses are not so much devalued in the whānau
as given two different values. On the one hand they are classified
as outsiders, people whose primary loyalty can be presumed to
be to their whānau of origin, until they prove otherwise. On the
other hand, that very fact gives them value. They are essential to
the continuation of the whānau into the future *because* they are
outsiders. Since marriage within the whānau is generally frowned
upon, outsiders must be brought in to be the fathers and mothers
of the next generation. As a Kōtare kaumātua once told me: 'Our
husbands and wives are important, because they have given us
our children.' In-married spouses and those adopted from outside
the whānau are also important as the means of alliance and
communication with other whānau; they are living links between
groups. Such links are utilised in crisis situations to mobilise
affinally related groups to provide back-up support for enterprises such as hui.

Finally, in-married spouses and adopted children are valued
contributors to the whānau workforce. It is a standard joke that
in-married spouses are often the hardest workers at the marae
and in whānau enterprises, perhaps because they must continually
prove their commitment.

Tensions between husband and wife

Emphasis on descent and inheritance of mana from tūpuna has particularly significant implications for relations within the parent-child family, between husband and wife.

While Māori value marriage as an institution for its production of children and its creation of alliances, they do not necessarily accept the principle embodied in New Zealand law that the marriage tie should take precedence over all other kinship ties. Instead Māori live with a very real tension, not to say conflict, between commitment to their spouse on the one hand and to their parents and co-descendants on the other. Even when both husband and wife accept the meeting of whānau obligations as an imperative, they have to work out, firstly, how much of their money, time and labour may be devoted to that end without shortchanging each other and their children, and secondly, how to balance their obligations to the whānau in which each is a full member by descent. Even greater difficulties arise when the partners have different views about meeting kinship obligations, especially when one rejects them altogether (Taiapa 1994: 39). This is particularly likely if one is Pākehā.

How couples resolve such difficulties varies according to circumstances, personalities and the strength of each spouse's feelings on the subject. Many feel impelled either openly to put the whānau's interests before those of spouse and children, or to attend and contribute to whānau hui despite opposition from their spouse. Those couples who put their relationship or family unity ahead of their commitment to whānau risk recriminations from kin and sanctions such as withdrawal of support in crises. Māori whose ties with their own parents and whānau have been weakened for any reason may compensate for the loss by attaching themselves to their spouse's whānau.

The tension between commitment to spouse and commitment to parents surfaces in its most acute form at times of birth and death, in relation to choosing the place where the placenta of each child will be buried, choosing where the deceased will lie in state for the tangihanga and choosing where the deceased will be buried.

Burying placenta and umbilical cord

When children are born, the traditional tikanga is to bury the placenta (whenua) and umbilical cord (pito) on ancestral land. This practice is validated by the myth of the origin of the human species. When the god Tāne was searching for the female principle to be the mother of humankind, his mother Papatuanuku told him to take earth from her pubic area, stained with blood when she was forcibly separated from Ranginui by Tāne himself. Tāne shaped this red earth into Hine-ahu-one and, mating with her, brought humankind into being. When she gave Tāne part of herself for this purpose, Papatuanuku told him: 'Ka puta tō hua tuatahi, whakahokia tōna whenua ki te whenua.' ('When your first child is born, return her whenua to the whenua', that is, return the placenta to Papatuanuku, who is at once land and ancestor.)[2] The place chosen for this purpose should be, as Moana Paiaka explained, 'a place where there is new life', a tree in a garden or open field. Often it is marked by planting a tree. The spot where their placenta is buried has special significance for the persons concerned: it is believed that they can identify it as special even when they do not know that their placenta is buried there.

As long as babies were born in their parents' home communities, Māori observed this practice of burying the placenta but when hospital births became the norm the majority of Māori parents were whakamā (embarrassed) to ask hospital authorities for the whenua and pito. Not only the practice but knowledge of it ceased to be passed on. Over the last ten to fifteen years, however, some Māori parents have revived the practice, even though it means flying the whenua back to the country by plane or storing it until the next trip home.[3]

Deciding to bury their children's whenua and pito involves parents in not one but a series of difficult decisions. In the past the choice of where to bury the whenua was linked with the naming of the child, an activity which was governed by tikanga and usually resulted in some being named by the father's whānau and some by the mother's (see pp 142-45). This meant that siblings' whenua were buried in different places. It was one of the ways in which whānau maximised their connections with other groups. Nowadays many parents prefer to bury the whenua of all their children in one place, but since they so often come from different communities this can be a difficult choice, especially if they maintain ties with both sides. Some iwi give the father's side priority over the mother's, but others feel that it is more appropriate for the whenua to go back to the land of the parent who is female like Papatuanuku.

Going home at death

When a Māori dies, Māori knowledgeable about tikanga Māori agree that the tūpāpaku (the body) should be taken home to lie in state on an ancestral marae and be buried in te ū kai pō. This phrase is variously translated as 'sucking milk at mother's breast' (Barlow 1991: 142-43) and 'the breast that provides sustenance in the night'.[4] There are varying views on how te ū kai pō should be interpreted. At a deep level, the breast referred to is that of Papatuanuku and the night is the long night of death. At a level closer to reality it is interpreted as referring to 'the land of one's ancestors'. This leaves open the question of which ancestors. Some hold that the deceased should be buried with his or her ancestors on the father's side, while others favour those on the mother's side, since it was she who got up at night to suckle the deceased as a child. One expert holds that the phrase identifies 'the place in which a person grew up, that is where he or she was raised on the "fat of the land", especially during childhood' (Barlow 1991: 142-43). There is no agreement on a standard rule. As Arahi Mahuru said:

> That is a matter which changes from person to person. Everybody has to make a choice. A lot depends on your childhood experience, who you would like to be buried with. There are no fixed rules. Te ū kai pō has to do with meeting up with your placenta in ancestral land; not just one particular cemetery but any of the cemeteries on your ancestral land.

In practice, decisions regarding where the deceased lies in state and is buried are matters of debate, with several whānau contending for the honour. In many cases, the deceased has several possible ancestral communities and marae, those to which he or she is attached through mother, father and perhaps a grandparent who brought them up, through long residence, and active participation in a whānau based there. Although the main emphasis is on connection by descent, spouses and their whānau also assert their interest in the decision. Some claims are advanced mainly as a matter of form, a symbolic way of honouring the dead and his or her family, but often there are real alternatives and speakers set out and debate a variety of factors before reaching a final decision, especially about the burial location. It is generally admitted that the wishes of the offspring should carry considerable weight, but they must be prepared to argue their case strongly and persistently.[5] However strong the attachment in life, husband and wife are often buried in different places.

To simplify matters, let us assume that the deceased was male. If he was living in an ancestral community and took an active part in a local whānau for many years before death, that whānau will almost certainly take charge of the tangihanga. They will take his tūpāpaku (body) to their marae, resist other claims from a position of strength, and bury him with one or both of his parents in a local cemetery. If the deceased's wife has already died and been buried in her home community, her whānau will come and ask for the tūpāpaku to take home to be buried with his wife, but they will have little hope of success. When the deceased's wife dies after him, the offspring of the marriage are likely to wish to bury her with their father but will face a strong challenge from her own whānau when they arrive to claim her body.

If the deceased has been living away from his ancestral community with his wife's whānau or in the city, the range of choices to be argued will be greater and the final decision less predictable. The deceased's children often want to bury their parents together and in a place where they can visit the graves easily.

Some couples attempt to prevent their whānau separating them in death by making their own dispositions beforehand. However, it takes courage and strong speech-makers to stand out against whānau in this way, and not all succeed. Maki and Ropata Huria came from Northland and the East Coast respectively, lived and raised their children in a city remote from either and made formal provision to be buried there together. When Ropata died, Maki and her children defended this choice successfully against all claims from kin.

Affiliation choices

In each parent-child family in a whānau, the offspring have access to two different sets of grandparents and possibly to two different whānau, their mother's and their father's. If the parents maintain membership in and contribute equally to both, their children may follow them in doing so or some or all may prefer one above the other. In the latter case, siblings may well make different choices, according to personality, compatability, their experience with different kin and a host of other considerations. Their choices may both reflect and affect their relations with their parents. Differences in the attachment of siblings to their parents' whānau create the fault-lines along which whānau segment when the time comes.

Conclusion

Whānau are voluntary associations: individuals are free to choose not only between whānau but whether to belong to one at all. Constraints of time and money, distance and compatability mean that even the most family-minded must make choices. As the years pass, whānau members grow apart as they become separated genealogically, geographically and by competing interests.

In the next chapter this process will be explored from the point of view of both individual members and the whānau as a whole.

Chapter 7

THE HAMIORA WHĀNAU
1955–85

Kua tupu tōu pā harakeke,
kua aroha ki te pīpī nei, ki te kākā.[1]

*Your flax bush has grown vigorously,
it has nurtured the fledgling and the full-grown kaka.*

Like the flax bush, the whānau in its maturity provides sustenance for all, young and old, small and great, with their varied needs. Like the flax bush, real-life whānau pass through a cycle of growth, decay and regeneration. Circumstances of time and place interact with members' personalities to give each its own particular character and history.

To highlight and illustrate the dynamism of the whānau as well as its defining features, I shall now explore the development of the Hamiora whānau of Kōtare between 1955, when I got to know its members, and 1985, when it held a large reunion hui.[2]

This exploration provides graphic evidence of the way in which Māori shift between different meanings of the word whānau.

When I lived in Kōtare in 1955, the Hamiora whānau was commonly referred to by local residents as 'the Samuels family'. When I wrote about the Kōtare whānau in *A New Maori Migration* (1964: 61-75), I used 'family' instead of whānau because that was the common usage in Kōtare at the time but enclosed it in single quotation marks to indicate that it had a special meaning. During the 1980s, however, the Māori form of the group name came to be preferred to the English form.

The Samuels 'family' in 1955

In *A New Maori Migration* I reported that the label 'the Samuels family' was applied, first and foremost, to a *descent group* with corporate functions, made up of adults and children who shared descent from Hamiora Takutai (deceased) *and* regularly participated in the activities sponsored by the 'family', including management of the 'family' marae at Hakea, a sub-district of Kōtare. Beginning with the grandchildren of Hamiora and his wife Atawhai, these descendants comprised three generations, a total of fifteen adults and forty-six children[3] living in Kōtare, plus nine adults living elsewhere. The 'family' name derived from its ancestor's baptismal name, a transliteration of Samuel, used by subsequent generations as a surname.[4]

I recognised that the label was also used, secondly, for an *extended family* consisting of this descent group with the addition of another twelve adults and four children, members' spouses and persons 'adopted' from outside the group, who were actively involved in the group's corporate activities but generally excluded from leadership roles.

I failed to point out (as I should have) that the expression was also used, though rarely, to refer to all the known descendants of Hamiora, a *descent category* which included many who neither identified with the descent group nor participated in its activities. Most of these lived outside Kōtare. (See Figure 1, p 116.)[5]

In 1955 the 'family' itself kept no formal listing of active 'family' members or of Hamiora descendants. My model of the Samuels 'family' in 1955 was built up from interviews and attend-

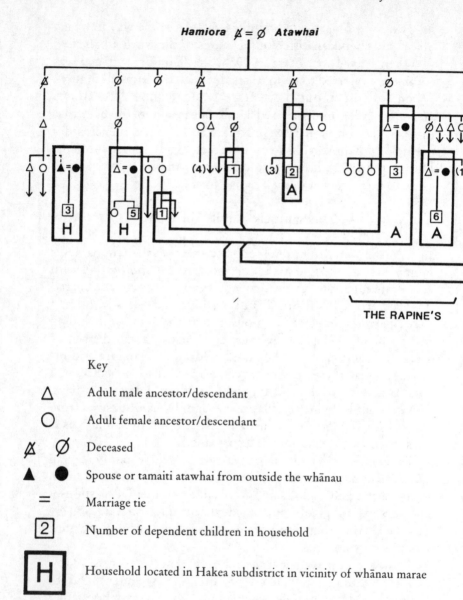

Key

△   Adult male ancestor/descendant

○   Adult female ancestor/descendant

⌀ ∅   Deceased

▲ ●   Spouse or tamaiti atawhai from outside the whānau

=   Marriage tie

2   Number of dependent children in household

H   Household located in Hakea subdistrict in vicinity of whānau marae

Figure 1. The Samuels 'Family'—The Hamiora Whānau 1955.
(From Metge, *A New Maori Migration*: 62, amended to include
subsequent correction in sibling order.)

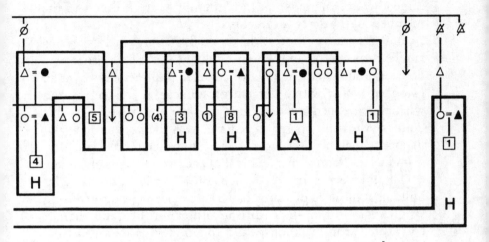

THE MATTHEWS'

A	Household located in another part of Kōtare
③	Number of descendants of Hamiora who live elsewhere but look to a home base in Kōtare
(5)	Number of descendants of Hamiora who live elsewhere and whose relationship with Kōtare is uncertain
↓	Indicates existence of descendants who live and look to a home base outside Kōtare

ance at 'family' gatherings. I concentrated on the membership of
the descent group and extended family and, while I recorded
remembered emigrants, did not attempt to track down all the
members of the descent category.

For practical purposes, the Samuels 'family' in 1955 was a
single corporate group which could be described either as a
descent group with a number of attached non-members or as an
extended family with a descent group core. It was, in short, a
whānau as defined and described in Chapter 4 (pp 62-64). This
'family' was firmly based in Kōtare, with the large majority of
members, including the most active, living on inherited land surrounding the 'family' marae at Hakea and in other parts of Kōtare.

The marae was in frequent use for 'family' purposes. Its
buildings consisted of a large hall used as meeting-house (during
tangihanga), dining-hall (during other hui) or dance-hall, a
corrugated-iron cookhouse, and toilets. It was managed by a
kōmiti marae composed of all active members of the 'family',
including spouses, with an elected executive confined to
Hamiora's descendants.

Internally the Samuels 'family' was subdivided on the basis
of descent from Hamiora and Atawhai's children into groups of
very unequal size. The two largest were also sometimes referred
to as 'families' and distinguished by surnames, as 'the Rapines'
and 'the Matthews'. These 'branches' as I described them (Metge
1964: 63) stemmed from two daughters, Aorangi and Rongopai
(sixth and seventh in the sibling order and both deceased), were
identified by the surnames of their husbands, and looked for ceremonial leadership to their eldest sons, who headed households
located in Kōtare on inherited land. The Rapines comprised two
households, the Matthews five. The rest of Hamiora's children
had relatively few descendants in Kōtare. Four were represented
by (respectively) an adopted son, a grandson, a widowed daughter
and a granddaughter, with their families, a fifth by a teenage
granddaughter staying with cousins. The sixth had several grandchildren in Kōtare but they had been brought up by members of
another Kōtare 'family' and in 1955 did not identify with the
Samuels 'family'.

In each generation, a considerable number of Hamiora
descendants had left Kōtare and given their primary loyalty to

'families' based elsewhere. One of Hamiora's sons, a grandson
and two great-granddaughters had married and settled in Te Puna,
a settlement some eighty kilometres away; these frequently sent
their children to stay with relatives in Kōtare for holidays and to
attend secondary school in the nearby town. Five such students
were included in Samuels 'family' households in 1955.

The various households of the Samuels 'family' in Kōtare
managed their everyday affairs separately but regularly exchanged
the products of gardens, orchards and seashore garnering, joined
forces to run the 'family' marae and hui celebrating members'
life crises (twenty-firsts, weddings, tangihanga and unveilings)
and provided other support as necessary. Sometimes, however,
the Rapines and the Matthews acted independently even in these
matters. Knowledge about family history and whakapapa was
kept by the kaumātua of these branches, other members applying
to them as necessary. In 1955, it seemed clear to me, the 'family'
was on the verge of segmenting into several independent groups
(Metge 1964: 63).

The Hamiora Whānau in 1985

At Easter 1985 over five hundred people gathered in Kōtare on
the marae at Hakea for what the organisers called 'the Hamiora
Whānau Hui'. For four days they enjoyed a varied programme
which combined the exploration of family relations with holiday
activities catering for all age groups. Besides swimming, fishing
and sunbathing, there were organised sports, treasure hunts,
housie sessions, discos and talent quests. There were religious
services (karakia) each evening and on Sunday morning, a session
on whakapapa, and a climactic reunion hākari (feast) on the last
day. The organisers produced a printed booklet titled *Hamiora
Whānau Hui*, which set out whakapapa from a famous northern
ancestor to Hamiora and from Hamiora and his wife Atawhai to
all their known descendants. The highlight of the hākari was the
ceremonial cutting of a reunion cake and the presentation of ten
smaller ones to representative descendants of Hamiora and
Atawhai's children. The hui was recorded on video film. Those
attending had a wonderful time, and the organisers ended up with
a credit balance.

In 1985 then, the Samuels 'family' was still in existence but the situation had changed in significant ways. The Māori forms 'Hamiora' and 'whānau' were generally used in preference to 'Samuels' and 'family', though they were still joined in the word order typical of English as 'the Hamiora whānau'. The number of Hamiora's descendants living in Kōtare had decreased to thirteen adults and seventeen children with twelve attached spouses. The number of households involved had increased from eleven to twelve, but their average size was much smaller, most consisting of parent-child families or grandparents caring for grandchildren. (Figure 2, below.)

Some of those who were living in Kōtare in 1955 had died; many had emigrated in search of jobs or after marriage. Some of these emigrants had dropped their allegiance to the Hamiora whānau, transferring it to whānau based elsewhere or dispensing entirely with whānau support. A considerable number, however, came back regularly on holiday visits and for life crisis hui, staying on whenever work was available. They attended marae committee meetings when in the area and several served on the executive. The practice of their children and grandchildren varied widely; some shared their parents' interest in and visits to Kōtare but many more visited Kōtare for the first time for the reunion. In general, those who were still actively involved in Hamiora whānau affairs were those who had parents or siblings in Kōtare and could use their homes as their physical base there. Although the proportion of active whānau members who lived outside Kōtare had increased significantly, leadership in whānau affairs remained with Kōtare residents.

The buildings of the 'family' marae at Hakea had been destroyed by a hurricane in 1958. They were uninsured: rebuilding seemed an almost impossible dream. Since then Hamiora hui had been held at the main Kōtare marae a couple of kilometres away. After fifteen years in recess, the Hakea komiti marae was finally revived in the 1970s and started fundraising. It consisted (as before) of an elected executive and any Hamiora descendants, spouses and adopted children who cared to turn up at meetings. The Annual General Meeting was always held in the holiday season between Christmas and New Year, when it attracted twice as many members as ordinary meetings.

The Hamiora descendants who lived in and regularly visited Kōtare in 1985 were divided into three main groups which were descent groups or extended families according to context. Two, the Rapines and the Matthews (sometimes called the Matius), were clearly continuous with the two branches with those names contained within the Samuels 'family' in 1955. Both had lost two kaumātua since then. Eru Rapine, son of a former kaumātua, was in the process of growing into leadership of the Rapines, while the Matthews looked to Rahera (eldest surviving daughter of Rongopai and Nika Matthews) as chief adviser, and to her husband Tamati as their formal speech-maker. The third group, the Hakaraias, derived from a set of siblings who had been children living with their parents in Kōtare in 1955. Two had set up homes in Kōtare while the rest had emigrated, but though their father (their point of attachment to the Samuels 'family') had died, they remained focused on their widowed mother and the parental home as their tūrangawaewae. Of the remaining 'family' descent categories, three had lost the representation they once had in Kōtare, one had acquired an additional household when a descendant who was raised in Te Puna but often visited Kōtare as a child built a home on inherited land there, and a fifth acquired a representative where it had had none when a lost descendant decided to acknowledge his Hamiora heritage. Too few to form groups of their own, Kōtare residents belonging to these other categories attached themselves to one or other of the three main groups for whānau activities.

The Rapines, the Matthews and the Hakaraias were markedly more independent than they were in 1955. Kōtare people referred to them as whānau. In 1985 these three groups organised hui marking their members' life crises independently of each other. They expected and accepted offers of help from each other in the running of these hui but did not rely on or always receive the promised support. The Rapines and the Matthews maintained a lively interest in the 'family' marae at Hakea and provided most of the ordinary and executive members of the marae committee but were not always in agreement. It would be more accurate to describe the three groups as whānau which formed alliances with each other than as branches of one whānau. They had segmented as I foretold, but retained special links with each other of the

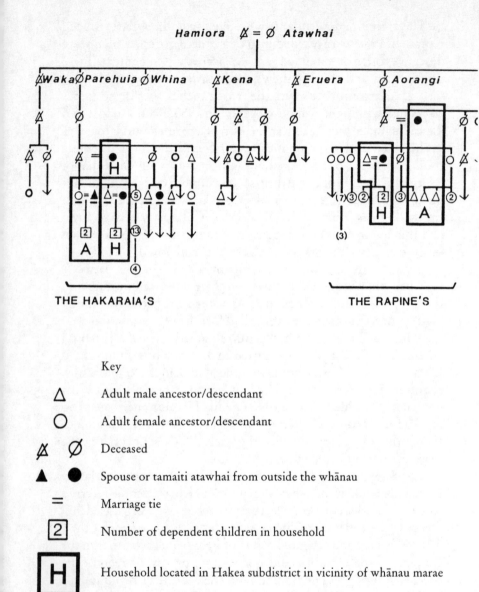

Key

△   Adult male ancestor/descendant

○   Adult female ancestor/descendant

⌀ ∅   Deceased

▲ ●   Spouse or tamaiti atawhai from outside the whānau

=   Marriage tie

2   Number of dependent children in household

H   Household located in Hakea subdistrict in vicinity of whānau marae

Figure 2. The Samuels 'Family'—The Hamiora Whānau 1985.

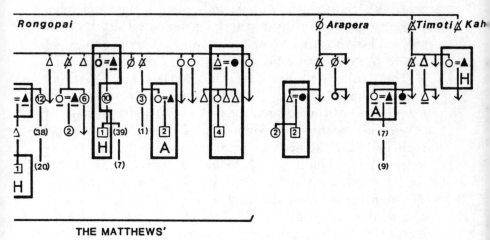

THE MATTHEWS'

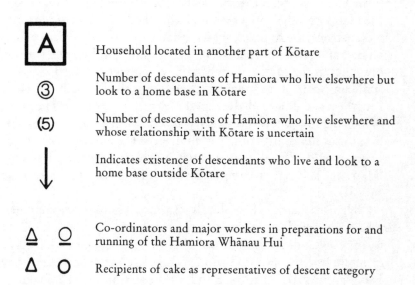

	Household located in another part of Kōtare
A	
③	Number of descendants of Hamiora who live elsewhere but look to a home base in Kōtare
(5)	Number of descendants of Hamiora who live elsewhere and whose relationship with Kōtare is uncertain
↓	Indicates existence of descendants who live and look to a home base outside Kōtare
△̲ ○̲	Co-ordinators and major workers in preparations for and running of the Hamiora Whānau Hui
△ ○	Recipients of cake as representatives of descent category

kind the Samuels 'family' had with related 'families' in 1955 (1964:
63). Many members of the oldest generation alive in 1955 had
died, but a few were left. With the addition of one and sometimes
two new generations by birth, the genealogical depth of the
whānau had increased overall, but most members belonged, as
before, to a three generational range.

The Matthews whānau was (as in 1955) larger than the other
two, with more members living in Kōtare and more emigrant
members who regularly returned. It was at a similar stage of
development to that of the Samuels 'family' in 1955, with several
branches which sometimes acted in concert and sometimes
independently. One of these branches was located in Kōtare but
the other two were in Auckland, a striking new development.
The branches often referred to themselves as whānau and were
identified as such by others. When the marae committee placed a
levy 'on each whānau' to meet marae expenses, these branches
insisted on paying separate levies instead of paying one jointly.
As the kaumātua of one branch said, it was a matter of identity.

To sum up: in 1985 the people of Kōtare commonly used the
term whānau to refer to groups of three different kinds and levels:
the Hamiora Whānau, which no longer had any ongoing corporate existence; the Rapines, the Matthews and the Hakaraias, which
all had an active but 'occasional' corporate life; and the various
branches of the Matthews whānau, which were in the process of
achieving corporate independence. As I shall shortly show, a
fourth usage emerged during the organising of the Hamiora
Whānau Hui, when the word was also applied to the descent
categories stemming from the children of Hamiora and Atawhai.
From now on I shall give whānau a capital letter in the phrase
'Hamiora Whānau' to emphasise its difference from its various
sub-divisions.

Whānau at each of these levels stemmed from a married couple,
who were equally ancestors to their descendants and kaumātua
to their extended families. But the linkage between whānau at
different levels was through one of these kaumātua only, the other
being an in-married spouse and a potential point of linkage to
other whānau. A significant proportion of the links between
whānau of different levels were women, as can be seen clearly in
Figure 2.

The Hamiora Whānau Hui

The Hamiora Whānau Hui held at Easter 1985 was the product of a growing perception that the Hamiora Whānau no longer existed as a functioning entity and that the descendants of Hamiora and Atawhai were widely scattered and often unknown to each other. The clearly stated aim of the hui was to bring these descendants together in order to get to know one another and to learn about their ancestors and kinship connections.

The idea of holding a Hamiora reunion developed over several years. The 75th anniversary reunion of the Kōtare primary school in 1978 attracted many emigrants home and stimulated interest in kinship connections and the past. Assembling material for the reunion booklet, Eru Rapine's wife Rangi discovered the names of forgotten Hamiora descendants in school rolls and committee minutes and began to ask questions about them. In 1982, stimulated by a school project, Eru and Rangi's son Heta collected information on family relationships from his grandmother (Eru's mother, an in-married spouse) and enlisted the help of his parents in ordering the results. They in turn discussed the task with friends from neighbouring districts, many of whom they knew as cousins without knowing the links in the chain of connection. Determined to correct their ignorance, the cousins decided to organise a reunion and set the date for Easter 1985. Meanwhile, the older members of the Matthews whānau had also become concerned that many of their young folk were strangers to each other. They agreed to support the Hamiora reunion but also decided to hold one of their own combined with an unveiling already planned for Christmas 1984, stressing their descent from Nika Matthews as well as Hamiora's daughter Rongopai.

An Organising Committee for the Hamiora Whānau Hui was formed in June 1984 and held monthly and later weekly meetings in various Kōtare homes. About one half of those attending lived in Kōtare or were active members of whānau based there. The rest were about equally divided between Hamiora descendants who had once been active members of such whānau but had dropped out and others who had never been members. In particular, a strong contingent came from Te Puna, where several Hamiora descendants had settled on marriage. Jesse Peters,

kaumātua of the Rapines, was elected Chairman of the Organising
Committee; when he died suddenly his nephew Eru Rapine was
elected in his place.

It was early decided to organise the hui on the basis of descent
from the children of Hamiora and Atawhai, at least from the
eight who had issue: Waka, Parehuia, Kena, Eruera, Aorangi,
Rongopai, Arapera and Timoti. The resulting eight groups were
quickly identified and thereafter referred to by the organisers as
whānau. They were not corporate groups but descent categories.
In every case, their members were widely dispersed residentially,
did not all know each other and were distributed among several
different whānau of the descent group/extended family type,
including some based outside Kōtare. Many had never been
to Kōtare, let alone lived there. The Hakaraias, Rapines and
Matthews formed the core of three of these descent categories
respectively, while the Te Puna descendants of Hamiora's son
Timoti formed a focus for the fourth. The descendants of the
remaining four ancestors were relatively few in number: for
organisational purposes they attached themselves to one of the
four main groups.

By July 1984 the main tasks had been defined and allocated to
coordinators drawn from the three Kōtare-based whānau and
from a fourth group consisting of people from Te Puna, which
was quickly dubbed 'the Te Puna whānau', though in fact it
included people from three descent categories. These coordinators, most of whom lived in Kōtare, mobilised the support of
their own whānau and any other accessible co-descendants,
forming sub-committees to handle their allotted tasks. In this
way whānau saw to hiring and erecting marquees to serve as
sleeping quarters and as dining-room and kitchen; making timber
tables which could later be dismantled; assembling kitchen and
dining-room equipment; gathering mattresses, sheets and pillows
from homes and neighbouring marae, including Te Puna; constructing a drainage system and temporary toilets and showers;
and organising the various entertainments.

In addition, Hamiora descendants living in Auckland set up
two 'whānau committees' to coordinate their contributions and
travel arrangements. One was organised by a second cousin of
the Hakaraias who had been brought up in Te Puna but stayed

in Kōtare while at secondary school, the other by a grandson of Kena, whose descendants were no longer represented in Kōtare. A third 'whānau committee' was set up in the central North Island town of Kawerau and combined families which were offshoots of the Rapines and of the Matthews. These three whānau committees had no prior existence but were action groups formed to support the Hamiora Whānau Hui. Each drew together people who were active members in Kōtare-based whānau and others who were not. Two combined descendants from more than one of Hamiora's children. Their description fits that of the groups I have called 'kin-clusters' (Metge 1964: 166, 169-70; also p 42, above).

The Organising Committee assigned the task of compiling a booklet of Hamiora Whānau members to Heta and Rangi Rapine, who had already assembled a substantial body of material. Questions about family membership and descent on registration forms brought in more details and Heta and Rangi enlisted the help of key members in each descent category in checking and amplifying their whakapapa charts. In the booklet *Hamiora Whānau Hui* a wealth of whakapapa information is ordered under the names and photographs of Hamiora and Atawhai and their children, an innovative numbering system making it a simple matter to trace both descent and kinship connection. Significantly, these whakapapa include the names of spouses and identify those who are adopted (without regard to the legality of the adoption) and their birth parents where the latter are also Hamiora descendants.

The expenses of holding the hui were covered by a combination of fees (for registration, accommodation, meals and a copy of the whakapapa booklet), awhina (assistance) in both cash and kind, and the sale of tickets to the various entertainments. As awhina, the two whānau committees in Auckland, for example, supplied one hundred chickens, several trailer-loads of vegetables, twelve stainless steel sinks, numerous stainless steel trays, plastic plates and -film, obtained at a discount through city contacts. The whānau committee in Kawerau (a timber processing town) contributed numerous rolls of paper for tablecloths, paper plates and plastic ground sheets. All the meat and vegetables required were donated before the hui began, so that the main expense in the food line was the hire of a freezer truck to keep it fresh.

For the hui itself, descendants of Hamiora and Atawhai gathered from all over New Zealand and five families came from Australia. A busload of travellers from Auckland were given a formal welcome ceremony by those organisers who were on hand when they arrived but most came by car in small groups and were welcomed informally. All those attending were given name tags embedded in rosettes colour coded to indicate which of Hamiora and Atawhai's children they were descended from or attached to as spouses or tamariki atawhai: light green for Waka, dark green for Parehuia, red for Kena, magenta for Eruera, pink for Aorangi, blue for Rongopai, pale blue for Arapera and yellow for Timoti. Purple and salmon were allocated to Whina and Kahu who died without issue. These rosettes were worn throughout the hui: they acted as an aid to placing each other and, marked with coloured dots, as entry tickets to the entertainments paid for.

These eight sub-divisions were used as the basis for organising a number of activities, those with few representatives present being amalgamated with the larger ones. A roster drawn up by the catering sub-committee delegated responsibility for cooking, serving and cleaning up after meals to one or two of these categories in turn. They were the basis for seating arrangements for the main commemorative religious service and for group photographs. Finally, they were highlighted during the hākari (feast) on the last day.

The hākari was presided over by Eru Rapine in his capacity as Chairman of the Organising Committee. Those present were seated in their eight whānau descent categories, with the senior representative of each sitting at the top table.

The climax of the hākari was the cutting and presentation of the cakes. A tiered cake representing the whole Hamiora Whānau was cut by the two eldest living descendants of Hamiora and Atawhai, Puhata (daughter of Aorangi) and Tenga (son of Timoti). When that was done, ten small cakes, each bearing the name of one of the ten children of Hamiora and Atawhai and decorated with their distinguishing colour, were presented to representatives of the descent categories concerned. The latter were chosen by the organisers on the basis of age and/or seniority of descent. Waka was represented in this way by his son's son's daughter (currently living in Auckland), Parehuia by her daughter's daughter (Auckland), Kena by his son's daughter (Huntly), Eruera by his daughter's son (Auckland), Aorangi by her daughter Puhata, in her nineties the oldest person present (Whatuwhiwhi), Rongopai by her daughter Rahera (Kōtare), Arapera by her daughter's daughter (Auckland) and Timoti by his son Tenga (Te Puna). Whina and Kahu were represented by their namesakes from other lines. On receiving the cake, each representative had to make a speech and at its end their whānau joined them in 'singing for their cake'.[7]

While the Hamiora Whānau Hui was organised on the basis of descent from a common ancestor, in-married spouses were not overlooked. Their names were included in the whakapapa booklet, enrolment and attendance were by parent-child family, spouses from whānau based in Kōtare and Te Puna were heavily involved in the Organising Committee and its sub-committees (as indicated in Figure 2), and visiting spouses were subsumed under descent category labels in the assignment of activities.

In-married spouses were also important as a source of differentiation within the whānau, giving their children and other descendants access to other kinsfolk, to other whānau and if male to other surnames. The three main whānau within the Hamiora Whānau in 1985 were differentiated by their descent from the sisters Parehuia, Aorangi and Rongopai, but this was reinforced by the differences in the surnames, land base and kinship connections inherited from these sisters' husbands. Parehuia and Aorangi had married men from outside Kōtare and lived for much if not all their married life in their husbands' home settlements: only one or two of their children felt and passed on attachment to land and kin in Kōtare.

Rongopai on the other hand had married a man from another Kōtare whānau, Nika Matthews. Most of her children remembered living on their father's land in another part of Kōtare when small, and though Rongopai took them to live in Hakea on Hamiora land after Nika died, several of them also lived on Nika's land as adults, keeping warm their rights in it. While Rongopai's descendants identified themselves as an integral part of the Hamiora Whānau in 1985 through membership in one of its major sub-divisions, they also said they 'felt aroha' for their ancestor

Nika and were moved to emphasise their descent from him as distinct from their descent from Rongopai. Hence their insistence on holding a Matthews' reunion as well as supporting a Hamiora one, and combining it with the unveiling for their previous kaumātua, who for many years had farmed the land inherited from Nika.

The 'Founder' of the Hamiora Whānau

The reunion hui firmly established Hamiora as 'founding ancestor' of the Hamiora Whānau. The first page of the *Hamiora Whānau Hui* booklet sets out a whakapapa tracing Hamiora's descent from Nukutawhiti, rangatira (chiefly leader) of the important northern canoe Ngātokimatawhaorua. Underneath are the words: 'This whakapapa is the foundation of our past, present and future. The very roots of our existence.' The whakapapa of the whānau itself begins with a photograph of and reference to both Hamiora and his wife Atawhai, but the formula used ('Ka moe a Hamiora i a Atawhai'—'Hamiora married Atawhai') and the setting out stress the primacy of Hamiora. In discussion Hamiora and Atawhai are sometimes mentioned as a couple, but more often than not the reference is to Hamiora alone. It is Hamiora's name which is used as the Whānau's identifying label.

Yet in 1958 one of the Whānau's most knowledgeable kaumātua told me that Hamiora did not belong to any of the Kōtare whānau or hapū by descent nor even to Te Rarawa iwi.[8] His inherited land base was in the territory of a neighbouring iwi. He had settled in Kōtare well after his marriage to Atawhai at the invitation of Atawhai's mother's brother Aperahama, a rangatira who wanted members of his whānau living on the land to ensure recognition of his ownership by the Māori Land Court. Members of the Hamiora Whānau properly derive their rights as tāngata whenua in Kōtare not from Hamiora but from Atawhai. The kaumātua said that Aperahama had 'adopted' Hamiora as his heir. If true, this leaves unanswered the questions why it was considered necessary and why Atawhai's key position has been forgotten in recent years. Atawhai was elusive as a personality, but so was Hamiora. Even in 1955 I met no one who could provide a character sketch, heard no stories of his doings. By 1985 he was only a name and a photograph.

The word 'founder', with its connotations of deliberate planning and strong leadership, seems less than apt for Hamiora. His main contributions to the whānau would seem to have been the begetting of a large sibling set and a name suitable for use as a group symbol. Instead of 'founder', he is better described as the eponymous or foundation ancestor of the whānau, neutral terms which leave open the degree of active leadership involved.

The way in which the Whānau has elevated Hamiora to the position of foundation ancestor over his wife Atawhai is not unusual in the Far North. A number of reunions in neighbouring districts in the last ten to fifteen years have given similar prominence to in-married husbands of women who belong to local descent-lines, some of them Pākehā. It is possible that the hui organisers did not investigate the relevant whakapapa thoroughly enough to discover that the husbands were not of local descent, but that would not account for the Pākehā 'founders'. The most likely explanation is that they were acting on the belief that in pre-European Māori society leadership roles were a male prerogative. This view was presented by early ethnographers like Best (1924) and more recently by Hiroa (1949), Schwimmer (1966) and Orbell (1978). Its general applicability was challenged by Apirana Mahuika (1975) with particular reference to the history and practice of his own people of the East Coast. Examining early European accounts in conjunction with the oral traditions and tikanga of many iwi, Anne Salmond concluded that the pre-European pattern of leadership was not a simple matter of male dominance. Summing up, she wrote:

> Regional variations in the relative status of men and women are difficult to sort out retrospectively, because the records are very uneven in quality and quantity for different districts, but it does seem clear that women in all tribes had property rights, played co-ordinate roles in many rituals with men and often had great influence in practical affairs. Agnatic preferences were probably always stated, but the principle of balance between men and women both in theory and practice was also very strong. (1991: 340)

Whatever the pre-European practice was or is believed to be in the Far North, the identification of men as foundation ancestors was strongly reinforced by Government insistence on patronymic surnames and by the emphasis placed on male dominance by the Pākehā population until fairly recent times.

In my experience, leadership in contemporary whānau in the Far North is a matter of considerable complexity. While the making of speeches to welcome visitors to the marae is mostly carried out by men, kuia distinguished by high descent, strength of character and oratorical ability do sometimes make such speeches, mostly within limits which they impose on themselves, speaking from the shelter of the meeting-house porch or inside the house, after male speakers have opened the way, and on their own ancestral marae. Once visitors have been welcomed, women take a full and active part in the subsequent discussions, in so far as they wish to do so. When visitors are not present, kaumātua of both sexes provide personal leadership in ways governed mainly by the occasion and by their status as descendants of the whānau ancestor or as in-married spouses. In particular, when the emphasis is on the whānau as descent group, as in discussions relating to whānau assets, the kaumātua descended from the whānau ancestor have the decisive voice, whether male or female. This was certainly true of Rahera, kuia of the Matthews whānau, in the years when she was the only member of her generation of the whānau living in Kōtare.

Conclusion: the Hamiora Whānau as process

Since 1955 the corporate group that was the Samuels 'family' has been continually in the process of growth and change. The original 'family' and its branches have segmented into new groups of the same kind, groups which consist of a core of members descended from a common ancestor plus their spouses and adopted children, organise 'occasional' group activities and manage inherited group property. In each generation, some members of these groups have been lost through migration and the transfer of their allegiance to other groups, along with the potential members who are their descendants. On the other hand, some have returned home to live and become active in whānau affairs.

As these new whānau have grown progressively further apart and shown signs of segmenting themselves, there has developed a countervailing desire to get back together again. The Hamiora Whānau Hui reasserted the idea of the descendants of Hamiora as a whānau by repeated use of Hamiora's name as a rallying call. The logo on the cover of the *Hamiora Whānau Hui* booklet emphasised the oneness of the Whānau and its identity with a home base in Kōtare, using symbols representing the Whānau sheltered between sacred mountain and beach. But the Hamiora Whānau thus asserted is a descent category, not a descent group. Its identity is conceptual, not actively corporate, its eponymous ancestor important more for his symbolic than his personal headship.

Today the descendants of Hamiora continue to identify the descent category defined by descent from this ancestor as a whānau, the Hamiora Whānau, while also applying the term whānau to a series of smaller groups contained within it: to descent categories stemming from Hamiora and Atawhai's children which first became significant at the Whānau Hui, and to descent groups and extended families stemming in most cases from their grandchildren.

So far no one has suggested that they attach the prefix Ngāti- to Hamiora's name or recognise the Hamiora Whānau as having the status of hapū. Such a move is unlikely, firstly because the existence in print of *Hamiora Whānau Hui* helps make 'the Hamiora Whānau' a familiar phrase, and secondly because the Hamiora Whānau is a purely conceptual entity. The descendants of Hamiora individually and as members of whānau are too widely scattered to have or pursue common aims. Management of the one piece of common property left, the marae, has effectively been assumed by a committee of descendants living in Kōtare and its vicinity.

In Kōtare the process of whānau developing into hapū has not occurred and probably never did occur. But the segmentation of old whānau into new can still be observed as new generations of descendants are born and existing whānau become too large or too scattered for effective operation.

Chapter 8

SHARING THE CARING

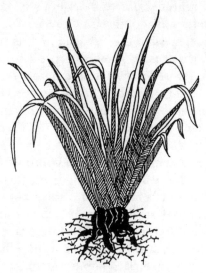

Parapara waerea a ururua, kia tupu whakaritorito te tupu o te harakeke.[1]

Clear away the overgrowth, so that the flax will put forth many young shoots.

L ike the flax bush, the whānau is most productive when cultivated purposefully. Like the rito, children need space and light to grow tall and strong.

Continuing the horticultural metaphor, the Māori word for raising children is whakatupu, literally, 'to make to grow'. With the addition of a noun ending, whakatupu becomes whaka-tupuranga (generation), identifying descendants the same number of steps from a common ancestor. The children born to whānau members are at once descendants of the whānau ancestor and potential whānau recruits. When a whānau functions as a unity, adult members describe each other's children as 'ā mātou tamariki' (the children of us many), as distinct from 'ā māua tamariki' (the children of us two), and take an active interest in their raising.

Māori child-raising has been the focus of interrelated research studies reported by Ernest and Pearl Beaglehole (1946) and by Jane Ritchie and James Ritchie (in publications ranging from 1956 to 1989). The conclusions reached in these research studies have been illustrated, illuminated, challenged and amplified by numerous short stories, novels and biographies by Māori writers, especially since 1970.[2]

In view of the rich literature available, I shall not attempt to cover the whole field but, after a brief overview based on the Ritchies' research studies, I shall concentrate on two particular aspects of Māori child-raising from the perspective of the whānau, namely, the parts played by parents and other kinsfolk relative to each other and the Māori practice of adoption. The propositions advanced are grounded in my own observation and participation in real life whānau, tested and illuminated by the contributions of kai-whakaatu reflecting on their own experience.

Children and young persons

Beliefs about children and the phases of childhood are reflected in the vocabulary for describing them and the way it is used.

The Māori words *tamaiti* (singular) and *tamariki* (plural)[3] correspond fairly closely in definition to the English words *child* and *children*, but there are some significant differences in usage. Like child, tamaiti is used with several overlapping meanings.

First, tamaiti is used generically to refer to a young person below the status of adult. In this generic sense tamaiti is defined by opposition to kaumātua (or its synonym pakeke), which has the general meaning of 'adult or grown-up', as well as the familiar meaning of 'person of senior age and status'.[4]

Within this generic category, tamaiti is defined (secondly) in opposition to taitamariki,[5] distinguishing a young person below the age of puberty from one who is between puberty and full adulthood, the English 'adolescent'. This distinction is similar to that made in the Children, Young Persons, and their Families Act 1989 between 'child' and 'young person', except that the Act draws its boundaries in terms of age, defining child as 'a boy or girl under the age of 14 years' and young person as 'a boy or girl of or over the age of 14 years but under 17 years'. In the vocabulary of many Māori, especially the younger ones, taitamariki has been largely replaced by rangatahi.[6]

Tamaiti is also sometimes used (thirdly) to describe a child in the 'middle years' between kohungahunga (infant) and taitamariki, roughly between three and twelve years of age.

The boundaries between the generic categories tamaiti and kaumātua and between the various sub-divisions of tamaiti are not associated with a particular age or life event but shift backwards and forwards according to context and individual maturity. Early European observers made no mention of any rites marking puberty or entry into adulthood among the Māori, though they may have failed to see them.[7] In classic Māori society this function was probably fulfilled by a boy's first war expedition and a girl's first child. Nowadays Māori often stage a hui to mark a young person's twenty-first birthday but this usually occurs well after the transition to adulthood is complete.

In contexts emphasising physical maturity and competence, Māori adults accord young people the status and autonomy of adults at a relatively young age, at fifteen or even younger. In contexts emphasising social maturity and the acquisition of cultural knowledge, on the other hand, they continue to identify young people as tamariki, taitamariki or rangatahi until they are well into and even out of their twenties (Metge 1964: 198-202). Under the entry 'young', Ngata's *English-Maori Dictionary* gives the example: *'You're still young at thirty, lad*. Kai te tamariki tonu koe i te toru tekau, e tama.'[8]

As in most societies, adults and children often have different understandings as to when the boundary has been crossed in particular cases.

In general, Māori see the relation between child and adult as relative rather than absolute, the term they choose in particular contexts making a statement about relatively higher or lower mana. Significantly, native speakers of Māori use the word kaumātua as a verb to indicate not simply the passage from childhood to adulthood but any significant advance from one developmental stage to another, during childhood as well as adulthood. Thus the mother who says 'Kua kaumātua taku tama' or 'my son has/is grown-up' (using 'grown-up' as the English equivalent of kaumātua) *may* be saying that her son has graduated from childhood into adulthood, but she may equally well be referring to his transition from kōhanga reo to primary school *or* to his acceptance into the company of the elders at around fifty years of age!

In these chapters, for the sake of brevity, the terms child/ children will be used with the generic meaning of tamaiti/tamariki to refer to all children and young persons in the care of adults, from babies to adolescents.

Words for relatives

The modern Māori kinship vocabulary includes both Māori and English terms, many of them matched as translations. It is important to realise, however, that, in modern Māori usage, Māori terms are used with meanings modified by acquaintance with their English counterparts, while most English terms are used with meanings influenced by their Māori counterparts.

In the following pages I use English terms the way Māori use them. Thus the terms parent, mother and father refer to a person's own or adopted parent, mother and father. Grandparent, grandfather and grandmother, are used to identify not only a person's parents' parents but also the latter's siblings and same generation cousins. Grandchild, grandson and granddaughter refer to the grandchildren of all identified as grandparents, that is, to a person's own children's children and the latter's cousins of the same generation. Uncle and aunt refer to parents' brothers and sisters and also to the latter's same generation cousins and to the spouses of those so identified. Niece and nephew refer to the children of a person's cousins as well as their siblings.

The Māori pattern of child-raising

Drawing on team and individual research in Māori communities both rural and urban, Jane and James Ritchie have studied and written about Māori child-raising for nearly four decades. In that time, their theoretical and methodological approaches have changed with changes in the social sciences, and their interpretation of the evidence with advances in understanding (Jane Ritchie and James Ritchie 1989: 96-103). Their most recent

publications (1979, 1989) demonstrate a balanced appreciation
of the kinship context in which Māori child-raising takes place,
its aims and achievements, and its relationship to child-raising in
other parts of Polynesia.

Describing the Māori pattern of child-raising as they observed
it in Māori rural communities in the 1950s and 1960s, Jane and
James Ritchie focused, firstly, on a significant shift in the way
adults and in particular parents related to babies and to children
past babyhood. Babies lived in a golden world, the focus of continuous, loving warmth and attention; they were fed on demand,
continually picked up, nursed and carried around by parents,
siblings and surrounding adults. When babies became toddlers,
often about the time the next baby was born, parents pulled back
from close interaction, assigned them to the care of older siblings
for much of the time, and encouraged them towards independence. Discarding the early labelling of this process as rejection,
Jane and James Ritchie characterised it as involving not a
withdrawal of love but a reduction in the frequency, degree and
directness of its expression, a shift from continuous to intermit-
tent interaction and socialisation. In response, children turned
to others for continuous interpersonal warmth, especially grandparents and peers, learnt to pay careful attention to social signals
and developed marked 'skills of social vigilance'.

Relations between parents and children were worked out
(secondly) in community, in the midst of a 'surrounding world
of kinsfolk'. As long as they caused no disturbance children were
admitted everywhere into the adult world and adult relatives
participated actively in their care. Parents and adults generally
approved independence in pre-school and school children within
wide bounds, confident that they would come to little harm,
because any siblings and adults in their vicinity would keep an
eye on them. This pattern of 'multiple parenting' reduced the
burden of responsibility borne by parents, enabled children to
form a variety of emotional ties, provided them with many
models, and prevented their being locked into restrictive or
punitive relations with parents.

Jane and James Ritchie laid particular stress (thirdly) on the
importance of peer socialisation. This took place both within
sibling sets and in loosely structured neighbourhood play groups

involving children of varying ages and mostly from related families. Put in charge of the younger ones, older siblings assigned the bulk of day-to-day chores, dealt with minor misdemeanours, gave training by word, command and act, and also supplied solace, comfort, consolation and companionship.

The transition to adolescence involved young people for a short time in a reorientation towards their parents as models and mediators of adult life. Parents took renewed interest in teenage children, expecting more work from them but also allowing them to share more in adult activities. They exerted more control over their behaviour, especially in the case of girls, but lifted it once the teenagers were recognised as adults by the community. The final transition to adulthood was rapid and usually completed well before sixteen years.

Writing in 1970, Jane and James Ritchie summed up the positive features of this pattern of child-raising:

> The early warmth of the mother-child relationship, the added security of a number of parent-like adults, the special relationships with an older brother or sister, and the ever-present, always-accepting group, provide both the basis and the structure that enable the Māori individual to keep his balance in a changing world. (1970: 132)

At that time they made a less favourable assessment of the reduction of direct parental involvement with children past babyhood and the prominence of socialisation by peers. As their perspective has widened to include all Polynesia, they have come to appreciate the way these features fit into the total pattern and contribute to the development of a strong sense of togetherness, a high valuation on consensus, and the capacity to set conflict aside, when necessary, in favour of cooperation.

Jane and James Ritchie examined and rejected the possibility that the child-raising pattern they described was sufficiently explained by rural residence, large family size, low incomes and limited socio-economic differentiation. Their contention that it was cultural in origin was confirmed by comparable results from research studies in other parts of Polynesia (1970: 129-45).

Underlying principles

Underlying the Māori pattern of child-raising is a set of principles which are not taught as a formal code but are mostly taken for granted and absorbed in the context in and for which they were developed, that of a community of overlapping and interlocking whānau.

The first principle is that children are to be valued not only for their own sakes as unique individuals but also as the uri (descendants) of recent tūpuna (grandparents and great-grandparents), as links in lines of descent that stretch from the beginning of time into the future, and as nodes in the kinship network which connects living individuals and groups. They are frequently described as taonga, treasures given by God and the ancestors, to be held in trust and cared for, as members of whānau, hapū and iwi and as inheritors of ancestral names and gifts. Teacher Kowhai Hardy once told me with passionate intensity that when she looks at a Māori pupil she sees not that child only but the line of ancestors who stand behind him or her and whom she must take into account in her dealings with that child. She was highly critical of Pākehā teachers who see and treat children only as individuals, in isolation from their background.

The second principle is that children belong, not to their parents exclusively, but to each of the whānau to which they have access through their parents. Belonging in this context is a matter of identity, not possession. It derives in the first place from whakapapa but should be confirmed and strengthened by regular social interaction. As Atakura Waru put it:

> We see children as belonging to us regardless of whether they come from our own womb. I feel as close to my nieces and nephews as to my sons and daughters, but then I call them tama and tamāhine. There is no such thing as owning or possessing children.

The third principle is that rights and responsibilities for raising children are properly shared by the adult members of the whānau to which they belong and in some cases reserved to particular senior relatives. What these are will be explored in this and following chapters.

The fourth principle is that children also have rights and responsibilities. They have rights to their genealogical identity, to love, to support and to socialisation in tikanga Māori, from other members of their whānau as well as and sometimes instead of their parents. In their turn they are expected to honour reciprocal responsibilities to their parents, their ancestors and the whānau as a group. Their rights are held in balance with the rights of other whānau members, especially the kaumātua, and of the whānau as a whole. Their rights to their parents' attention and support must compete with their parents' responsibilities. Whānau value children but are not child-centred.

These principles differ radically from those held by past and many present policy-makers and embodied in all but one of New Zealand's family laws (Durie-Hall and Metge 1993: 58-79). The current Guardianship and Adoption Acts (1968 and 1955) especially are based on the assumption that rights and responsibilities for children belong to their parents to the exclusion of others, as long as they discharge them faithfully. If parents cannot or do not do so, legal procedures are provided for their rights and responsibilities to be transferred to one or at most two other guardians as *substitutes*. Other relatives are not legally recognised as having either rights or responsibilities unless these are transferred legally to them as guardians or adoptive parents by the (birth) parents.

The Children, Young Persons, and their Families Act 1989 greatly widened the legal framework when it provided for family or whānau members to participate in Family Group Conferences arranged to develop management plans for children and young persons in need of care and protection or charged with offences against the law. However, its provisions apply only to limited categories of children and limit whānau members to a responsive rather than an initiating role. In the years since *Puao-Te-Ata-Tu* the Department of Social Welfare and other government agencies have modified their interpretation and implementation of several family laws to accommodate cultural difference and major changes in the kinds of family found in the population at large. Several of the out-dated laws are currently under review.[9] But there can be no certainty about policy until the laws themselves are changed.

Naming

Prominent among the rights traditionally held by whānau members was the right to give a child a name. Over the years the exercise of this right has been undermined by the law which makes parents responsible for registering a child's birth and name, by the scattering of whānau members in migration and since the 1960s by the increasing independence of the younger generations. While many young people do not even know about this right, those who wish to recapture their Māori heritage are beginning to revive it. My kai-whakaatu recollect it fondly as a way of reinforcing kinship bonds within and between whānau.

Older Māori regard naming children as a serious matter which requires the wisdom which comes with age and life experience. As Donald Owens explained:

> Children's names are taonga [treasured possessions] placed on their tinana [bodies] and rama mō ō rātou waewae [lamps for their feet].

Kaumātua usually choose Māori names which have been borne by relatives and ancestors or commemorate happenings in their lives. Such names have mana as a result of previous associations; recipients are believed to inherit some of the qualities of the original possessor along with the name. Many are taonga which belong to the whānau and often also to hapū and iwi. In several Muriwhenua whānau I know, women's names in particular are often bestowed every second or third generation, reinforcing the links between recipients.

In choosing names, the kaumātua have to know the tikanga (rules) governing their allocation and the repertoire of names on which it is tika (right) for them to draw. They need to know which names carry blessings and which are tapu (prohibited) because they have been associated with aituā (misfortune) of some kind. They also have to be careful to bestow them where they will be treated with respect. Inappropriate application and disrespect directed at name or bearer are breaches of tapu which are believed to have disastrous consequences for child and whānau.

For this reason and to make life easier for the child at school, parents usually add a more ordinary name for everyday use. Māori children typically acquire nicknames early in life and may be given others to commemorate some major family event. Many kai-whakaatu remember being given English names by Pākehā schoolteachers who found their Māori names too difficult to pronounce. When Māori today change the English names by which they have been known for Māori ones, they are often reviving names given them by relatives whether at birth or later.

The detailed content of the rules governing the allocation of naming rights varies between and within iwi. One common pattern gives the right to name all the sons in the family to the father's side, the right to name all the daughters to the mother's. According to another, the firstborn son is named by his father's side, the firstborn daughter by her mother's, and the other children in alternation without regard to sex. The rules of allocation, however, include provision for waiving them to meet special needs.

By conferring names on their mokopuna, kaumātua attach them firmly to a particular descent line and, as Roimata Wiremu pointed out, 'make sure that they are not lost to another whānau'. Rules governing the naming of boys and girls, especially the firstborn in their family, ensure that the claims of both parents' whānau are met and by doing so strengthen the ties between them. Awatea Hardy explained:

> We are Tainui. In our family the first son is always named from the father's side. The first daughter is always named by the mother's side, and that daughter must go back to her maternal grandparents. I asked Dad what the reason for that was. He said, 'When your sister was born she was named by the Ngāti Whātua people and she went back to Ngāti Whātua, to her grandmother. It was right for them to name that girl. She went back to her grandmother.'

In Moana Paiaka's experience, names were given for many reasons.

> Names were given for political reasons as well as cross ties to other families. Some were for succession to land, some

were thank-yous for favours, some were to do with whakapapa links, to show you were not nothings. People today do not understand, there is mana attached to a name.

She herself had three names: one from her mother's side, one from her father's and a third bestowed by a childless relative of her father's who had wanted to adopt her. Though the adoption did not proceed, her name guaranteed her rights of succession to his land (according to her iwi's tikanga) and his continuing interest in her welfare and achievements. Every time she departed for boarding school he waited at the bus stop to see her off and pressed a gift of money into her hand.

As is typical of Māori social practice, the professed rule is often set aside in response to higher imperatives. Thus kaumātua may transfer their naming right in order to strengthen ties with in-laws, especially if they come from another tribe, or name a child after a relative who has recently died, regardless of whether the connection is on father's side or mother's. In 1992 Arahi Mahuru of Te Rarawa gave up his right to name his daughter's firstborn daughter to the baby's paternal grandmother, at one stroke honouring the distant iwi from which she came and enabling her to commemorate her recently deceased mother.

When tohu (signs) mark out a child as special, kaumātua may actively compete for the right to name him or her. Roimata Wiremu, who was born in 1942, recalled:

This is what I was told about my naming. In those days, no one encroached into one another's territory, and that included names. When it was almost time for me to be born, my grandfather had gone away. After he left, this old kaumātua came by horse from a neighbouring community and awaited my arrival. When I was born he named me and he was leaving when my grandfather met him on the road. A few words were exchanged between them and they were not good words. My grandfather, having arrived home, asked my Dad had the old man named me and my Dad said yes. He got a good telling off from my grandfather but it was too late, because in those days those kaumātua's word was law.

Taken as a child to a hui in another part of the country, Roimata
was surprised by the rapturous greeting accorded her by the hosts.
Years later she learned that the old man had given her an ancestral
name which made her a link between tribes.

Naming a child has important psychological, social and even
political implications. Bearing an ancestor's name gives a child a
special emotional link with that ancestor, an interest in him or
her as a role model and a special attachment to his or her descent
line. It also attracts a special share of that ancestor's mana. This
affects the way relatives behave, causing them to treat the child
more politely than is usual, to mute discipline and to set higher
standards of achievement. Partly as a reminder and partly to light-
en the burden of responsibility, the name itself is often replaced
in use by a kinship term (Koro, Kui) as nickname. Wai Tahiwi
recalled that her grandmother's sister, Nanny Erena, 'always
called me "Mum", because I was named after her Mum'.

The 'weight' of a name is increased when it comes from
another tribe. Awatea Hardy recalled a painful episode from his
youth when Auntie Maata, the wife of his mother's younger
brother, asked him to name and be godfather to their fourth child.
Living at a distance from her natal iwi, she appreciated his interest
in her older children. Only twenty years of age, he accepted her
invitation without realising how great an honour it was. When
the baby was eighteen months old, Maata was visited by an older
brother from her distant home community. He told his sister to
change the name Awatea had given the baby to that of their
maternal grandmother. Because he was mātāmua (eldest) in her
sibling set, Maata felt constrained to obey him. She knew nothing
of deed poll, so the change was just one of usage. Six months
later, the little girl died. At her tangi relatives in the mourning
party which came from Maata's iwi asked how the child had got
her name. When Maata told them, 'there was dead silence', then
they laid the blame for her death on Maata's brother, saying that
he had been whakahīhī (arrogant) to change the name given by a
relative of the child's father, one who was moreover from a
tuakana line. Awatea said he 'felt terrible'. His father warned
him: 'Don't do that again until you know exactly what you are
doing.'

That was not, however, the end of the story. Many years later the eldest brother of the dead girl asked Awatea to name his firstborn son with Awatea's own name. Awatea refused but was then summoned by his uncle. When Awatea arrived at his uncle's home, his uncle gave the talking over to Maata (his wife). Awatea recalled:

> She said, 'It wasn't your fault. It was my fault and the fault of my family, not yours. You blessed that little girl and my family came down and took that blessing away from my little girl, and that's why I lost her. Nepia wants you to name his boy, and I want you to name him. That little boy is a sickly boy. I have faith that if you name that little boy, he is going to become well.

Now much more mature, Awatea agreed to name the child with the name he bore himself, but insisted that he was naming him not after himself but after the child's great-grandfather, Awatea's mother's father, for whom Awatea himself had been named.

> I said to my uncle and aunt, 'I'm going to give your father's name back to the Waaka family.' They were really pleased. My aunt said to my cousin, 'Now your grandfather's name has been given back by your tuakana, I want you to respect it. Never a bad word will be said about that baby. When you are angry with him you are never ever to use a swear word to him.' That baby got well and grew up into a robust young man.

Today, the right of senior relatives to name a child is not always exercised and when exercised may be resisted by parents refusing to register it. They may do this to assert their rights as parents against the whānau or in rejection of tikanga Māori in general. Or, respecting the name's tapu quality, they may not wish to burden the child with the responsibility it represents. Parents who seek such a name should realise that it entails a commitment to raise the child to be competent in Māori language and tikanga.

Primary care-givers

According to the Māori way of thinking, parents do not have an indisputable, exclusive, 'natural' right to bring up their children themselves nor even to choose alternative care-givers. Up until the 1950s, and even later in some communities, kaumātua often made decisions about who would raise the children of the whānau with little or no reference to their parents. Talking to a conference on child and family policy, Tamati Cairns recalled:

> I grew up in a little place called Ruatahuna which is still around fifty years behind the way we live in Wellington . . . I was raised by my old people, my kuia and koroua. I was a whāngai by way of Māori adoption. In the processes that were explained to me as to how I became that whāngai, the discussion was not made between my natural parents and my kuia and koroua, rather it was between my kuia and koroua and my adopting parents . . . the decision-makers for my destiny were not my parents. I was taken at one week old to my adopting parents by my grandmother and grandfather. My grandmother simply said: 'Here is your child', nothing terribly complicated, simply that. (Cairns 1991: 100)

Māori parents living in rural communities found it difficult to stand out against decisions made by the kaumātua because they were often dependent on older relatives for a living and the kaumātua had the support of the community. As, from the 1950s on, young people became more independent economically, migrated and settled away from their home communities, they became better able to resist the efforts of senior relatives to take their children. Nevertheless, Māori generally continue to recognise the right of grandparents to share in decision-making regarding their mokopuna and grandparents commonly play important roles as negotiators, advisers, and advocates of particular solutions. Tamati Cairns went on to relate how he helped to carry the pattern of whāngai on into the next generation.

My sister fell pregnant some 20 years ago and at that time

she was excelling in her career . . . My wife and I had no children. We saw an opportunity. However, I did not negotiate with my sister, I negotiated with my mother and father, the grandparents of the unborn child. The reason why I went to my mother and father is because I related to the process that I had come through and the decisions that had been made for me. Having made the negotiations, my mother and father told my sister: you are giving your child to your brother. (Cairns 1991: 101)

Even though parents now play the major role in the decision-making, Māori children are still considerably more likely than Pākehā children to be brought up, for all or part of their childhood, by their grandparents and other senior relatives as primary care-givers. There are many reasons why parents agree to let a child be brought up by grandparents or other relatives, and many reasons why grandparents want to assume that responsibility. These will be explored more fully in the section on atawhai adoption.

Sharing the caring

Regardless of who the *primary* care-giver is, Māori who belong to functioning whānau expect whānau members to act caringly towards children belonging to the whānau whenever an opportunity presents itself, without waiting for permission. Māori parents and other primary care-givers not only allow but *expect* other adults in the whānau to do for their children whatever they would do themselves, in their presence as in their absence, in ordinary situations as in crises. To their way of thinking, adult relatives should feed children when hungry, put them to bed when sleepy, treat and comfort them when hurt or distressed. Nor should their care stop there: they should also give whānau children instruction and direction, correct their mistakes, and reprimand and if necessary punish them for bad behaviour.

Until the late 1980s I described the acting out of these expectations as 'shared parenting', a phrase suggested by one of my kai-whakaatu, but I have since found it necessary to replace it with 'shared care-giving', for three reasons. Firstly, 'shared parenting' has been taken over by social workers and media commentators to describe the situation where a divorced couple share the custody and care of the children of their former marriage by an alternation between homes established with other partners. Secondly, the word parent has such pronounced specificity for Pākehā speakers of English that extending it to other relatives results in ambiguity and confusion. Thirdly, I began to suspect that the Māori pattern of child-raising included a division of labour between parents and other relatives with respect to certain tasks. This hypothesis will be explored more fully in the next two chapters.

The greatest opportunity for shared care-giving occurs where several generations and nuclear families live together in one household or in households located close to each other in the same or neighbouring settlements.

Growing up after World War II, Rahera Anderson lived in a large extended family household consisting of twenty-two persons, comprising several elderly couples and four families with children. Though there were a number of small bedrooms, most of the time they all slept in the big living room. Meals were cooked and eaten round the long table in the kitchen. As Rahera commented wryly: 'Where discipline was concerned, everybody gave you a hiding. It wasn't just the one person.' Growing up about the same time, Arahi Mahuru lived in a household presided over by a grand-aunt and two uncles. He recalled how they took in relatives whenever there were problems.

There were times when there would have been at least half a dozen families in the house and only two sets of parents looking after them. Families came and went; there was a turnover due to families moving away to Auckland and coming back.

Sometimes in such households particular relatives assumed or were given responsibility for particular children. As Hera Hikuwai recalled:

My sister, my brother and I were brought up by our Nanny. We slept with her in a big double bed and she got

us up, washed and dressed us, she heard our prayers at
night, and she fed us. Our other brothers and sisters slept
in the other bedroom with Mum and Dad. I must have
been six or seven before I realised they were our parents.

Harata Solomon had her own personal attendant:

> I had long hair as a child . . . It was very curly and wiry and
> I couldn't comb it myself. We had a little old lady, we called
> her Aunty Pua and I don't remember much about her,
> except she was alone, and she didn't have a home and she
> lived with us and her whole time was to bathe me and dress
> me and comb my hair. (Fyfe 1990: 90)

Most of my kai-whakaatu grew up with ready access to several
households and were perfectly at home in each. Recalling his
childhood in Muriwhenua in the 1920s and early 1930s, Rongopai
Russell told how:

> If we were too far away from home when lunch time came
> we went into the nearest house. We accepted that as our
> right. More often than not our own table at home had a lot
> of visitors. We children tended to gather at a particular
> place, especially after school. At weekends we would turn
> up at one of the relations' homes, about twenty children,
> and we'd play together there as a group. When it came to
> meal times, then the burden fell on the particular auntie at
> the time, whoever she was. Sometimes at night we just
> bedded down with these other people too. 'Your home is
> my home and my home is your home' is the attitude we
> had.

Wiki Thomas, who grew up in the same decade in a neighbouring
tribal area, described her home settlement as 'full of kōtīti (wan-
dering) children—if you got a beating from your mother, you
took off to another house, to Auntie Ani, Auntie Rihi, Auntie
Whoever.' Another contemporary, Nancy Whaiawa, said that
'the continual trekking of the mokos' had worn a pathway between her parents' and their grandmother's, because 'Granny

always had something for us when we visited her.'

In such settlements, no less than in extended family house-holds, everyone kept an eye on everyone's children, providing care as and when necessary. Otene Reihana, who grew up on the East Coast in the 1920s and 1930s, recalled:

> Finding kai moana was our fun. For us kids, when it was decided we were going to the beach, everyone had to bring a potato in each pocket and some waterproof matches. We'd go out and spend the weekend. Our parents would call others and ask if we were there. Someone would have seen us going to the beach.

Growing up in the 1950s in the same settlement as Wiki Thomas, her sister's son, Nika Hall, found it unchanged in this respect:

> The houses were open to all the children. Everybody moved around, we moved together . . . you didn't worry where you had your meals, the closest house was where you went. They were all the same people. Anyone who went past was invited in for a feed.

Living in a schoolhouse next to a marae settlement in the central North Island in the 1960s, Matiu Waimea observed that after school, when their chores were done, the children would play around the houses.

> If some one knocked a peach from a tree on the way home, one of the aunts would lay into them for it. It didn't matter which one. An offence against one was an offence against all. It wasn't uncommon for Auntie Raiha to chase someone else's child with a stick—it was threat more than punish-ment but a very important social control. A kid wouldn't hive off and plunder someone else's tree or eggs, because he would get the same treatment from the nearest aunt. Parents had an understanding, they delegated rights to other relatives. At mealtimes if kids were at their grand-mother's place she would just as likely give them a meal and a bed.

In many cases, children were and are hard put to single out one household as home. Recalling his boyhood in the 1950s, Karena Tipene said:

> As children we had so many homes to go to. We weren't always with Mum. Most times we were with our grandfather. He was widowed, a lovely, gentle old man.

As a boy in the 1950s, Will Nopera lived in a Māori settlement six miles out of a small town. He regularly went to town on Friday nights to stay with his grandparents, spent Saturday helping them around their house and garden and visiting relatives, and went to Mass with them on Sunday before walking home. He spoke of an aunt who lived in the same settlement as his parents as 'very much like a mother'.

> We could go into her home at any time and help ourselves to any food in the cupboard, or we would sleep there. I can remember, when I was about six or seven, going to her place and having a bath with her children, all in the bath together. This was the way things were. We were very, very close.

Yet another contemporary, Harry Waimiro, travelled by bus from a country settlement to secondary school in the nearby town. Most of the time he lived with his grandparents, but he often 'popped in' to his parents' home across the road and after school he often boarded the bus for another settlement where he stayed overnight with an uncle. It depended, he said, on which bus he came across first, and whether or not he was in trouble at home.

Though rural-based whānau regularly lose constituent families by emigration, those which remain reasonably accessible to each other, whether in town or country, have maintained this pattern of shared caring for children through the years to the present day. In the mid 1970s, when her youngest child started school, Wai Tahiwi felt able to work fulltime because 'there was always someone around to look after the kids.' After naming ten 'nannies, aunties and uncles' on whom she could call, she added:

Even Auntie Lovey, who worked at the hospital, she'd say, on her day off, 'drop the kids off to me, I'm lonely, I want some mates!'

In 1982 I met nine-year-old Tammy, who divided her time between her parents' home and that of her mother's mother's sisters, attending school from both homes. She loved being an only child cossetted by her kuia, but sooner or later missed her brothers and sisters and went home to see them. She addressed both her mother and her oldest grand-aunt as 'Mum' and told the latter: 'I am very lucky, because when you die I'll still have a Mummy to go to.'

This sharing of care for related children extends from childhood through adolescence into adulthood. A kuia of over sixty, Hera Hikuwai explained that her sister Winika's grandchildren were 'our mokos' and she did what had to be done for them without any fear that Winika would consider such action interference. When Winika's unmarried granddaughter became pregnant some years ago, her 'other grandmother' (her father's mother) offered to take the baby when it was born but Hera talked to the girl, advising her to think seriously about keeping the baby. She also spoke to the other grandmother, explaining that if everything was made too easy for her the girl would 'never learn'. Hera and Winika visited their granddaughter together after the birth and cried with joy when she announced her intention to care for the child herself. For the next twelve months she lived with Hera. Then, having proved herself a good mother, she moved into a place of her own, where Hera and Winika were frequent visitors.

Caring at hui

Up to the 1960s, it was standard practice at hui on marae for two or three kaumātua to assume control of all the children attending, keeping them occupied with chores and games, making sure they did not make too much noise, and seeing that they were fed at appropriate intervals. Their parents were thus released to devote their energies to the work of whānau hospitality. This practice has lapsed in many places, but where kōhanga reo have been set up at marae, those in charge often open the kōhanga reo building and gather both local and visiting children there under their supervision during hui.

Where children are not supervised as a group, they are attended to as necessary by whichever relative is closest or quickest off the mark. Will Nopera recalled that, during his childhood in the 1950s:

> At hui, the parents took on a very general role of parenting. If they saw other parents' kids getting into trouble or into mischief or about to do themselves an injury, they will take up the mantle of parenthood and reprimand or help or whatever. At the marae you often see women picking up other people's children, nurturing and caring for them, even suckling them.

Sharing a whānau occasion with a set of siblings and their spouses and descendants in 1981, I noted that all the adults had a child on their knee, and that in each case the child was not their own child or grandchild but that of one of their siblings. When two of the children began to quarrel over a toy, the two nearest adults intervened to distract them, though their parents were sitting only feet away.

Filling the gap

Where one parent is missing for any reason, the lack is supplied by other members of the whānau. This was clearly the case for Miriam Norton.

> I did not know I was illegitimate till I went to boarding school. Until I was thirteen I had never heard the word. I had grown up with my Mum's family. With uncles and grand-uncles, I never once felt the lack [of a father]. I felt the most loved child. I couldn't have got any more love if I had had a father. . . . It is not that I did not know. I knew who he was. But it wasn't till I got to school that I learnt *that* word.

Neri Paiaka, whose father died overseas in the Second World War, felt the same.

> We were always called the war babies, by everybody in the community. They would say, 'Oh, here come the war babies!' I never felt anything missing. I knew my father had died, but *they* were all there.

When parents cannot supply the material needs of their children, especially in crisis situations, other members of the whānau feel an obligation to help, often in substantial ways. Many of my kai-whakaatu went to boarding school equipped by the whānau rather than their parents. When Ngawai Lancaster won a scholarship to boarding school, her widowed father could not meet the cost of the clothing required on his own. He showed the list to his cousins and sisters and she set off fully supplied with 'a somewhat motley assortment' assembled from their contributions. Once established as a teacher, she reciprocated by helping equip her nieces and nephews and more recently her great-nieces and nephews:

> I have always bought them something, whichever ones I have heard about. Three went last year, so that cost me three pairs of shoes.

Visiting

Whānau members expect and are expected to accommodate each other's children on both short and long-term visits.

Children in strife or under stress at home often take the initiative and remove themselves to another home for 'time out'. Growing up on the East Coast in the 1940s, Niho Waata recalled how:

> If you wanted a break, you went and stayed with Auntie or with Uncle. We were able to escape to [my uncle's] farm, seven miles riding by horse. But you couldn't escape very far. It was a controlled escape. It didn't matter where you went, you connected up with your family again. It was going from one family to another.

Often the 'time out' is as important to the parents as it is to the children. Also from the East Coast but ten years younger, Kiwa Paki recalled that 'my mother used to have time out by us just moving down the road and being taken care of by other families.'

Often also such visiting takes place on a reciprocal basis. The children of Kiwa's mother's half-sister 'all came to stay with us from time to time and we went and stayed with my aunt and her husband, not for long periods but mostly over the school holidays. We sort of swapped families.'

Parents concerned about their children's need for wider experience, firmer discipline, more achieving role models or access to higher education than they can give often send their children to relatives for longer periods. After Kiwa's parents settled on the rural verge of a regional urban centre they had cousins staying with them almost all the time. It was mostly boys who came to stay, particularly in the difficult years between fourteen and sixteen years. Their parents sent them because they had difficulties communicating with them and making them work. They would stay from six to twelve months and then return to their parents.

> We had a cow and wood to chop and all those sorts of things. . . . My father was seen as someone who was fairly strict, who had guidelines but was always fair . . . it was because my father was adamant that we were always to be busy, always doing things that were helpful, so we all had to play sport, we all had to stay at school, we always had to talk with our parents. Some parents found they just weren't able to talk to their children.

The less rebellious girls came for shorter periods, at a younger age, as part of the normal exchange of visits.

For generations, children from homes in remote areas have been sent to live during the week or even for a term at a time with relatives closer to schools. Moihe Eruera, in his eighties when interviewed, grew up in a coastal settlement accessible only on horseback. For five years from the age of seven, he lived during the week with his grandfather's brother, so that he could attend primary school. In 1955 eight children from Te Puna lived with relatives in Kōtare during the week in order to attend secondary school in Kaitaia. The special ties developed in this way often continue throughout life. Several of the Te Puna children who lived in Kōtare during their school years have returned to settle on inherited landholdings there, instead of in their parents' community, and others played significant roles in the organisation of the Hamiora Whānau Hui in 1985 (pp 125-27).

Conclusion

If they were brought up in a whānau in close touch with relatives, Māori parents do not expect to carry the whole responsibility for raising their children. They are accustomed, by their own childhood experience, to sharing the caring, with their own older children on the one hand and with older relatives of their own and their parents' generations on the other.

This pattern of shared child-raising is grounded in beliefs and values which stress the importance of descent and kinship connection as the basis for organising social life, value children as links in and between descent lines, and see them as belonging not to their parents only but also to their parents' whānau.

Chapter 9

PARENTING: EMPHASES AND AVOIDANCES

Ka mate kāinga tahi, ka ora kāinga rua.[1]

If you have two houses and one tumbles down,
the second remains to shelter you.

In pre-European times, a whānau had several kāinga (dwelling-places) located near different resources and moved between them in the course of the seasonal round. Metaphorically, this proverb endorses diversification of social and economic investments. Applied to child-raising, it stresses the importance of enabling children to build relationships with other relatives, so that if their parents die or cannot meet their needs, they have other sources of nurturing.

Māori relatives who share in child-raising are often described as acting 'like parents', sharing in tasks regarded in the first place as parental responsibilities. Jane and James Ritchie use the chapter title 'Many Parents' and the phrase 'multiple parenting' in writing about this feature of child-raising in Polynesian societies (Jane and James Ritchie 1979: 27-38; 1989: 110).

Over the years, as I observed whānau in action and talked to numerous kai-whakaatu, I began to question the assumptions implicit in this usage that the full range of child-raising tasks is assigned to parents in the first place and that other relatives *share* in these tasks, carrying out the same functions in the same way as parents. I noted that, especially in earlier decades, relatives of kaumātua status often pre-empted parental decision-making with regard (for example) to naming, residence, schooling and career choice. I became increasingly aware that parents tended to avoid certain aspects of child-raising, and that these were carried out by other relatives, especially grandparents. I wondered whether

158

these tasks might traditionally have been omitted from the definition of the role of parent and assigned to other relatives as part of their own proper role.

A division of labour?

I had my first intimation of a possible division of labour in Māori child-raising in 1979 when Kiwa Paki, talking about her childhood, commented almost as an aside that 'my parents never praised me'. She stopped suddenly, with a startled look on her face, as the implications of the comment struck us both. Kiwa is a mature and well-balanced woman, who has successfully raised a family and worked for many years as a family counsellor. She has clearly not suffered from emotional deprivation. If her parents did not praise her, from whom did she get the assurance of her own worth which is a feature of her personality? Reflecting on this problem, she realised that it came from the other relatives who were an integral part of her childhood environment.

In the years since, many other kai-whakaatu have commented on the lack of parental praise, in almost the same words. What is more, most have added the observation that in their experience lack of parental praise was coupled with a stress on correction. As Ruia Wylie said:

> My parents rarely praised anything we did—but they came down on us like a ton of bricks if we did not do things right.

Why this embargo on parental praise, coupled with this emphasis on parental correction? Remembering his own upbringing in the 1930s, Eru Paiaka suggested a combination of 'the social environment of the time' and the large size of families, which led parents to avoid trouble by treating all their children 'with equal firmness'. While these factors undoubtedly played a part, they do not account for the pervasiveness of the pattern in families of all sizes. Awatea Hardy supplied the key to parental avoidance of praise, when he said:

> Of course, our parents couldn't praise us. It would have been like praising themselves.

This analysis was confirmed by Eru Paiaka. Remembering how his adoptive father praised the achievements of all the children of the whānau except those he brought up, Eru commented:

> There was a kind of whakaiti [humbleness] in there, a preference for other members of his peer group to do the praising.

As we have seen (pp 103-4), Māori disapprove strongly of behaviour that is considered whakahīhī (conceited or arrogant). Talking about one's own achievements is described as 'skiting' and attracts critical comment. At the same time children are closely identified with their parents. In close-knit country communities they are often referred to by their father's forename or nickname in place of the family surname. To criticise a child as whakahīhī is to criticise his or her parents, implying that they have set a bad example or failed to check conceited tendencies. Consequently parents feel impelled to take pre-emptive action. They avoid praising their children not only in public but also in private, and they commonly reprimand children for expressions of confidence or pride in achievement. Kai-whakaatu working as teachers and counsellors report that the parents of Māori students commonly minimise or ignore their achievements and exaggerate their faults in discussions about their progress at school. Keri Waipapa remembered:

> When I was a counsellor, I would ask the parents to come in. They'd say: 'I don't know what to do with this rotten kid.' They'd complain about their kids. All their dealings with them were negative.

Such deprecating behaviour is very close to the way Māori respond when praise is directed at themselves.

Repeatedly through the years the failure of Māori parents to foster self-esteem in their children has been interpreted as indifference and lack of parenting skills. Close acquaintance with particular parents shows that such explanations are often wide of the mark. Parents' reluctance to praise their children can be more comprehensively accounted for by the inhibiting effect of

The Hamiora Whānau Hui, Kōtare, 1985: The hākari.
The Whānau Hui cake waits to be cut by the eldest living
descendant of Hamiora and Atawhai. The ten small cakes were
given to the eldest living descendants of their eight sons and
daughters who had issue and to the namesakes of the other
two.

The Hamiora Whānau Hui, Kōtare, 1985: the descendants of Aorangi.

Whānau summer at the seaside, Kōtare, 1960s.
A group of cousins and their uncles about to set off on an
expedition.

internalised disapproval of conceit. Matiu Waimea described this reluctance as 'a mechanism to negate whakahīhī'.

Whatever its causes, the withholding of praise by parents hurts children and if not countered damages their self-esteem. Māori parents often try to convey indirectly the pride they cannot put into words by stratagems such as telling others about their children's achievements when they know the conversation will be overheard by or relayed to the children concerned. On its own, this is not enough to reassure children of their worth; many fail to get the message. When the whānau is functioning effectively, the deficiency is made good by other relatives who express interest and pride in their nieces, nephews and grandchildren with questions about their activities, words of praise and small gifts. As Eru Paiaka summed up: 'The compensatory aroha came from Nanny or from our uncles and aunts.'

When Arano Martin came home on holiday from secondary school in the 1950s, he recalled that:

> Dad would hardly say anything about what I had done, but I noticed he was pretty proud. When I first went to boarding school, he'd talk about it but as I got older and more successful he didn't. The others did. He wouldn't say anything about it until the others asked.

Moana Paiaka had much the same experience in the 1960s. In her case it seemed as if her father and uncle had an unspoken agreement to encourage each other's children.

> Your parents never told you directly, 'Well done!' You never knew [what they thought]. My father and his brother used to wait at the store for the mail to come in. They would study our reports [from boarding school] and have a discussion about their children's progress. The other kids lived past our place. As they went by, there's our father leaning over the gate, waiting for them, and he'd say, 'A word with you, young man!' 'Yes, Uncle?' 'I understand you didn't do so well — do better!' He would supply support and comfort to his nieces and nephews. Their father Uncle Ned would come to our place and say, 'I hear you

have been doing very well!' and maybe he would slip me
half a crown.

While raising a large family in a community setting in the 1970s,
Wiki Martin noted:

As soon as our children start putting themselves up, we
start saying things to level them off. It is the other relatives
who praise our children, and we give praise to our nieces
and nephews. With others the children are on their best
behaviour because they want to be well thought of by their
relations. At the marae you'd think they were all perfect,
they know how to do things, and they get plenty of praise
for it, too. At home we are always correcting them, saying
'How do you know?' and so on.

Although increasing numbers of Māori parents make a
conscious effort to build up their children's self-esteem, they are
not always comfortable doing so and the children still need and
appreciate support from other relatives. Early in 1994 Moana
Paiaka visited her brother's household in another city. Her
brother had said nothing about his son's School Certificate results
(issued in January) and she was afraid to ask in case they had
been poor. Catching her nephew on his own, she asked how he
had fared; his face lit up and he rushed to fetch his results slip,
which showed that he had passed all his subjects with very good
marks. He talked to her at length about the examination papers,
especially the difficulties he had had. He had not discussed them
with his parents.

This discussion of who praised children produced insights
which led me to pay particular attention to the roles of grandparents, aunts and uncles (using those terms with the wide
meanings Māori give them) in relation to that of parents. Talking
to kai-whakaatu who had had a thoroughly Māori upbringing, it
became clear that, while there is no explicit rule, no tikanga as
such, Māori parents do tend to concentrate on certain child-
raising tasks and to leave others to relatives of their own and
their parents' generations.

Parents: emphases and avoidances

In all cultures, the role of parents in child-raising varies according to the parent's sex and the developmental stage of the child. In the Māori case, these variations have been described in detail by Jane and James Ritchie (1970, 1978, 1979). Here I propose to concentrate on the parental role as a unity and on those aspects of care-giving which parents emphasise on the one hand and avoid on the other.

When the relationship is not distorted by economic worries, ill health or social isolation, Māori parents are characteristically close and loving to their children while they are babies (piri poho, literally chest clinging), nursing and carrying them around in their arms. Far from keeping their babies to themselves, however, they share both physical closeness and care with relatives of all generations. In particular, busy mothers place babies in the care of older children, beginning a process of bonding between pairs of siblings which continues into adulthood.

My own observation, reinforced by the recollections of my kai-whakaatu, suggests that parents with children past the baby stage are preoccupied with satisfying their children's physical needs (for food, clothing, housing, transport, etc) and making sure that they acquire basic physical and social skills. Especially if they have many children, much of the parents' own time and energy is absorbed in physical activity (mahi) on the land or in waged employment, in the house, at the marae, and in social interaction with other adults. Parents involve their children with them in appropriate tasks, imparting skills mainly by expecting them to watch and imitate. Once the children are reasonably competent their parents leave them to work and play on their own. They do not see them as needing constant supervision or cosseting but encourage them into early independence.

When interacting with their children, parents typically maintain a stance of authority. They make frequent use of the imperative mood (giving directions and orders) and negative forms (rebuking or warning against wrong behaviour). Earlier generations were particularly strict and insistent on obedience and the regular performance of chores. Violet Rongonui recalled that when she was growing up in the 1930s:

I never used to answer back. In my time we were seen and not heard. My Mum was really strict . . . our teatree broom had two purposes, to sweep the floor and to hit our legs when we didn't listen. We each had to cart water before school and at night, and to get a sack of bark for firewood. We all helped with the planting of potatoes—one of our duties was to split the potatoes set aside for next year, with an eye on each side.

The chores were often demanding. In Lilian Nikau's family, her eldest sister worked chiefly at 'kitchen duties': at the age of eleven she competently assumed responsibility for ordering stores and preparing meals when her mother was in hospital having a baby. Lilian's second sister saw to the washing and care of clothes for the family and helped in house and cowshed. Her eldest brother, who worked in the cowshed with his father and cousins, was responsible for making sure the cream was ready to be picked up and the shed up to standard in case the dairy inspector called. All these jobs had to be done before the school bus came at 8.15 a.m.

Parents were often terse in criticising what they considered useless activities. Otene Reihana remembered:

At that time I read a lot. I was reading science fiction. My people didn't understand science fiction. I was a dead loss because of those books, I was told I'd do no good.

However, as parents of those generations grew older and their eldest children passed out of their care, they relaxed their guard and were less strict with the younger children. Lilian Nikau, who was one of twelve children, reflected that with the 'first batch' of children in the family her parents 'seemed to be establishing themselves, establishing the laws within the family and the boundaries, and enforcing them'. The 'middle run', to which she belonged, had these rules passed on by her older sisters and brothers, who took care of them. When the younger ones were growing up, their parents had moved from the farm into town and the three eldest had married and left the family home.

My mother and father treated the younger ones more like what I consider friends. They were able to have their mates at home after school, something I never saw when I was growing up. They were able to have friends home for the weekend and even take billets, people who came to the school for sports events and festivals. My parents would open up the house and go about making their stay comfortable.

Though he was grateful for his father's training, Karena Tipene remembered him as 'blimmin' strict':

My older brother Nikora is fifty-three but he still won't smoke in front of our father. But with my younger sisters and my young brother, Dad used to teach them counting games and nursery rhymes in the morning. It used to be the thing, when they were little, they would go and hop into the parents' bed. Pop would chant away, then you'd hear the little kids.

In the last twenty to thirty years, as the social climate has changed, Māori parents have become markedly less strict in controlling their children's behaviour, especially with regard to chores and not answering back. In spite of these changes in the detail of practice, however, the general outlines of the pattern persist in most cases. Keri Waipapa, a long-serving community officer, was intrigued by the way a Pākehā friend asked her children how they got on at school every day when they came home, and sat down to talk about it. She commented to her friend:

Māori parents wouldn't do that. They would say, Go and change your clothes, do this, do that. It is all instructions and directions.

While Māori parents place particular emphasis on caring for their children's physical needs, imparting basic skills, and re-proving bad or whakahīhī behaviour, they typically refrain from behaving in certain ways in relation to their children. These avoidances are not consciously articulated as taboos but they are so common in practice that identifying them in conversation evokes immediate comprehension, agreement and illustrations from Māori who grew up in Māori settings.

Avoidance of praise

Reference has already been made to the way in which parents avoid praising and expressing pride in their children. Matiu Waimea's experience was typical. As he said:

> My Dad was never one for telling me straight out that he was pleased with me. He would come and watch me play rugby but he never got excited on the sideline or yelled things like 'Well played!' Afterwards, if I had played well, he would say that the *team* played well—he would never identify my performance.

Once, when Matiu played in a curtain raiser before a big match, a bystander impressed by his performance asked his father who he was.

> Dad went to great pains to let me know that he told him I was a Waimea, not letting on that I was his son. He himself was known to the local Pākehā by an English surname.

When Matiu became a parent he found himself doing the same thing.

Will Nopera worked hard in the garden as a child, cleaning up, mowing lawns, cutting hedges and so on, in an effort to please his father.

> Strangely, it is not until recent years that I can remember getting praise from my father. In recent years my Dad has actually come out and said how good some of the things I have been doing are, but I don't recall getting that when I was young.

This avoidance of praise applies particularly to progress at school. Summing up his own experience as child, parent and teacher, Eru Paiaka said:

> Parents are always reluctant to talk with their children
> about their school reports. I know, with my own children,
> I never talk too much, just say, 'That's a nice report.' Nor-
> mally you leave it to the extended family to express praise
> or reprimand or both in terms of school reports.

In many cases parents get round their inhibitions about
praising their children indirectly, commenting favourably on
achievements within earshot of the subject or to third parties
who can be relied upon to relay the message. As Otene Reihana
perceptively noted, calling on children to perform tasks is itself a
way of indicating approval and pride in their competence. When
one of Otene's older brothers was picked for the hapū's haka
team, a great honour, his father and uncles did not congratulate
him in so many words but they were 'always asking him if he
knew this haka or that and getting him to demonstrate it'.

At the time, children often feel resentment at the lack of praise
and encouragement from their parents. More often than not they
fail to recognise the hidden messages of approval. It is only when
they become parents themselves that they realise how inhibited
their parents felt in this connection and begin to understand why.

Not infrequently, parents go beyond avoidance of praise to
engage in active criticism, belittling and putting their children
down. This often involves the sort of deprecatory remarks they
use to pre-empt or respond to praise aimed at themselves. When
Eru Paiaka passed School Certificate, the congratulations came
not from his mātua atawhai but from an uncle.

> He was loud and definite in his praises of that achievement,
> saw it as only the first little step and spelt out immediately
> the other hurdles I must aspire to. Whereas the fellow who
> brought me up, his contribution to the conversation was,
> 'He'll probably end up like the rest of the boys, on the
> farm dagging my sheep' and 'He'll probably decide to get
> married tomorrow.' While one praised, the one who was
> very close to me would not support that praise.

Eru remembered attending several weddings at which a speech-making father made disparaging remarks about bride or groom, saying (for example), 'I don't know what you see in my daughter' or 'My son was never efficient with his tasks on the farm.'

> I asked my matua, 'Why do they continually put down their children?' He laughed. All he said was, 'Te mana tangata, te mana o te whānau. Kei motu.' [Personal mana, the mana of the whānau. Lest they separate.]

By disparaging his offspring, the father was avoiding being thought whakahīhī and protecting the mana of the whānau by making sure that it could not be accused of deceit if the couple later separated.

Children's personal development need not be adversely affected by lack of parental praise, as long as they receive enough encouragement from other sources. But where such affirmation is not available and where parents are consistently disparaging, children's self-esteem may be irreparably damaged. When Keri Waipapa was teaching at a city school, she found many Māori students so lacking in self-confidence they would not try anything difficult, such as tāniko weaving:

> The kids would say: 'Don't make me do this. I can't do it. I'm useless. My parents are always telling me so.'

Whatever the reasons for parental criticism in particular cases, the critical attitude displayed by so many Māori parents towards their children is best understood (I believe) as a deeply internalised habit developed in the process of growing up as a defence against accusations of whakahīhī and modelled on their own experience of parental behaviour.

Avoidance of discussion

My own experience and that of my kai-whakaatu, especially in the 1950s and 1960s, suggest that Māori parents living in a whānau context did not as a rule engage in extensive verbal interchanges with their children, interchanges of the kind required to develop children's linguistic skills, reasoning ability and understanding of their social world. Ngawai Lancaster, who was brought up by her father after her mother's death in the 1950s, spoke for many when she said:

> I can't ever remember having a discussion with my father. He just said what we had to do. . . . Right up until I was nineteen he was telling me whether I could go out or not. . . . There wasn't any real discussion, he just left it at that. I didn't have the gumption to argue with him, it was just not expected.

Most of my kai-whakaatu commented on this parental avoidance of discussion indirectly rather than directly, by talking about verbal interaction with grandparents in particular. Brought up by a widowed mother and grandmother, Keri Waipapa remembered interacting with them in different ways. Her mother spoke English all the time, but they always spoke Māori with their grandmother. When she and her siblings came home from school their mother would cut short their complaints (for example, about their lunches) with a pithy comment: 'You're lucky to have lunches at all!' They would then try to wheedle food out of their grandmother. She would not necessarily give in but she would discuss the issue in a soft way, explaining the value of *all* food.

> My mother would give it to us straight between the eyes, she would respond sharply. Everything my grandmother said had a teaching point to it, she always took the opportunity to get a point across.

While most adults, including her mother, actively discouraged children's questions, her grandmother would first disclaim special knowledge.

> Then I'd say, 'If you don't tell me, who will?' And she would tell me.

While there were exceptions to this general rule, they were special cases which served to emphasise rather than test it. Will Nopera, who grew up in a Taranaki rural community in the 1950s, was grateful to his father for the way he would sit and talk to him and his brother, helping them work out answers to their questions. Talking to his children like that was 'one of the things that set him apart from the rest of the community'.

When their older children had grown up and left home, so that making a living was no longer such a struggle, parents often began to treat the remaining young ones, as Lilian Nikau said, 'more like what I consider friends', talking to them, telling them stories, even playing games with them (p 165). Echoing many traditional stories, my kai-whakaatu commented wryly on the precociousness of pōtiki (the youngest in a sibling set), explaining that their parents indulged and talked to them a lot. Both comment and explanation pointed up how unusual such discussions were.

As increasing numbers of Māori parents have trained as teachers or participated in play centre and kōhanga reo training programmes, especially from the 1960s on, many have modified their parenting practice to include reading and talking to their children. Even so, the traditional pattern remains deeply entrenched in many Māori homes, reinforced by the ubiquity of radio and television.

Various explanations have been advanced to account for the 'failure' of Māori parents to talk with their children. Some lay the blame on the parents, suggesting that they are uncaring and neglectful or lack parenting skills. Some emphasise the disastrous effects on children of a life style which features excessive drinking of alcohol, gambling and violence (e.g. Duff 1990). Some focus on child-raising patterns of cultural origin: the practice of parents making older children responsible for the care of the younger ones, the large measure of freedom accorded children away from adult control, and limitations on children participating in adult conversation (e.g. School Publications Branch 1971: 16-27). Other explanations focus on the social and economic disadvantages under which Māori labour as a minority group. Thus it is suggested that Māori parents working in unskilled jobs to support large families do not have enough time or energy left to talk to their children, or lack the confidence to discuss school work because their own experience of school was limited or unhappy.

Explanations of these kinds lead to the formulation of remedies which mostly concentrate on changing parental circumstances and child-raising methods: for example, family planning, increased family assistance, budgetary advice, counselling for violence and re-start educational schemes. Such proposals are good in themselves but their effectiveness is limited by the assumption that language development is a task which belongs to and can be done by parents only.

While recognising that these explanations may apply in particular cases, I suggest an explanation at a deeper structural level: namely, that developing children's use of language and their understanding of tikanga Māori were traditionally seen as the responsibility of the senior members of the whānau and not as part of the role of parents as such.

Avoidance of talk about sex

For many Māori parents in the 1950s and 1960s, a third area of avoidance was anything pertaining to sexuality. Most of my kai-whakaatu reported receiving little or no preparation for or information about menstruation, developing sexuality or courtship from their parents. As Eru Paiaka summed up the situation:

> Sex is tapu. Mothers have great difficulty in talking about puberty to their daughters. Fathers have even greater difficulty with their sons. I don't think my brothers and sisters and I had any direct guidance from the guy who brought us up.

Regarding menstruation, Roimata Wiremu spoke for most of the women who grew up before 1960 when she said: 'my mother never discussed it with me, I never taught my daughters about it'. As Violet Rongonui recalled:

> I never knew—especially with my period. I thought I was dying—I didn't know what was wrong. I felt shy, I didn't know what to ask. I couldn't ask my Mum because she

never said a word to me about it.

If parents gave their daughters any instruction, it was to warn them of the taboos they must observe when menstruating: keeping the evidence hidden from males, not pegging under-clothes where others would have to walk under them, not riding horses and not working in the gardens or gathering shellfish. Observance of these taboos was reinforced by stressing the disasters (sickness, crop failure, the disappearance of shellfish) that would follow their breach, but there was no mention of the deeper reason for these prohibitions, the polluting tapu associated with menstrual blood. According to Ata Robertson: 'Mother only talked to me about the hygiene side, about not going near the beach or near food.' Brought up by a widowed father, Ngawai Lancaster managed virtually on her own.

> I didn't have a clue. When it happened, I didn't know what it was but instinct made me use a pad. Ignorance, however, made me leave it on my bed-side table where my father saw it. He gave me my one and only sex instruction and that was: 'You are a woman now, and the next time this happens, don't let me or your brothers see it. And don't get involved with boys or you'll get a baby.' I had no idea what he was talking about.

For Neri Paiaka, who grew up in the decade after World War II:

> The menstruation part was all right but when it came down to sex, my mother shied away from that. She didn't even mention the subject. I was shy to ask about those things.

Sometimes a crisis forced parents to provide the necessary information and instruction. Neri remembered her brother Otene coming home in the middle of the night and waking her mother up. He had climbed through the window into his girlfriend's room when her father came in and caught him there. He asked Otene : 'Kua raruraru kōrua?' (Have you two got into trouble?) Otene did not know what he meant and had come to his mother for enlightenment.

She asked him: 'Did you actually get into bed with her?'
He said no, he was sitting on her bed talking to her. So she
explained it to him then.

Most often, however, young Māori learned what they needed
to know about sexual matters from their peers and from older
relatives they trusted. Eru Paiaka explained:

The third party played an important role for us. In my
case it was an uncle. In the case of the girls it was an older
aunt in one case and for the others an older sister, the first
to get married. She became the transmitter of sex knowledge
to the younger girls in the family.

Roimata Wiremu received the help she needed from her older
sister; she in turn passed it on to her younger sister. Violet
Rongonui in desperation asked the person she trusted most, the
elderly uncle who lived with her family, and he explained. When
eventually she told her mother, she said, 'You don't talk about
things like that.' For Ata Robertson, it was her grandmother who
explained menstruation to her. Ata could not remember exactly
what she said, but 'she spoke to me alone. I remember how she
spoke to me about it, as a mysterious thing.'
    Roimata Wiremu suggested that Māori parents' failure to talk
to their children about sexual matters when she was young could
be traced to the tapu attached to the human body 'in those days'.
Growing up in Muriwhenua in the 1950s, she and her sisters were
taught to keep the basins they used for personal washing separate
from those used by the men of the family or for preparing food
and never to let their hair fly in the wind. Tapu beliefs and
practices do not, however, account fully for parental avoidance
of this task. Given the serious consequences of breaches of tapu,
it would have been more logical for parents to make sure that
children were well prepared and not likely to make mistakes.
Classical Māori beliefs and practice with respect to talking about
sex were far from prudish. Orators, storytellers and poets made
frequent and effective use of sexual metaphors and in the myths
key events were described in terms of sexual encounter, as in

Tane's creation of woman and Maui's death (Reed 1963: 43-45; Alpers 1964: 70).

This particular parental avoidance could also be attributed to the Victorian form of Christianity to which Māori were converted in the nineteenth century and the attitudes prevailing in New Zealand society as a whole in the decades when most of my kai-whakaatu were growing up. Their experiences in this regard are very similar to those recounted by Pākehā contemporaries. Both these explanations contain an element of truth but cannot be the whole answer because information and advice on sex *was* provided, by other relatives.

Parental avoidance of sexual matters can be most fully explained in terms of a division of labour which assigns the task of sex education to relatives other than parents. The underlying rationale for this is (as in the case of the avoidance of praise) the close identification of children with their parents. Given their closeness, physically and emotionally, there is wisdom in avoiding the discussion of sex between sexually active parents and adolescent children living in the same household. Taboos on the discussion of sex between or in the presence of particular kinds of relatives are common in other Polynesian societies, such as Tonga and Tikopia. Although there is no reference to it in the literature, an informal taboo on such discussion between parents and children made good sense in Māori rural communities up to the 1960s, when families were typically large, both parents were occupied with work outside the home, and older relatives were accessible and responsive.

Conclusion

When Māori parents do not praise their children, read or talk to them at length, or provide them with sex instruction, it should not be too readily assumed that they are lazy, indifferent or unskilled as parents. While such explanations may apply in particular cases, Māori parents may also avoid these tasks because they have inherited and internalised a pattern of child-raising which excludes them from the parental role and assigns them to other relatives.

Chapter 10

GRANNIES, AUNTS
AND UNCLES

*Nāu i whatu te kākahu,
he tāniko tāku.*[1]

*You wove the body of the cloak,
I made the tāniko border.*

One of the most admired of Māori cloaks, the kaitaka, consists of two contrasting parts. The body of the cloak is the honey-gold colour of treated flax; plain and unadorned, its value inheres in the firmness of the flax strands, the regularity of the weave and the close spacing of rows made by double-pair twining. The tāniko border catches the eye with geometric designs in several colours in the even closer weave achieved by single-pair twining. The beauty of the garment is enhanced by the complementarity of its parts.

The proverb at the head of the chapter is usually interpreted as a metaphor for child-raising in the whānau. Parents lay the ground-work, developing basic character and practical skills in their children; senior relatives complete the process by nurturing the children's self-image, linguistic competence and special talents.

The senior relatives who play this special part in child-raising are those identified as tūpuna or grandparents, and as aunts and uncles.

Relations with tūpuna

Whether Māori are speaking Māori or English, the terms *tūpuna, grandparent, grandmother* and *grandfather* are usually given a much wider range of reference than the three English terms generally have. As well as a child's parents' parents, they are used to refer to a child's parents' parents' siblings and cousins, to the latter's spouses, and to relatives from the previous generation if still living.

Most Māori prefer to use affectionate variations on the general terms both for reference and for direct address. In many cases these are applied equally to both sexes, for example, Tupu, Karani, Granny or Nanny, according to whānau or iwi usage. However, grandmother and grandfather are also distinguished as Koro and Kui among northern iwi, Pōua and Tāua among iwi of the East Coast and South Island.

As the diminutive form of many of these terms implies, the relationship which they call to mind is commonly surrounded with an aura of warm affection.

Love and support

With few exceptions my kai-whakaatu remembered relations with their tūpuna as warm, close and comforting. Throughout their childhood their tūpuna had been a source of love and support, expressed openly and consistently in words and actions. Remembering her childhood before and during World War II, Neri Paiaka said:

> They were always so happy to see you. There was never that angry look on their faces, always a bright smile, and

they really wanted to touch you and pull you to them. The
Nannies were always down low, sitting on the floor, cross
legged. It was nice to sit by them, and then they'd just touch
your hair or put their arm around your shoulder and chat
away.

Her husband Eru remembered the way they would awhi
(embrace) and mirimiri (stroke and rub) their mokopuna: 'They
would always touch you somewhere, on your leg or hand, and
then rub.'

For their part, the mokopuna liked to get as close to their
Grannies as they could. A contemporary of Neri and Eru, Ata
Robertson, recalled that when they went to stay with her grandmother, she put the mattress on the floor, because all the mokopuna wanted to sleep with her. 'They were all trying to get close
and cuddle her.' Rose Etana summed up her Grannies as 'patient,
tolerant people, kind and gentle. They always had plenty of time
for mokos, yet they were always busy doing something.'

Particular tūpuna left very special memories. Though his
grandfather died when he was seven, Arama Martin had vivid
recollections of the five years he lived with Arama's family.

He doted on me, carried me everywhere on his shoulders
when I was little, put me down by the woodheap and
chopped wood. He was pretty old then . . . He would talk
and sing to me, always in Māori. He brought us all sorts of
things we didn't get otherwise, like biscuits. He spoilt us.

Awatea Hardy's mother's mother played a central role in his
childhood.

My Nanny was a wonderful old lady. Quite often my
younger brother and I were left with my grandmother, and
that was a wonderful time of our lives. We got anything
that we wanted. She made sure we were tucked into bed
and things like this, which made us feel more secure. With
regard to kai, we got anything we wanted, within reason
of course. Everything which she had in the cupboard we
could have. She used to make what we called horarirari

paraoa, which is a form of porridge made out of lumps of flour. Whenever I was ill I would want horarirari paraoa made by my Nanny. It had to be made by her. . . . As compared with today, Nanny's food was very poor, but at that time, to us, it was absolutely marvellous. The freedom was there. You knew that whatever Nanny had you could selfishly have, as much as you wanted. But at home you couldn't do that . . . When I say that we were spoilt, I don't really think it was spoilt. We were being really loved and cherished by our Nanny.

Tūpuna outside the direct descent line were remembered no less warmly. Eru Paiaka and his siblings always looked forward to visiting their mother's aunt, a widow with white hair and a walking stick.

She was warm. We always nestled into her. She would say, 'Haere mai, mokomoko' and hug us. Often her first question was 'Kei te mate kai koutou?' [Are you hungry?] Out would come this tin of blackball lollies, for each of us. There was an air of caringness, a tenderness, a warmth. She'd take us to her orchard and point to the ones that were good. Then she'd boil up some koko [cocoa] and cut some papa koroua [damper bread]. When we left we always had a kit of something.

Several kai-whakaatu explicitly compared the treatment they received from their parents and grandparents. Ngaio Eruera, who grew up between the two World Wars, commented:

There is a lot of loving from your grandparents, whereas your parents are too busy working. The grandparents patted you like a little pussy. At your grandparents' you are far from being ordered to do this and that. When you go to your grandparents, you have a beautiful time, you are king of the castle.

Oriwa Tipene remembered:

My Mum was widowed for a long time. We lived with our grandfather. Mum did all the disciplining and we went to Granddad for the loving and the cuddling.

Will Nopera's experience was similar:

The physical disciplining was done by our mother. Koro and Kui, I could always go to them for sympathy and love when I needed it.

Gentle correction

Not that grandparents were overly indulgent. They set standards of behaviour, especially with regard to tikanga and tapu, and did not hesitate to check their mokopuna for faults, but they had more patience and either eschewed physical methods of punishment altogether or made minimal use of them. Awatea Hardy said that:

I can never ever remember the time when my Nanny punished me. I can remember her saying to others, 'Patua i te tamaiti ra', but she would never do it herself. My father never punished his grandchildren but he would say to me, or to someone else, 'Patua i te tamaiti ra.' Mum certainly never ever punished her mokopuna at all.

Nominating his grandfather as the person who influenced him most, Niho Waata said:

He never ever reprimanded us. If he did tell us off, he did it in a lovely soft way. It made you feel bad, it made you want to cry.

Miriam Norton recalled:

My grandmother was the one who taught us mokopuna what to do, with a little willow stick that just touched you. I don't ever remember her giving me a hiding. It was just a gentle reminder, it just tapped your foot. Nothing else, no words, but you *knew*. Or a look. She only had to look at you. Say it was on the marae. If you got up to cross when somebody was speaking, she just looked at you and you felt your knees go down.

Ngaio Eruera remembered the grandmothers of her childhood as always having a calm serenity.

You don't hear them screeching round the place. They don't shame you in front of people. They don't chastise you. They talk to you gently, but you can feel the sting.

Mutual caring

In many cases, my kai-whakaatu had had ready access to their tūpuna, because they lived in the same or adjacent houses. Sometimes the tūpuna were active heads of households, sometimes they were unable to do more than sit in the sun or by the fireside. Either way they were the source and the object of much caring. Maire Owens' earliest memories include the elderly grandfather who lived with her family.

I can remember waiting on him hand and foot. You cared for them. Whenever they wanted something you got it for them.

When his parents went off to the bush or coast to gather food, Muru Rata and his siblings

were always left with the Grannies. There were a lot of kuia in Waimiro in those days. I went to all our Grannies, I went from one house to another. You had to listen to what they said in their house.

Toro Karetai was one of nine children living with their parents in a house of four rooms in the 1950s. His father was a bridge-builder and was often away for one or two months at a time. Their grandmother helped by having her grandchildren to stay, two this week, another two next week.

Those who lived at a distance from their tūpuna saw them on holiday visits or when the widowed ones came to stay in the course of a regular family round or to help out in times of crisis. Referring to her father's father's sister, Akinihi Rata said:

> Granny Ngapine had a big influence on us. She had no natural children but lots of whāngai. She would appear and stay with us when Mother was hapū [pregnant]. Then she'd go to another relative's and then another. They moved around, those old kuia. We always had our grannies visiting.

Otene Reihana grew up moving between his mother's and his father's communities in the 1930s and 1940s. His widowed grandmother

> nursed most of us. We lived with her or she lived with us. She never stayed in the one place, she did the rounds ... She taught the little ones. I look back and I can see so many little ones holding to her skirts. I used to do a lot of hunting and I could tell by the bark of my dogs what sort of pig it was. So Granny could tell by the [mokopuna's] cry, she could interpret what the children said. She sang all the lullabies.

After she was widowed, Matiu Waimea's grandmother went to stay with all her children in turn.

> When she turned up she took part in the parenting all right. She would help with the smallest one who needed to be washed and dressed. She would comb my sister's hair, things like that. She would free my stepmother to get on with the daily domestic chores ... But she was never totally in our home. After a week or two she'd decide to pack up and go and stay with her other families and do the same thing.

Building up self-esteem

Grandparents were particularly remembered for the interest they took in their mokopuna's achievements and for building up their self-esteem with praise and affection, expressed quietly, in intimate moments together. Akinihi Rata's Granny Ngapine 'always complimented us if we brought back drawings from school. She would ask to see them.' Otene Reihana had no doubts that:

> It was always the Grannies that did it [the praising], more than the parents. It's only spoken between the Granny and the child.

Matiu Waimea received from his grandmother the praise his father ingeniously avoided expressing.

> Grandmother would always hear, secondhand from Dad, that in the Pākehā world we had done well at sports or in school reports or the like. She was the one who would say: 'You've done very well. You must keep working hard like that.'

Kōrero: talking and teaching

Generally less involved in active physical labour than the parental generation and more interested in kōrero (talking and verbal skills), the tūpuna of my kai-whakaatu played an important part in developing their language skills and store of knowledge. Keri Waipapa recalled a saying she often heard quoted as a child, especially by parents: 'Hoki ki tōu tupuna, māna koe e kōrero'. Literally, this means 'Go back to your Granny, he/she will talk to you', but the implication is that your Grannies are the *proper* people to 'talk' to you, whether to impart information or engage in the give and take of conversation. Keita Epuni commented that parents always had to worry where the food was coming from, whereas

> our grandparents were always there, they didn't have to worry about food. They lived for their grandchildren. If you went to them with questions, they had patience. If you went to your parents, they'd say, 'get outside and don't come back till next week'. On the farm, Mum used to fix

fences, dig drains, with Granddad. The only one home was my grandmother. She'd take time to listen to you. I'd go and get the kumara and sit down to peel them and Granny would talk, mostly everyday things, what they did last week.

Nuku Huatahi lived with his paternal grandparents till his grandmother died when he was nine. Looking back, he realised that his grandmother's greatest gift to him had been the way she had talked to him in Māori all the time, in the house and in the garden, while they did tasks like sorting kumara.

I cannot recall any formal teaching, it was always the talking, the talking, the talking, . . . telling stories, explaining things, giving a lot of love and patience . . . That was her thing, being able to sit there for hours and hours, and whenever I was with her, the talking.

When Api Awhitu was left a widow with five children still at school, she went out to work and her mother came to live with her and look after the children. They called her 'Mumma'. Even now, when they are all grown up, Api is constantly surprised at how often they come out with the comment 'Mumma told me that.' Even her sisters' children, who saw their grandmother only during holidays from their city home, often ask for more information about something 'Mumma told us'.

Grandparents did much of their teaching through the medium of stories. Sometimes they read stories, especially from the Bible, but more often they told them, stories about their own lives, the local pakiwaitara (fantastic, 'fun' stories), Bible stories, European fairy-tales and animal fables remembered from their own schooldays. In contrast with parents who gave instruction through instructions, Keri Waipapa noticed that the grandparents taught indirectly, telling a story in the third person, making it interesting and memorable.

When you asked them a question they don't answer directly, they give you an example. My grandfather would say, 'I rongo ahau [I heard that] somebody did this or that',

'I asked my auntie when I was young and she told me this.'

Describing his grandmother as 'a very strong old kuia', Toro Karetai told how

> she tells a story every night in the old days. Every night, she talks about our history, our tūpuna, marae protocol, how you should do this, why you should do that. She used to take us on the marae and show us what it is all about. It's a very different way of bringing up from Mum and Dad. The teaching was very, very old, very tapu, very Māorified.

It was from his grandmother that Toro learnt about the moon and the stars and their role in gardening and how to predict the weather from the sky and the clouds. Nuku Huatahi's paternal grandfather 'talked all the time about Māori mythology and about Te Kooti, his dreams and his kupu whakaari' (prophecies). Akinihi Rata recalled that as a child she and the other mokopuna heard a great deal of 'talk' from their grandmother. She did not gather them together for the purpose, but would tell them stories when they jumped into bed with her and when they sat watching her make kits. The vivid tellings kept the children enthralled. As Ngaio Eruera recalled: 'They told it their way. You'd just about be able to see the ghost creeping along.'

As grandparents and grandchildren grew older, the range of topics they discussed expanded. In particular, young people often confided to their grandparents secrets they were inhibited from discussing with their parents concerning their aspirations, achievements, anxieties and love affairs.

Teaching tikanga

In my informants' experience it was the tūpuna who assumed the task of teaching children tikanga in general and whānau knowledge in particular. They had the time, the knowledge and a mature understanding of children. According to Hana Reihana:

> It wasn't our parents who taught us about gathering kai

moana, it was the grandparents, the old people. Our father would have liked to teach us but he was too busy. It was old Eparaima across the road who taught us how to make paua hooks and the reti board. An uncle of Dad's taught us how to plant everything—kumara, strawberries. He did it the old way.

Hana's husband Otene added that in his family his grandmother was the main teacher for her grandchildren.

She was the one that taught most of the tapu things. She told the young people why, and what they should do if they broke a tapu. She taught the laws of the home—how you should receive food, how food should be given to a man or a woman, how you should present it.

Sometimes grandparents chose particular mokopuna (especially the eldest) and kept them close to themselves from an early age, exposing them constantly to subliminal learning, as well as teaching them directly. Teaching in a Wanganui River community, Matiu Waimea watched one of the kuia take her pre-school mokopuna everywhere with her. As a result, 'that kid could chant the Ratana litany—long passages of karakia—very accurately.' When she went to school she was articulate in both Māori and English. Then her grandmother took her younger sister around with her in the same way.

Hana Reihana's father had been chosen for special training by his uncle.

Uncle Wiri chose the ones he wanted and tutored them. He took my Dad. He took one girl from one family and boys from three other families. He took them and taught them. They went and lived with him [at his home].

Hana's husband Otene was one of the youngest in a large family. His granduncles took some of his older siblings away for training and his grandmother played the major role in teaching those who remained. She had them to stay with her and she told them stories in the meetinghouse at hui. Brushed aside as too young, Otene picked up what he could by listening in when supposed to be asleep. Sadly, his grandmother died before he was old enough to join her circle.

Sometimes tūpuna spent years watching their mokopuna at home and on the marae, until they had identified their particular abilities. Those children who actively sought particular kinds of knowledge they tested by delaying tactics to see if they were keen enough to persevere. Once satisfied that a child had both capacity and commitment, tūpuna took the initiative in proposing a particular training, whether in tikanga Māori or in Pākehā skills. Parents who had hitherto hesitated to encourage their children could then support what had become a whānau agenda. It was Moihe Eruera's mother's uncles who first proposed that he should be sent to train at Theological College. As Moihe said:

> The first to promote children of ability are the kaumātua. Only when that happens will the parents give their support. Not that the parents are not interested, but they don't want to promote their own children—that would be self promotion. They would sooner it was done by others.

Ihaia Iwirau, an expert in bush medicine, acquired his knowledge from his father's father after the latter chose him as a pupil. It was to this grandfather that he went for approval and support when he decided he wanted to train as a Christian minister. Tane Larsen, highly respected for his traditional knowledge, said he learnt about weaving from his mother's mother's sister. She took him and his siblings diving for kuta (a kind of rush) in the lake and taught them how to gather, dry and weave it.

Grandparents were often influential in the acquisition and retention of Māori language and knowledge. When Awatea Hardy's parents proposed to send him off to boarding school, his grandmother was 'dead against the idea' but his mother argued and cried, and in the end his grandmother gave in. But she sent for Awatea to visit her. As he told the story:

> So I sat there, all formal and stiff, and this was one of the very first times I was scared of my grandmother. She turned round to me and she said: 'Kia ora ana koe, e tama. Ko te

pīrangi o tō whaea kei te haere koe ki te kura kia mōhio koe i te mōhioranga Pākehā. Ae, e whakaae atu ana au, engari ko taku kōrero ki a koe, haere atu ki te Pākehā, engari kaua e hoki mai ki te kāinga nei ki te whakapākehā i a koe. Hoki mai koe ki konei he Māori koe. Haere, haere atu ki ngā mātauranga o te Pākehā, whakahokia mai ki kōnei, huihuia mai ki ngā taonga o te Māori, hei oranga māu.' These words have had a big effect on my life. My grandmother had said: 'O.K. Go to the Pākehā, learn the Pākehā education, but don't come back here to make a Pākehā of yourself. Remember you are a Māori. Go to the Pākehā, learn his ways, but bring it back here, combine it with the Māori ways, and build your future life on that.' Her philosophy had a big effect on my life in that I have tried to remember that I'm a Māori, and I can see now that not only my life but the lives of other people are influenced by the work I do.

Source of identity

Where identity in the Māori world is concerned, grandparents are more significant than parents. As Keri Waipapa said:

When doing your whakapapa, you are supposed to know who your grandparents are. You don't need to know more. You belong to them and they are responsible for you.

If a child's grandparents are known, knowledgeable adults can link them into known whakapapa. Grandparents rather than parents bear the responsibility for teaching children who they are, how they are related to particular relatives and how to behave towards them. When Keri Waipapa was growing up in the 1940s and 1950s, this responsibility was taken so seriously that it was used to control children's behaviour. She remembered children being constantly admonished to 'listen to your Granny kei whakamā tōu tūpuna' (lest your grandparent feel ashamed). An oft quoted proverb runs: 'Ka tangi te mokopuna, ka tangi te tūpuna.' (If the grandchild cries, the grandparent cries too.) A common variant is more explicit: 'He tangi tō te tamaiti, he

whakamā tō te pakeke.' (If the child cries, the elder feels ashamed.)[2] As well as emphasising the affectionate sympathy between
grandparent and grandchild, these proverbs were often used to
warn children against behaving in ways that pained or reflected
adversely on their grandparents. If children cried for wrong or
insufficent reasons (for example, out of boredom or anger at being
thwarted) or if they made a noise at the wrong time (for example,
during tapu proceedings on the marae), then the grandparents
suffered blame and shame for not having taught them better.

Sources of power and influence

Because of their age and wisdom, in spite of often failing health,
the tūpuna of my kai-whakaatu wielded real power in their
whānau, commanding respect as well as affection from all age
levels. Ata Robertson lived in a three-generation household on a
hill above the harbour. Her uncles had to go down the hill to get
water. They did not like her accompanying them, because they
had to carry her as well as the kerosene tins back up the hill, but
they always gave in when Grandmother told them to take her.
Whenever Matiu Waimea's grandmother was in the house, she
became the arbiter of disputes.

> If my generation got into a quarrel she wouldn't take sides
> the way my stepmother or Dad would. She'd let it occur,
> but she'd always protect the younger ones, and at some
> point she would make a stand and . . . [it] was unanimously
> accepted. Whoever was in error, the dispute was over. It
> was the same with the generation ahead of me, my Dad
> and uncles. She would hear them out and, at some point in
> the discussion, Grandmother would have her say and that
> was the end of the matter.

Despite a general decline in respect for authority, some
particularly strong-minded tūpuna can still command the
obedience of their families. When Ani Owens went to hospital
for an operation in the late 1980s, her husband's sister Mere
looked after her youngest child, but when Ani was well enough
to care for him again Mere refused to send him home. She brushed

off an aunt who remonstrated with her and started him at the kindergarten near her home. In desperation Ani spoke to her mother-in-law, at that time well in her eighties, 'and next thing the boy was home.'

Kai-whakaatu who are successful by worldly as well as whānau standards are quick to recognise the formative influence of their grandparents. It was from his grandmother that Matiu Waimea learnt the patience and open-mindedness that contributed to his success as a teacher and school principal.

> My grandmother was patient, you could take any subject to her and she would accord it space in her mind. I never saw my grandmother get angry. I learnt from her that conflicts can be resolved without recourse to anger.

Another teacher, Miriam Norton, said of her grandmother:

> She had the biggest influence in my mind, because she was the one who everyone used to look to in the family. My uncle and his wife and my cousins and other aunties, we were all living together, yet she was the one who guided everybody, she was the one who taught us, the mokopuna, how you behaved.

Exceptions to the rule

My kai-whakaatu recorded occasional exceptions to the general rule of warm relations with tūpuna. Some grandparents failed to mellow with age. Some favoured particular grandchildren and were unsympathetic to others. Some had so many children and grandchildren that with the best will in the world they could not give all of them all the attention they wanted.

Keri Waipapa had the warmest relations with the widowed grandmother who lived with her family but was on her best behaviour with her other grandmother, who was always ill and full of complaints. Though he admired her quick mind and wisdom, Matiu Waimea resented the way that his grandmother played favourites.

There was no doubt there were some of her mokopuna that she favoured, and I wasn't one of them. Not that I couldn't feel free to go to her and be heard, but I didn't get the kinds of rewards she bestowed on my younger brother and sister.

Ngawai Lancaster did not like her father's mother, for various reasons. Her dislike was so strong that once when she was sent to her grandmother's to borrow something, she hid instead and then reported that 'Tāua said to go and buy your own.' She knew she would be punished for such a blatant lie, but 'I just couldn't make myself go there.' No parent could disregard such disrespect for a tupuna. Ngawai commented ruefully: 'Did I ever get a belting for this?!! The only hiding I ever got, with Dad's shaving strop!! I never forgot it.' Disrespect for a grandparent was as serious as it was rare in the whānau my kai-whakaatu knew.

Aunts and uncles

Except in formal situations Māori generally use the English terms *aunt* and *uncle* or Māori transliterations of them to refer to and address relatives of the same generation as their parents. While they mostly restrict mother and father to their own (birth or adopted) parents, they extend aunt and uncle more widely than Pākehā speakers of English do to include parents' siblings, parents' cousins and the spouses of all those relatives.

According to my kai-whakaatu, aunts and uncles in this broad sense played a very significant part in their upbringing. As a group, they behaved in ways that placed them somewhere between parents and grandparents. They shared the authority of parents. As Otene Reihana put it: 'What my aunt and uncle said was as good as my father and mother telling me', while Tui Netana said: 'If we went to my auntie's place, that was our place too. We'd have to behave the same as at home.' Brought up by a widowed mother in the 1930s, Rahera Tipene remembered:

The uncles, they'd bring you up to the mark, whether they were your parents or not. They didn't stay in the back-ground. We used to all live next door to each other. My

Uncle Charlie, you only had to mention his name and the children obeyed. We were all one family.

At the same time, aunts and uncles were typically less critical and directive than parents, more encouraging and demonstrative of affection. Nieces and nephews turned to them for help and reassurance in preference to their parents. According to Wiki Martin:

Our aunts and uncles gave us more attention. In particular, when my mother's sister came to spend the weekend, I remember my auntie giving more attention to my brothers and sisters and me, and my mother giving her children more attention. There was less reserve with our aunts and uncles.

Will Nopera observed that 'kids behave better with their aunts and uncles than they do with their parents, especially on the marae.' Similarly, Piripi Davidson noted that his nieces and nephews sought his advice while his own children preferred to go to his brothers. Awatea Hardy recalled:

All my aunties and uncles really spoilt us, doted on us. Once they were married, they used to take us away for weekends and things like that. They were actually like mothers and fathers to us. Even when they had children of their own we got treated exactly like their own kids and in fact better, especially by Mum's younger brothers and sisters. We used to get royal treatment from them, better than their own kids, and my brother and I looked forward to going to stay with them.

Moana Paiaka recalled her mother's sisters with special affection.

They did special things, like giving us sweets for birthdays, pocket money for boarding school, watches for birthdays, because our parents couldn't afford them. Now we are continuing the circle.

Ngawai Lancaster, who could not remember ever having a

discussion with her father, could and did discuss issues with her aunties, especially one of her father's sisters.

To most of my kai-whakaatu, the homes of their aunts and uncles were as familiar as their own. Their parents sent them there to be looked after, for short or long terms, when they were otherwise occupied themselves, in order to attend school, or for a holiday. Ngawai Lancaster's widowed father supported his family mainly by seasonal work like shearing.

> When he went to whatever he was going to do, he just called on one of my aunts and said: 'You can look after these two for a couple of weeks' and we'd go off to her and think nothing of it. We didn't think we were deprived or anything. In fact, we quite liked staying with her, because tea was cooked as soon as we got home, we went to Ringatū services and we had a woman to look after us. I loved it, it was like a holiday.

Otene Reihana grew up in his mother's community along the East Coast but every year the family spent two months in his father's community further south, staying either with his father's sister and her family or at the marae. Every second year they spent a holiday at a coastal settlement with another of his father's sisters. Niho Waata was brought up by his grandparents in a household that included an aunt, and when he did not spend his holidays with his mother and stepfather he stayed with either Uncle Rapi or Uncle Muru on the farm. 'Uncle Rapi and his wife stayed with us a lot too', and though Uncle Muru's family rarely came to stay 'they were in and out of the house like yo-yos, them and their kids'.

Often, children sought refuge with an aunt or an uncle of their own accord, when they were in strife at home. Moana Paiaka chuckled as she recounted how she would 'pack my little suitcase and go on round to Uncle Ned's when I was fed-up with my parents'. Her father would eventually come and get her 'because the chickens wouldn't listen to anyone else'. Epa Huritau remembered helping his younger brother 'pack his swag' when he was 'having trouble with our mother'.

I gave him the bus fare to get to an auntie. He was there four months before Auntie Huria turned up at our place with him in tow. The cause of the trouble had been put in perspective.

Aunts and uncles often supplied support in situations where parents felt impelled to criticise. When a cousin of Matiu Waimea's fell in love, he asked his father's younger brother to speak to his grandfather, asking him to organise a formal visit to the girl's family to propose a match. The young man bypassed his father knowing that he would have offered criticism rather than support (p 168).

Special bonds

Many Māori children have a special relationship with a favourite aunt or uncle. This is based on personal compatability, often reinforced by appreciation of past kindnesses or other special links. As Awatea Hardy explained:

> I was the favourite of my mother's eldest brother and of the second eldest too, but my mother's younger brothers and her sisters favoured my young brother. I was getting so much attention from the ones older than Mum that they felt sorry for my brother and began to favour him. But my grandmother didn't have any favourites. We were all the same to her.

Niho Waata still mourns the loss of his Uncle Rapi, killed in World War II.

> Uncle Rapi was my favourite uncle. He was so close he was like a father, he was a father figure to me. When he went away to war, I wrote to him and he wrote to me.

Eparaima Arthur never forgot that his older brother left school early and worked in order to give his younger siblings a good education. Eparaima said that he had never thanked his brother: instead, 'I do my part by his kids.' Neri Paiaka had several favourite aunts to whom she could talk more easily than the others. They were the ones who had had her to stay for holidays when she was a child. She felt particularly close to one of these because she was named after her dead son.

Sometimes the relationship is an extension of one formed between siblings. When Neri Paiaka was young her older sister Tira was her 'nursemaid', deputed to look after her by their mother. After Neri and her husband settled in the city a succession of Tira's children came to stay with them.

> One daughter is very attached to us. She has almost become our daughter rather than my niece, her children have become almost our grandchildren. When she wants to know something or is puzzled about the twins, she'll ring and ask my opinion about taking them to the doctor.

When Tui Netana was a child her older brother looked after her: now he takes a special interest in her children.

> My daughter Nina, my brother is like a father to her. She writes to him in Australia. When he comes home on visits he buys things for her as well as his own children. She was always hanging round his neck, and he took her everywhere. When his daughters got married, he said to her: 'Nina, when you get married I'll give you away.'

Such favourite aunts and uncles are called upon to act as buffers between children and parents in conflict and as go-betweens relaying messages and information. As a single adult Moana Paiaka finds that:

> We are always getting landed with our brothers' and sisters' and cousins' children when they can't get on with their parents or their parents split up. The kids will listen to their aunts and uncles sooner than their own parents. Parents are more understanding with their nieces and nephews than with their own children.

While Moana received praise or reprimand for her school reports from her uncles without a word from her father, her father performed the same service for her cousins. One of the latter, Eru Paiaka, recalled:

> He did it all the time. He stands there with his shovel in his hand and he says, 'I want to see you, young fellow.' So I had to go and see him. He said, 'Congratulations!' and we had a hongi. It's quite strange having a hongi with your uncle, because I suppose it is my first hongi with him. I was then I suppose a young man in his eyes.

Teacher Hone Paraone remembered an outstanding essay written by a student about his father's exploits in World War II. The writer told him that the information was obtained, not from his father, who never spoke of his war experience to his children, but from his father's brother, with whom he was on more intimate terms.

Where there are special bonds, those who feel excluded may react badly. Niho Waata and his brother were brought up by their grandparents. While he had a special bond with his Uncle Rapi, he recalled:

> There was a little bit of envy and jealousy from my other uncles. One uncle in particular, he would wait until I was out of sight of the old people and he'd grab me by the ear for no reason.

Aware that the uncle who was good to him was favoured by his grandparents, Niho thought that was probably why the other uncles 'took it out on me'.

Aunts and uncles as teachers

Because they are easier to talk to than parents, uncles and aunts play an important role as educators for their nieces and nephews. As Awatea Hardy said:

> The discipline certainly came from Mum and Dad, but many of the other things were taught us by our aunts and

uncles, through talking. We'd open up more freely with the uncles and aunts, they were quite uninhibited and would tell us a lot of things. So a lot of learning came from my aunts and uncles, and very, very much from my grandmother.

Tui Netana learnt a great deal from her father's sister Ruia, who came to help when her mother had her babies.

We were all pretty close together. Auntie Ruia was sometimes there for a long, long time. She wasn't married. Aunt Ruia worked—she always used to bring things back for us.

For Nuku Huatahi, living alone with his grandparents miles from the nearest neighbours, his uncles were the source of insights into the outside world, the world of modern machines and strange exotic places.

One of my uncles was in the army. He would come back with his uniform and his rifle and tell me about the battles taking place overseas. . . . I followed him round like a shadow and he would tell me all these wonderful things.

Other uncles told him stories from other cultures, including Greek myths.

However, the openness of the relationship with aunts and uncles can be modified by status considerations. Awatea Hardy remembered:

Mum's eldest brother was always very formal when he discussed anything with my brother and me . . . he was the eldest one, the rangatira and the tohunga of the family, a person to take notice of and be reckoned with. And so his discussions were formal. But all the other aunts and uncles, there used to be a lot of good humour coming through the discussion, so that you didn't feel as though you were inhibited at all . . . We just completely opened up and told all our little secrets, and we knew many of theirs.

In his experience, the same pattern continues today. When his brother's eldest son wanted to get married, his brother asked him to head their family group at the tono (the formal meeting at which the match was discussed and approved).

> This had to do with the uncle and aunt business. You have a lot of say in the running of the family, a lot of say in the selection of marriage [partners] and all that sort of thing. And so the honour was given to me, I was spokesman for the family, because I was my brother's elder brother.

The older aunts and uncles are, and the more knowledgeable, the more like grandparents they become. In particular, they may pass on special kinds of knowledge. When Violet Rongonui was a child, their household included an uncle, a cousin of one of her parents. He was the one who did the whai-kōrero at the marae. As she recalled:

> He was blind, older than my Dad. We really loved him. Everytime we went to bed he'd come in and tell us stories, Māori stories . . . The other thing he used to do was to make us sing a lot, Māori songs, pātere, pao, the old ones. He'd say, 'if you go to a hui, be prepared to stand up and sing.' He just kept singing them over and over and we had to try to pick it up. He would just sing, just start up. We used to hang around him a lot at night; I think that way he knew we were interested . . . Most of the time he tells a story there is a song connected to the story. To me he was the best uncle out . . . Most of my education came from him.

He took her with him to the bush to gather plants and let her help him prepare rongoa (plant medicines). She credited him with 'teaching' her to karanga, by encouraging her to try and providing advice and criticism.

Conclusion

Within functioning whānau, grandparents, aunts and uncles share
with parents in the raising of children, providing supplementary
care and accepting responsibility for tasks which parents avoid.

Far from being jealous of the part that grandparents, aunts
and uncles play in their children's lives, most Māori parents are
grateful for and capitalise on it. When a child becomes rebellious
and 'won't listen', parents call in one or more of these older
relatives to 'talk' to him or her or send the child to stay with
them for a spell. When an older relative chooses a child to inherit
their knowledge or endorses his or her choice of an ambitious
career, parents accept the selection, freed to provide as whānau
members the support they feel inhibited from initiating as parents.

The sharing of child-raising by parents and other relatives has
certain inbuilt problems. As the number of their mokopuna
multiply, grandparents have difficulty maintaining the same
loving relationship with them all, especially those who live at a
distance. The financial implications can become burdensome. As
life expectancy and health standards rise, grandparents remain in
employment and pursue interests of their own to a more advanced
age than formerly, so that they have less 'free' time. Uncles and
aunts have difficulty balancing their responsibilities to their nieces
and nephews with those to their own children. These problems
are exacerbated by migration, which scatters whānau members
from one end of New Zealand to another and overseas, reducing
the frequency of interaction between children and many relatives
in these categories and changing its quality.

Reflecting on the conflict between competing responsibilities,
Eru Paiaka summed up:

> We talk about it [the conflict of interest], it does exist. My
> own brother when he separated from his wife, my sister,
> when she and her husband separated—we had a conscience
> about what role we should play in terms of their children.
> You wonder if you can split your allegiance with your own
> children or whether they would see you as paying too much
> attention to others and not to them. The same with our
> cousins' children. They come to Wellington and stay with

us—our house is bursting at the seams, every bed chocker-block, top and tail. It's a fine line we are treading, yet this is an obligation we accept.

The preferred—and most successful—way of resolving competing responsibilities is through reciprocity, the division of labour extended over time. Grandparents who have filled a special role in the lives of numerous grandchildren are likely to have a choice of companions who are willing to come and care for them in their own homes, and of caring homes to go to, in old age. Even when living at a distance from each other, siblings and their children find services to perform for each other. Looking after their cousins' children in the city, Eru and Neri Paiaka know that they can count on the cousins living in their home community to look after their house there. These cousins regularly send their son to mow the lawns, and when Eru and Neri return for holidays and tangihanga they open the place up and have a meal ready for them. When whānau bonds are strong, even difficulties can be overcome.

Coda

WHAKATUPU TAMARIKI

The traditional pattern

Reflecting upon their own experience, my kai-whakaatu provide illuminating insights into child-raising as they experienced it in Māori rural communities, especially the important part played by relatives other than parents. Within the whānau, relatives of senior status monitored and sometimes overrode parental rights of decision-making with regard to children. Grandparents, aunts and uncles (widely defined) contributed extensively to the care and socialisation of children, supplementing and in some cases complementing that provided by parents. Apart from providing the basic necessities of shelter, food and clothing, parents tended to concentrate on providing instruction in practical and social skills and correcting faults, while other relatives fostered self-esteem, language skills and special abilities. My kai-whakaatu also bore witness to parental encouragement of early independence, the frequent assignment of young children to the care of older siblings, and the importance and socialising influence of children's peer groups.

This pattern of child-raising was not formalised, discussed and taught as an articulated set of tikanga but was learnt mainly by example and role modelling. It was traditional as defined in Chapter 2 (p 49, above), passed on from generation to generation but adapted in each to meet its circumstances and needs. Taken for granted as familiar and right, it was developed in and generally well adapted to the social and economic life of small rural communities where most people were kinsfolk of similar socio-economic status grounded in the local district by ancestral association and inheritance. It was a pattern which helped to compensate for differences, for example, in the number of children born to the same parents, the size and composition of households, illness and mortality rates, access to economic support, and personal compatability.

The participation of other relatives in child-raising in small rural communities had many strengths. Accepting such participation relieved parents of the full weight of responsibility for their children, no small consideration when families were large and included new babies. Parents did not have to provide continuous supervision for their children but could allow them to play out of sight or go visiting on their own, secure in the knowledge that related adults and/or older children would watch over them and take responsible action if it became necessary. When problems arose, parents could count on older relatives for practical help as well as advice. Grandparents, aunts and uncles provided both children and parents with time out from each other and acted as intermediaries in the resolution of conflicts. When parents were too critical, too busy or too heavy-handed, children could turn to these other relatives for reassurance, information or temporary refuge. With access to a wide range of kin, children were well supplied with confidants and role models. Though it could not be eliminated, the trauma of losing a parent was reduced when children were already attached to the relatives who assumed some or all of the responsibility for their care. The interest of adult members in the children of the whānau was a safeguard against neglect or abuse.

On the other hand, while shared care-giving relieved some of the pressure on the relationship between parents and children, it reinforced the close personal identification which made it difficult for them to talk to each other on intimate matters. Some children were disadvantaged by being born into small or exceptionally large sibling sets, others because their parents had few or no siblings, were immigrants in the community or had offended against community norms. In large sibling sets, those who were in-between in age and/or unexceptional in personality sometimes missed out on the attention they needed. In spite of watching eyes abuse could go undetected or unpunished for a long time if the offenders were clever at concealment or of high mana.

In general, this traditional pattern of child-raising produced adults who were well prepared for life in predominantly Māori communities, with developed social sensibilities and a preference for group over individual action (Ritchie 1970: 134). In my experience, it also fostered a wish to escape from watching eyes

and a taste for exploration and adventure. Interest in 'new places
and new people' combined with and sometimes pre-empted
economic necessity to take both individuals and parent-child
families out into the wider world (Metge 1964: 106-7). Sometimes
they came home to live, bringing spouses and ideas with them;
more often they settled elsewhere, returning on periodic visits.
Before World War II this out-migration was mostly between
rural areas; after the war it was increasingly directed to towns
and cities.

Urban adaptation in the 1960s

Reporting on interviews with mothers living in urban areas in
the 1960s, Jane and James Ritchie noted varying modifications
in their child-raising practice (1970: 139-45).

Mothers who had recently moved to a small town not far from
their home communities showed signs of anxiety and stress as
they coped, in isolation from kin, with close and prolonged
contact with their children, a restrictive environment and the
expectations of Pākehā neighbours and landlords. Striving to
comply with Pākehā practice as they conceived it, they concentrated on surface features such as dress standards and toilet
training but continued to adhere to Māori principles at a deeper,
unconscious level, encouraging early independence and seeing
no need to supervise or shape all their children's learning. They
relieved their anxiety and re-affirmed traditional practice by
frequent visits home.

The city mothers interviewed were much further removed
from their ancestral communities, many having grown up in small
towns and the city itself. Some, absorbed into the mainstream of
New Zealand life, conformed in general to the Pākehā pattern of
child-raising but afforded glimpses of the traditional pattern.
Among those who emphasised their Māori identity, however,
the traditional pattern was still clearly discernible. More
sophisticated and self-assured than small-town mothers, they recreated in the city a model of the Māori community they missed.
Concerned about their children's future, they continued to
believe that children needed independence to grow properly and,
instead of intervening to set successive goals, allowed children

to make their own decisions. This was often interpreted by Pākehā as neglect, especially in the case of poorer and less well educated Māori parents, who carried the traditional pattern mainly at an implicit level.

Summing up, Jane and James Ritchie suggested that the traditional pattern had proved its resilience by surviving under difficult circumstances and predicted that Māori mothers would work out their own adaptations, grafting new practices on to the old, provided that their confidence in their capacity was not undermined. However, they expressed concern at the high stress levels shown by those interviewed and underlined the need for more social support and companionship.

Child-raising in the 1990s

Since 1970, the continuing growth of the Māori urban population and its stabilisation at a high level have combined with other developments to modify the contrast between urban and rural populations and to increase the diversification of both, not least in the organisation of family life and child-raising (see pp 75-76, above). After decades of urbanisation most Māori families have as many if not more relatives living in the same town or city as they would have in their home community in the country. Urban and rural residents alike have been affected adversely by increases in the cost of living, unemployment and the introduction of the Domestic Purposes Benefit, which requires sole parents to set up separate households. Differences in experience and outlook are mediated by constant visiting between urban and rural areas, return migration, influences transmitted through television and radio, organisations with national networks (from the pre-school movement to gangs) and shared pride in the Māori cultural heritage.

Like all social and cultural change, change in child-raising is not a simple matter of replacing items of belief and practice separately and completely but a complex process in which traditional ideas and practices are modified in encounter with introduced ones, those chosen for adoption are modified to suit local conditions and goals, and a new pattern is born out of the interplay between the two.

A series of linked research studies is needed to explore the range of variation and the complex adaptations which have taken place in Māori child-raising over the last twenty-five years. My own research has been exploratory, concerned more with the past than the present, and focused mainly on one particular aspect, the relative contribution of parents and other relatives. On this basis I put forward several tentative conclusions for further investigation.

Firstly, I suggest that the traditional pattern lives on, with varying degrees of modification, adaptation and coherence, not only in Māori rural communities but wherever Māori have settled, not only among those who consciously seek to espouse it but among many who are not consciously aware of its existence. Whether it is visible to participants and observers depends a good deal on their knowing what to look for and how to interpret what they find.

Secondly, I suggest that whether the modifications made are effective and adaptive or not depends to a considerable extent on whether parents are able and willing consciously to access and reflect upon their experience and understanding of child-raising on the one hand and on current social and economic conditions on the other.

Over the last twenty-five to thirty years, Māori parents in rural as well as urban areas have in fact been thinking and talking about these issues in increasing numbers. They have been stimulated to do so by encounter with people with different ideas, as neighbours, spouses, and professionals of various kinds, by publicity about the perceived underachievement of Māori students in formal schooling, and by exposure to theories of child development and education in teacher and pre-school training courses. Until the development of the Kōhanga Reo curriculum in the 1980s, almost all the information and advice available in books or courses on child development and child-raising was drawn from Pākehā and international sources. In the last ten years, as part of the drive to affirm Māori cultural identity, Māori have begun to explore, articulate and communicate the beliefs and practices inherited from their own forebears.

While some Māori parents have adopted new theories and practices in their entirety, most have responded by thinking more deeply than before about their own experience, weighing the old and the new against each other, reaffirming what they value about the former, adapting what they find convincing and useful about the latter, and weaving the two together. Such developments have been particularly encouraged by Kōhanga Reo and Kura Kaupapa Māori movements, after initial attempts in some quarters to exclude anything of non-Māori provenance.

Conscious reflection usually results in parents accepting more responsibility than was characteristic of the traditional pattern of a generation ago, reclaiming the right to make child-raising decisions from older relatives, undertaking more supervision of children's activities or making formal arrangements for others to do so, and accepting functions that earlier generations of parents tended to avoid. Extending the definition of the parental role in this way arises partly from parents' desire for greater autonomy for themselves, and partly from their recognition that other relatives are less frequently available because of residential scattering and other commitments. As parents extend their own role, they limit to some extent the rights and responsibilities traditionally exercised by other relatives. In general, however, they affirm the idea that relatives should share in their children's socialisation and rely on their doing so whenever possible. While they mostly accept limitation of their decision-making powers, grandparents, aunts and uncles continue to provide care, encouragement and correction for young relatives whenever opportunity presents, whether the parents are present or not.

In adapting their conception of their role to present realites, Māori parents often vary their practice to fit different contexts. Many accept full responsibility for their children when other relatives are not present, which is often but not always the case in the home, but revert to sharing that responsibility with relatives whenever they become accessible, during visits to each others' homes, in informal whānau activities and meetings, and at hui. When most relatives, or the most important ones, live too far away for frequent contact, parents keen for their children to have strong ties with their kin take or send them to stay with grand-parents, aunts and uncles on holidays, for a school term or even longer. The resulting alternation between close contact and little or none needs careful handling, especially if parents are not present. Even if the reasons are carefully explained, children unsure of their parents' affection may feel abandoned; elderly relatives may have difficulty controlling active youngsters without parental support; and repeated short-term changes can have adverse effects on children's development and schooling. If these problems are understood and dealt with, this strategy can greatly enrich children by giving them access to a wide range of relatives and to aspects of tikanga Māori they might otherwise miss.

Accessing implicit knowledge on any subject is far from easy. So deeply internalised is much of the traditional pattern that even the most thoughtful parents have difficulty bringing all aspects of their experience to consciousness or recognising that their approach is not universal. Brought up in a rural whānau by a grandmother and trained as a teacher, Miriam Norton recalled the difficulties of being a young parent in an urban suburb. In particular, she frequently felt angry when her Pākehā neighbours telephoned to tell her that her sons were up to mischief down the road. Why, she asked indignantly, could they not simply open the window and growl at the boys, especially if they were doing something dangerous like throwing stones? By the time she arrived to deal with them, the boys were miles away. In maturity, years later, she could recognise that she and her neighbours were motivated by different understandings about the role of parents, especially vis-à-vis non-parents, but at the time she felt aggrieved at what seemed like criticism directed at her parenting and a denial of support.

In adjusting their behaviour according to context, parents often idealise their ancestral community and overlook the changes that have occurred there over the years they have been away. Bringing up children in the city, Will and Noeline Nopera developed their own style of child-raising, drawing on experience overseas as well as teacher training. They fully realised the need to monitor their children's leisure activities and contacts in their urban neighbourhood but when they went back to Will's home community for holidays, Will gratefully relaxed control, assuming from his own experience that there would be other adults around who would keep an eye on the children and intervene if necessary. Slowly it dawned on him that changes in population and employment had greatly reduced the number of adults available and their capacity to act as watchers and nurturers.

While increasing numbers of Māori parents consciously and effectively adapt their parenting practice to current circumstances, others go on doing what comes naturally, apparently giving little thought to their child-raising practice or the ideas on which it is based. Such behaviour is often perceived as selfish and neglectful, especially when their children come to official notice as needing care and protection or for anti-social behaviour. In particular cases this may be a fair assessment but other explanations should also be explored. The parents may be fully occupied with the struggle to survive. They may resent and be unwilling to accept help from outsiders unfamiliar with their problems. They probably do not know that they have implicit knowledge nor how to go about accessing it. Above all, they may be acting in terms of a limited, traditional definition of the parental role, internalised in the course of their own upbringing. As we have seen, this was characterised by several avoidances, including avoidance of reflection, especially in the early stages of family building.

In the small, kin-based rural communities of past decades, avoidances were compensated for by the support and advice provided by older kinsfolk, who were able to draw on reflection as well as experience. Under modern conditions, however, when supportive kinsfolk are not always available, practices which were effective when integrated into a larger pattern can become inappropriate and even counter productive.

This is particularly the case with shared care-giving. Encouraging early independence in children, providing only limited supervision and allowing them to spend much of their time with peers works well when they are surrounded by numerous kinsfolk who take an active interest in their raising, but it can turn into a recipe for disaster in situations, whether urban or rural, where kin are few in number and reluctant to accept that degree of responsibility, and where children have access to many other sources of instruction and entertainment. If, for whatever reasons, parents continue to behave in terms of the traditional pattern without making sure that other relatives are playing their part effectively, their children receive only part of the care they need and would formerly have received. As well as additional protection from physical and moral danger, they are deprived of access to a variety of role models and escape hatches, and the opportunity to build up supportive kin networks of their own.

Because the traditional pattern of child-raising was built on a partial division of labour, the sharing of complementary roles between parents and other relatives, children who are brought up by *either* parents *or* grandparents without ready and frequent access to the other party may be short-changed with respect to key aspects of their nurturing, unless the parties concerned realise the problem and take steps to overcome it. Brought up by parents with only occasional contact with grandparents, they may miss out on praise, opportunities for learning and encouragement to pursue their aspirations, with adverse effects on their self-esteem and capacity for relating to people of kaumātua status. On the other hand, those brought up by grandparents without ready and frequent access to their parents may run a higher risk of becoming spoilt, self-centred and undisciplined. In both cases children are likely to rely heavily on their peers for companionship and support.

Important aspects of the traditional pattern of child-raising are most likely to be maintained and adapted in beneficial ways when parents and children are active members of a whānau with an ongoing corporate life, whether located in one place or linking kin at home and away. Formed and driven by a shared desire to keep kinsfolk together, an effective whānau encourages shared care-giving as an expression of whānau values and for its reinforcement of whānau solidarity. By bringing kinsfolk together for informal activities, whānau meetings and hui, the whānau provides opportunities and settings in which shared care-giving can take place. It ensures that growing children have access to kin of all ages and to the guardians of relevant knowledge. Both in rural and urban areas moves to set up whānau on a formal basis often originate with parents who want to give their children access to kin support and their ancestral heritage.

While access to kin in an active whānau does not guarantee that children will not become victims in need of care and protection or engage in anti-social activities, it does I suggest improve their chances and if things go wrong can be of major assistance in helping them and their parents deal with their problems, provided of course that the whānau concerned is working well and on the right side of the law. Sharing the care and responsibility of children may help to define the membership and limits of particular whānau. Concern for the whānau's children provides a strong incentive to keep the whānau working well or to pull kin back together after scattering. Nurturing the rising generation strengthens the whānau and its capacity to perform its other functions.

Conclusion

The social and economic changes of the last twenty-five years have presented Māori with many challenges with regard to child-raising, but none which cannot be overcome by conscious reflection, discussion and adaptation of the traditional pattern.

Chapter 11

ATAWHAI ADOPTION: 'BORN OF MY HEART'

Ka āpiti hono, hei tātai hono.

Groups join, (to get) a shared descent line.

T he values of aroha, whanaungatanga, mana and whaka-papa, so important in the structuring and operation of the whānau, also inform and shape the Māori view of adoption. As a result, Māori adoption differs in fundamental respects from adoption as embodied in New Zealand law and understood by Pākehā, in spite of recent changes in attitudes and practice (Durie-Hall and Metge 1992).

Atawhai, adoption and fostering

Differences in the way Māori and Pākehā think of adoption are reflected in the words they use and the way they use them when discussing the subject.

Pākehā generally equate adoption with *legal* adoption and set it in opposition to fostering. Under the current adoption law (Adoption Act 1955 and Amendments), adoption is a legal process which transfers the legal status of parent to a particular child from one set of parents to another. Thus Pākehā use the verb *adopt* to mean 'pursue the legal process of adoption', the adjective *adopted* to refer to children who have been the focus of this legal process, and the adjective *adoptive* to refer to adults who have acquired the status of legal parent as a result. The opposition between adoption and fostering is clearly set out in the *Heinemann New Zealand Dictionary*, which defines the verb to adopt as 'to make a member of one's family by legal means' and to foster as 'to bring up a child who is not one's own son or daughter without legal adoption' (Orsman 1979: 14, 429).

For their part, Māori use three Māori words, *atawhai, taurima* and *whāngai* when speaking English as well as Māori. They also use the English adopt and its derivatives, attributing to them their own meanings rather than their standard English ones.

Atawhai, taurima and whāngai are alternatives favoured by different iwi: atawhai by the iwi of Tai Tokerau, taurima by those of Taranaki and whāngai by the rest. The ordinary meanings of these three words are similar but not identical: atawhai means 'show kindness to, be liberal, foster; be inclined to, desire', taurima means 'entertain; treat with care, tend' and whāngai means 'feed; nourish, bring up' (H.W. Williams 1971: 19, 402, 488). In the context of child-raising, however, they are completely synonymous: all three are used *generically* to refer to *all* cases where children are brought up by other than their birth parents, without regard to the legal status of the relationship. The three alternatives all serve both as verbs and as adjectives attached to kinship terms: to tamaiti (child), tama (son), tamāhine (daughter), kōtiro (daughter in Tai Tokerau), whaea (mother) and matua (father in the singular, parents in the plural mātua). They are also sometimes used on their own, as nouns, to refer to the child being cared for: he atawhai, he taurima, he whāngai. None has a form which corresponds exactly to the abstract English noun adoption.

Because most of my informants are from Tai Tokerau, I shall henceforth use the Tai Tokerau term atawhai, on the understanding that everything said under that heading applies equally to taurima and whāngai. To clarify the discussion, I shall refer to the Māori concept of adoption as atawhai adoption and to the Pākehā concept as legal adoption.

While some Māori have assimilated Pākehā usages in this area, most use the English words adopt, adoption, adopted and adoptive with the broad, generic meaning they give to atawhai. Pressed to translate atawhai, they choose adopt and its derivatives, and vice versa. When relevant, they distinguish atawhai who have been the focus of the legal process from those who have not by adding the modifier *legally* to *adopted* or by using one of several Māori coinages: 'kua hurihia ia' (he or she has been turned over), 'he huri ia' (he is a turned over one), and 'nā te ture' (according to the law). Most of the time, however, their use of 'adopted' leaves the legal status of the person referred to undetermined. In the *Hamiora Whānau Hui* booklet 52 whānau members are identified by an A for 'adopted'. Some have been legally adopted and some have not but the compilers of the whakapapa considered the distinction irrelevant. In effect, Māori treat legal adoption as a sub-category of adoption, instead of equating the two as the law does.

Significantly, Māori have *not* developed Māori words to identify the concept and practice of fostering. Even when dealing with children who have *not* been legally adopted by their care-givers, they use the generic term atawhai (or whāngai or taurima). The motto of the New Zealand Foster Care Association is 'Foster a Child'; Māori advisers translated this into Māori as 'Atawhaitia he tamaiti.' When the Departments of Māori Affairs, Justice and Social Welfare cooperated to set up a nationwide programme to place Māori children in need of care and protection with relatives for fostering, without legal adoption, they chose the title Mātua Whāngai. Māori tend to reserve the English expression 'foster child' to refer to children from outside the whānau whose fostering is arranged and supervised by the Department of Social Welfare.

Māori attitudes to atawhai adoption

Māori place a positive value on the process of atawhai adoption and the status of *all* the parties involved. Far from seeing it as a strategy for handling failure on the part of birth or adoptive parents, they emphasise the element of aroha in the behaviour of both. The connotations of *atawhai, taurima* and *whāngai* are warm and positive. In *Te Paipera Tapu* (the Bible in Māori), *atawhai* is one of two phrases used to translate 'the grace of God'.[2] The other is *aroha noa*, love without limit. *Atawhai* is the kind of love which is given freely, without counting the cost and without guarantee of return. In the context of adoption, *taurima* conveys the idea of special care and attention, such as that given to guests,[3] while *whāngai* has the connotations of English *nurture*, implying the feeding of mind and spirit as well as body.

As long as they give them to relatives, birth parents who give up children for atawhai adoption are not criticised for shirking their responsibilities or not loving their children but instead are praised for their generosity. They retain and may actually enhance their mana vis-à-vis the adoptive parents in the eyes of the adults in whānau and community. (How the children feel remains to be adequately explored.) Placing children secretly with strangers, on the other hand, is severely frowned upon, for it means that they are lost to grandparents and whānau as well as birth parents.

In theory and usually in practice, tamariki atawhai are children who are sincerely wanted. Speaking from experience, Mere Ratapu commented that 'you have a special feeling for an atawhai, not necessarily deeper than for your own, but very strong'. Eparaima Arthur said that an atawhai 'though not born of my womb is born of my heart'.

In Māori communities, men and women who have brought up large numbers of atawhai are pointed out and admired. Even though their financial resources were stretched to the utmost, the atawhai they reared recall their homes nostalgically as happy, caring places. The uncle and aunt who brought up Eru Paiaka raised twenty-seven children altogether.

> They had sixteen of their own and they brought up five of us and six others as well. The older ones got married. There were fourteen or fifteen of us there at one time. No trouble to us, three in the same bed, two up, one down. There were other people there too, our grandfather and grandmother and an uncle.

Like other grandparents, such mātua atawhai may raise more than one generation. Wai Tahiwi remembered:

> When Mum died, anybody that she'd brought up came home to her funeral, and she had twenty-one. There was me and another young boy Barney, he was the last one: when we were at home all the others had grown up. Barney's father was another atawhai, Mum brought him up too. My own father, my natural father, was one of her atawhai; he lived with them a long time before he married my mother ... On top of atawhai she had teachers boarding with her and numerous others would come in for a couple

of weeks and then go. She was that type of person ... always
open house, always food on the table, always hot bread.

Atawhai: kin and non-kin

With very few exceptions, Māori who assume the primary care
of children other than their own do so for children who are related
to them by birth. Atawhai adoption means looking after your
own, as well as looking after *as* your own. As Nora Waaka
commented:

When you take a child, it's only your own relatives. You
are not taking a child from another family.

As Rahera Tipene put it:

It's your own flesh and blood really. I would only adopt
someone who has some connection with me. If I were
adopting, I'd like to know their background, their parents.
You wouldn't hesitate so much if you knew that.

Children taken as atawhai are not only related to their mātua
atawhai but in most cases are very closely related. The most
common form of atawhai adoption, accounting for a third of all
cases or more, is that in which grandparents atawhai one or more
grandchildren. Other mātua atawhai care mainly for the children
and grandchildren of their own siblings. In effect, most atawhai
relationships are contained within effective or potentially effective
whānau.

In the *Hamiora Whānau Hui* booklet, twenty-seven of those
identified as 'Adopted' were both born to and brought up by
Hamiora descendants. Cross references make it easy to work out
how they are related to their mātua atawhai. Ten of the 27 were
adopted by grandparents (a parent's parent or parents), eight were
adopted by a parent's sibling, seven by a grandparent's sibling,
and only two by relatives from outside their birth parent's branch
of the Whānau. The remaining twenty-five were born to relatives
of spouses married to Hamiora descendants.

While occasionally an atawhai is cared for by someone who is single (widowed, divorced, separated or never married), most mātua atawhai are married when they accept this responsibility. When a couple atawhai a grandchild, he or she is related to both of them by birth. In all other cases, however, atawhai are related to only one of their adoptive parents by birth. In such cases, there is a tendency, especially in the early stages of the relationship, for the mātua atawhai, their relatives and associates to think of the related parent as the adopter.[4] This tendency disappears, or more accurately becomes submerged, as the emotional attachment between parents and atawhai is reinforced in daily interaction. It may, however, resurface if the atawhai birth parents and their relatives single the atawhai out for special treatment above his or her adopted siblings or if disputes develop about the inheritance of land and other taonga.

It is not uncommon for a married couple to create a family of adopted children by taking some from the husband's side and some from the wife's. Wai and Ruka Tahiwi (for example) have three tamariki atawhai: the eldest and the youngest are the children of Wai's sister Hera, the middle one is the son of Ruka's sister Heni. Widowed Ngaire Eruera has five atawhai: two are the children of Ngaire's sister, two are the children of her deceased husband's brother and sister respectively, and the fifth is the child of his first cousin. Differences in the origins of adopted siblings may or may not be important in childhood but they often become so in adulthood, when siblings may choose to affiliate with or give their major support to different whānau.

Far from being a rare phenomenon, as it is among Pākehā, the transfer of children between close kin in atawhai relationships is and always has been a common and characteristic feature of Māori family life. The frequency with which children are given and taken as atawhai within whānau limits is illustrated by the following two examples from Kōtare, chosen out of a range of similar cases.

Wiki and Rua Thomas married in the 1930s and had seven children. Wiki's mother took their firstborn at birth and brought her up until she left to further her education in the city. Their fourth child Wai was legally adopted by Wiki's oldest sister Pare and her husband Nat, who was a cousin of Rua's. While their two youngest were still with them, Wiki and Rua brought their eldest daughter's firstborn home to raise. In the *Hamiora Whānau*

Hui booklet she is listed as their eighth child and as their daughter's first, with a linking cross reference and the annotation 'Adopted'. After Rua died, Wiki lived in Auckland for several years with her youngest daughter, helping care for her grandchildren. Eventually she returned to Kōtare taking two grandchildren with her; when her fourth daughter died she took one of her boys as well. These three atawhai remained with her until her death. By that time, the two eldest were in employment and able to look after themselves. The youngest returned to his mother; when he could not settle in the city she sent him to live with her brother on the family farm.

As well as their own twelve children, Adam and Marara Matiu brought up their firstborn grandson as an atawhai. The son of their second daughter was atawhai'd by their eldest daughter and her husband. Their third daughter and her husband gave their fifth child (a daughter) and their ninth (a son) to Adam's brother Maka and his wife, who had only two of their own, and their sixth (a daughter) to Adam's youngest brother Wiri and his wife Katarina, who had none. Wiri and Katarina also atawhai'd the son of Wiri's sister's daughter, the daughter of Katarina's sister and an unrelated child placed with them by Child Welfare. Later when their daughter's first marriage came to an end, they assumed the primary care of her two children for several years.

This practice of taking closely related children as atawhai continues a pattern handed down from generation to generation. Wiki Thomas, who atawhai'd four grandchildren, herself grew up in a household presided over by her widowed grandmother Ruta and containing her widowed mother Hana, Hana's other children (Wiki's siblings), Hana's unmarried brother Nepia, and four atawhai. Two of these were Ruta's daughters' daughters taken when their mothers died young; one was Ruta's sister's grandson taken for the same reason; and the fourth, the only one to be legally adopted, was a less closely related cousin. When Ruta died, Hana took over responsibility for her mother's atawhai until they left home, raised Wiki's eldest daughter and nearly always had one or two other grand-children staying with her for a spell, especially her third daughter's eldest son, who spent half his time with her until he went away to boarding school.

While atawhai adoption is focused primarily on the adoption

of close kin, mātua atawhai do occasionally take atawhai who are more distantly related. The reasons given usually include a desire to strengthen ties between whānau which had a common origin but have grown apart, genealogically and socially, over the years.

Though rare, it is not unknown for Māori to take unrelated children as tamariki atawhai. Such children are sometimes described as mōkai rather than atawhai. This word may be used with the meanings of slave, captive, pet bird or animal, as a term of opprobrium, or applied to the youngest in a sibling set (H.W. Williams 1971: 207); writers sometimes use it to refer to themselves when concluding a letter. It is, to say the least, ambiguous. On the one hand, it stresses inferior, dependent status; on the other, it often indicates a particularly strong bond, based entirely on affection.

Remembering the mōkai brought up in her community before World War II, Keri Waipapa was of the opinion that they were taken mainly to provide cheap labour and always treated as inferior to atawhai taken from within the kinship circle. On the other hand, the few cases with which I am familiar involve strong bonds of affection between adoptive parents and children. While they were living in Auckland, Roimata and Ned Wiremu became friendly with a woman from another tribe who was pregnant but experiencing difficulties in her marriage. When her daughter was born she asked Roimata and Ned to care for her. Though 'not keen at first', Roimata found that 'that bond became so important that we wanted to adopt her permanently'. The birth parents eventually agreed to legal adoption because they had separated and neither could care for her as well as Roimata and Ned. Now that daughter is closely bonded to Roimata and Ned and their children, with a special relationship with their eldest (birth) daughter and their two youngest, who are also atawhai.

In the 1950s and 1960s many Māori accepted unrelated children placed with them by the Department of Māori Affairs. Two brothers placed with Wiki and Rua Thomas settled in well, helping with the farmwork after school, as their own children did. Wiki and Rua were upset when the boys were removed when they reached school-leaving age. Until her death forty years later the brothers kept in touch with the widowed Wiki and she referred to them as atawhai and to their children as mokopuna.

Wiri and Katarina Matiu's second youngest atawhai was placed with them at the age of five years by Community Officers from the Department of Māori Affairs. He settled down so well with Wiri and Katarina that they considered adopting him legally but were advised against it by social workers. Later they regretted not doing so, because he felt odd man out in the family, with a different name from the others. When he set out in his teens to find his birth mother, Wiri and Katarina assured him they would welcome him home and adopt him legally if he asked them to do so. Eventually he held them to their promise. Now he shares their name with their own children.

Atawhai relationships in which there is no prior kinship connection are generally more brittle than those involving kinsfolk. They differ from atawhai relationships proper in that they are essentially relationships between individuals. They do not involve the whānau nor do they give the atawhai access to whānau rights. Atawhai of this kind are more likely to be resented by other whānau members.

The duration of atawhai relationships

Though in most cases atawhai relationships are established at birth and involve the provision of primary care throughout childhood, the word atawhai is also legitimately applied when the association begins later and lasts for a shorter time.

To a greater extent than legal adoption, an atawhai arrangement is open to reassessment and alteration when circumstances change. Ideally this is a matter not for the mātua atawhai only but for the whānau as a whole. If mātua atawhai cannot fulfil the responsibilities they have assumed, other members of their whānau should take them over.

When children are atawhai'd by grandparents or relatives of that generation, it is not uncommon for the mātua atawhai to die before their atawhai reach maturity or for them to have difficulty managing lively teenagers. At the same time, birth parents with a growing family are often in need of the support those same teenagers can provide. When Kiwa Paki was growing up in a Tai Rawhiti community in 1940s, it was common for children who had been living with their grandparents to return to their birth parents when they became old enough to help on the farm and/ or difficult for their mātua whāngai to manage.

The end of primary care-giving does not however necessarily spell the end of an atawhai relationship once it has been established. Children who receive loving care from mātua atawhai for a limited period often continue to entertain a special affection for them and to describe them by that term, even when settled in another home. When Roimata and Ned Wiremu were first married and living on the family farm, before they had any children, they had the daughter of a neighbouring couple living with them for a while, the third eldest in a family of twelve. Her father was an uncle to Roimata on her mother's side. According to Roimata:

> There was a whānau link there. She was about seven when we started to atawhai her. We had her about eighteen months, then we left for Auckland and she went back to her parents. Whenever she was allowed, there was no question, she always came back and forwards to us.

Roimata and Ned always include her when listing their children and refer to her as 'our atawhai'.

In Māori eyes, it is the quality, not the duration, which identifies an association as an atawhai relationship.

Reasons for atawhai relationships

Atawhai relationships are established for a wide variety of reasons and under a variety of circumstances. Underlying most of this variety and tying it together are three closely related themes— concern for the welfare of whānau children, concern for the welfare of whānau adults and the building up of whānau strength. Aroha in the sense of altruistic love is combined with aroha in the sense of kinship commitment.

The need to provide for children born to unmarried mothers has always been a major reason for atawhai adoption, both before and since the availability of the Domestic Purposes Benefit, but a significant proportion of atawhai also derive from parents who

are married to each other. Of the twenty-seven children recorded
in the *Hamiora Whānau Hui* booklet as belonging to the Whānau
by both birth and adoption, fifteen were born to unmarried
mothers and twelve to married couples.

When birth mothers are single

Reflecting the views of their generations, most of my kai-
whakaatu prefer children to be born after their mother has settled
down in a legal marriage or a stable de facto relationship. They
feel that the birth of children to single women diminishes the
mana of their parents and whānau, especially if it happens more
than once. At the same time, since they value all children born to
whānau members as descendants of the whānau ancestors, they
reject abortion and stranger adoption as courses of action when
a single woman becomes pregnant.

Up until the early 1970s, when both de facto relationships
and ex-nuptial births were frowned upon by Māori and Pākehā
alike, kaumātua would often push unmarried parents towards
legal marriage (and hence a home and name for the child) by
arranging a tomo, a formal meeting between whānau to discuss
marriage (Hohepa 1964: 82-84, Metge 1964: 66, 71, 184-85). If
that strategy did not work, the only acceptable alternatives were
for one set of grandparents to support mother and child, atawhai
the child themselves, or approve placement of the child with other
relatives as an atawhai.

Because of whakamā, reinforced by the advice of social
workers, unmarried Māori mothers sometimes concealed the
birth of a child from their whānau, spending their pregnancy in
a city well away from home and placing their babies for adoption
with strangers. (Under the Adoption Act 1955 only the consent
of the birth mother is required for legal adoption.) Others,
however, relied on the support of their families, supplemented
by the Child Allowance.

As long as they knew about the birth, most grandparents
actively sought to assume responsibility for the child, taking him
or her into their own home or arranging placement with relatives.
While the mother mostly accepted the support of her own
parents, the father's parents usually made an attempt to claim

the child as well. Where grandparents were concerned, any whakamā over the circumstances of the birth was overridden by aroha for their new mokopuna. Anticipating that her parents would be upset at her having a baby outside marriage, Tui Netana went to stay with her father's sister when she left hospital after her son's birth. Acting as go-between, her aunt broke the news to her parents. As soon as he heard it, her father came straight to her aunt's house. According to Tui, he told her:

> This child is my mokopuna, he is carrying my name. If you want to stay here, you can, but this boy is coming with me.

If she agreed, grandparents usually supported their daughter along with her baby but sooner or later she moved off again to take a job or to marry, often leaving the baby behind. Some mothers later tried to reclaim children left with grandparents but others decided not to disrupt the bond that had developed between child and mātua atawhai.

If her parents were dead or she was not on good terms with them, a single mother turned to other relatives, usually those to whom she was most attached. When Roimata Wiremu's brother's daughter had a baby at a young age, welfare workers strongly advised her to make the baby available for adoption. As Roimata reported:

> She refused to give the baby up. She kept calling for me to adopt the baby. She didn't want it adopted out of the family. So I had to take that baby.

Raiha Huriwai acquired her first atawhai when her husband Nika's younger sister gave birth while visiting them. Because she was unmarried, her brother Nika had 'the biggest say' over what happened to the child, but it was Raiha who decided they would keep the child themselves.

> I never thought of legal adoption, I just took her. The man who married her mother later came and asked for her, but we said no.

Some years later, Raiha's cousin brought her new-born son to Raiha after her marriage broke up. Raiha did not adopt him legally either: 'I had that feeling that my cousin wouldn't come and demand her son back.'

Introduction of the Domestic Purposes Benefit in 1973 offered single mothers an alternative, enabling them to support themselves and their children in a separate household. Nevertheless, some still prefer to give their children to their parents or other relatives to care for, because they sincerely believe it is best for the children.[5]

If a single mother is very young or gifted, grandparents may insist on assuming primary care of her child, with or without a whānau conference, so that she can complete her schooling or take other training. They reason that qualifications will improve her ability to contribute to the support of the child, along with any others she may have. When Violet Teira had a child while still at school, her father's sister collected the baby from the hospital with the knowledge and approval of both sets of grandparents. They intended that Violet should continue her studies, but she did not want to return to school. Instead she went to stay in the city with another aunt, got a job, married and eventually settled far from home. When the aunt who was raising her son died, the boy at first remained with his surviving mātua atawhai, but when the latter wanted to leave the district, Violet's parents claimed him and raised him as theirs.

When single mothers fail to care for their children responsibly or are overwhelmed by circumstances, close relatives feel obliged to step in. Though she had four children without a husband, Roimata Wiremu's youngest sister Peggy remained a 'dizzy lizzie who wanted her good times'. When her seven-year-old son was taken into care in a Welfare home, Roimata said that:

> I felt so sorry for my nephew and my sister that I asked her to let me bring him up. I took him from the Welfare Home. The parents in that Home were very good but because blood is thicker than water I couldn't leave him there. He lived with me until he was fifteen, when he wanted to go back to his mother.

In the course of time Roimata's eldest sister took Peggy's eldest daughter and her brother and his wife atawhai'd her third child, leaving only the youngest with Peggy.

> Because of her way of living we as a whānau were concerned about our nieces and nephews. There was no question they would go to anyone else. We felt it was our responsibility. We let them go back to their mother for holidays, and they know that she is their mother. It was our responsibility or I am sure Social Welfare would have taken them off her.

When birth parents are married

Close relatives also atawhai the children of married couples because the children's birth parents cannot care for them and/or because the mātua atawhai want children to care for.

Close relatives often take over the primary responsibility for the children of married parents in response to crises in their care, for example, when one or both parents become ill, die or desert them or when neglect or abuse comes to notice. When Raiha Huriwai's widowed sister died leaving seven children, Raiha and her sister Wini divided the children between them. When Eru Paiaka's father died, his mother returned with her children to her own people and re-married there. When word filtered back to his father's whānau that the children of her first marriage were being neglected, two of his father's brothers rode across the hills to investigate and brought the children back with them. One brother, whose family had all left home, took five and the other, who was still raising several of his own, took two. Never legally adopted, Eru spoke of the uncle with whom he lived from the age of ten as 'the most important influence in my life'.

Sometimes older relatives in leadership positions in the whānau decide that prevention is better than waiting for crises to happen. If young parents are struggling to make ends meet on a low income, have had several children very close together, or have health or marital problems, they may direct or advise them to give one or more children to relatives eager to take them. When Nora Waaka's mother had twins, she 'could only look after one,

so her brother took me; that's all there was to it'. Tamati Cairns'
account of his adoption has already been quoted on p 147.

Whether the parents face difficulties of these sorts or not,
relatives may also ask for children as atawhai to fill a gap in their
lives, usually because they have none of their own or because
they feel bereft and lonely after their own have left home. Even
when they are perfectly able to care for their children themselves,
parents may feel obliged to accede to such requests from relatives
out of respect for their mana in the whānau and aroha for their
loneliness and longing. Often the request is made during pregnancy, while the child is still without a name and personality.
According to Kiwa Paki's experience:

> As you were having a baby, for one reason or another that
> baby was bagsed. Someone said, 'I'll take this child, because
> you can have more', or 'I'll take this child if it's a boy'.
> People made the decision as you were carrying, that they
> would have that baby ... It wasn't necessarily the grand-
> mother who came. It could be a grand-aunt or a cousin
> [but] it was more than just an immediate friend.

Māori cultural purposes

Besides practical reasons and aroha for kin, there are also
specifically Māori grounds for establishing atawhai relationships.

By virtue of their seniority, older whānau members are
generally held to have claims on the children of younger ones.
Grandparents in particular have a claim on their first grandchildren, to ensure that they receive the education befitting their
status and to be the repository of whānau knowledge. Atakura
Waru, for example, was taken at birth by her mother's parents.

> I was the only child in the household, living with my
> grandparents and a whole lot of adult uncles and aunts.
> They were from the generation before, all mātua to me.

Until he died when she was eight, Atakura's grandfather took
her everywhere with him, all over the farm and to hui, introducing
her to her relatives and sharing his knowledge of tikanga,

whakapapa and waiata. As she said:

> We used to always sit with my grandfather. Wherever he
> sat, I sat, wherever he was, I was.

Sometimes the younger generation do not wait to be asked but recognise and fulfil the obligation to give a child to his or her grandparent of their own accord. In Patricia Grace's novel *Mutuwhenua* (1978), the central character Linda hears of her father's death shortly after the birth of her first child, names the child after her father and takes him home to her mother to rear.

Taking place as they do among close kin, atawhai relations both reflect and strengthen existing ties. Reflecting on the transfer of children between close relatives in her home community, Kiwa Paki recognised that it 'helped to keep the extended family together'. A junior member of a large sibling set, Otene Reihana was convinced that one of the main reasons why grandparents take grandchildren to live with them as atawhai is 'trying to bind the parents back to their parents'. The transfer of atawhai between siblings also strengthens the links between them and their families. Otene recalled:

> My own niece and nephew, they lived with us as brother
> and sister after their own parents parted. Those two were
> the ones strong on the family. When they grew up, they
> were the links between their families and the rest of our
> family and the aunties and uncle.

Relatives who have named or whose name has been given to a child often claim the right to ask for that child as an atawhai. Sometimes a couple without issue seek an atawhai in order to give the child a family name that would otherwise be lost. As Kiwa Paki said:

> You'll find that a lot of children who had been whāngai'd
> got the name of someone in that family, it might be a parent,
> it might be a grandparent, it might be a tupuna way back.
> They've taken that child to give that child that name.

Older kai-whakaatu recall that children whose birth was marked by unusual signs (a comet or freak storm, being born feet first or in a caul) or who were identified by matakite (seers) as having certain gifts were sent to appropriate elders for training, whether direct grandparents or grandparents' siblings or cousins. Though the third in his sibling set, Nuku Huatahi was chosen before birth by his father's parents as the child of the family to be fed with the tikanga and history of the tribe. His earliest memories are of being brought up by his koroua and kuia in close association with sea and bush.

> For the first six years of my life I internalised very deeply those Māori things, culturally I was very much a Māori, in the way I felt about things, the way I was brought up, the cooking of the kai, and sleeping with my grandparents . . .
> I remember, before I went to school, my koroua taking me to the side of the puna [spring], doing a karakia there, and the iriiri, the sprinkling of water on my head, a sort of dedi-cation for the purpose he wanted me to have in life, to be a repository of information for the people. I recall him saying, 'Give this child the wisdom and the ability to be able to understand the world he is going into, to bring peace to other people.'

Going back to the places where he grew up and to church and tribal hui, he can to this day faultlessly repeat the karakia and waiata he learnt living with his grandparents as a child.

Some iwi describe grandchildren brought up and kept constantly in their company by grandparents as 'he taura moko'—a mokopuna who is attached to the grandparent as by a rope. Such taura moko 'hear everything' and are 'very mature in Māori things'. In later years other members of the whānau seek them out for the knowledge of whānau history and whakapapa they acquired in the course of the association.

Finally, older kai-whakaatu also remember atawhai relation-ships being approved because they revived or established an alliance. A child might be given to mātua atawhai belonging to a different whānau or hapū in order to bring together descent lines which stemmed from a common ancestor but had grown apart.

In Kiwa Paki's experience, Tai Rāwhiti kuia sometimes gave a mokopuna to a best friend to whom they were related only distantly.

> They had had a close relationship as young girls and they wanted to keep that tie. They said to their daughters, 'Hoatu tēnei!' 'Give her this one!' Then that kuia would come and get that baby and that kept the links to that family.

Atawhai given in such circumstances were cherished by both families, linking them in a special way.

Occasionally kaumātua took the radical step of giving a child to non-relatives with whom they wanted to establish ongoing relationship. When they did so, however, they made sure that the terms of the arrangement and the obligations involved were discussed and agreed to at a formal meeting of the two sides, so that they would be clearly understood and communicated to ensuing generations.

Chapter 12

ATAWHAI ADOPTION: PROCESS AND CONSEQUENCES

Whakautua te aroha ki te aroha.
Let love be given in reciprocation for love.[1]

E kore e ngaro ngā mana o ōna tūpuna; he tukunga iho ki a ia.
The mana of a person's ancestors are not lost; they are gifts
passed down to him (or her).

E stablished in most cases as an expression of kinship aroha, an atawhai relationship results in an exchange of aroha of an intensely personal kind: the generous gift of love calls forth love in return. Atawhai adoption does not, however, abrogate connection by descent, which remains a fundamental value for Maori. Adoptive and natural parents, adoptive and natural siblings, and the atawhai themselves work together to achieve a balance between aroha and mana which is suited to their circumstances.

The process of establishing atawhai relations

The ways in which atawhai relationships are established are as varied as the reasons for establishing them. The initial suggestion may come from the child's birth parents, the would-be mātua atawhai or the kaumātua of the whānau. Agreement may be reached by informal communication between the two sets of parents, by the mediation of the kaumātua or by formal discussion in a whānau hui.

The approval of the rest of the whānau is valued but not essential. If the child is a member of the whānau by descent, approval is unlikely to be withheld: the only issue is whether the adopting parents have the most right and are the most suitable persons available to care for the child. If the child comes from outside the whānau, some whānau members may express resentment but they rarely interfere if the two sets of parents have agreed. Like in-married spouses, atawhai from outside the whānau are valued ambivalently: negatively as outsiders, positively as additions to the whānau workforce and links with other whānau. (The resented atawhai is an insider in the whānau of the other parent.) Forceful opposition may strengthen rather than weaken the resolve of mātua atawhai. When Pare and Nat Rangi atawhai'd Pare's sister's daughter, Nat's siblings used intemperate language in voicing their objections. Angered by their lack of aroha, Nat decided to adopt the child legally to protect her status. Though suppressed at the time, resentment can resurface and cause unhappiness later, usually in connection with inheritance of property.

If the two sets of parents are closely related to each other as parents and children or as siblings, agreement is usually reached with very little discussion. When the mother of the child is single, it is generally accepted that grandparents have first claim to the child, that this includes father's as well as mother's parents, and that the mother's parents have a stronger claim than the father's because of the closer bonding between mother and baby. (Under the Guardianship Act 1968 only the mother of a child is a guardian as of right; the father must apply to the Court to be recognised as a guardian.) If those involved in particular cases accept these principles, there is no need for argument. Either the mother takes the child to her parents or the latter go to collect it as soon as they hear of its imminent or actual birth.

However, this simple scenario can be complicated by other considerations, such as tensions in the mother's relationship with her parents, competing attachments, and who arrives first to press their claim.

Tilly Teira lived with her mother's mother until she was of school age and became particularly attached to her mother's younger sister Rahera Tipene. As Rahera said:

She was our baby, the eldest mokopuna, she was just like a sister. She never forgot that, even when she went back to her parents to start school and when she went away to work. She was more attached to us than to her mother and father.

When Tilly became pregnant in the 1940s, she stayed in the city until the baby was born and then took her, not to her mother, but to Rahera. When Tilly's mother heard this she went to her sister's home and claimed the child, to Rahera's great distress. Nevertheless she admitted, 'she was the real grandmother, te whaea o te kōtiro' (the girl's mother). When Tilly had a second child without a husband, she was so whakamā she did not contact any of her relatives. Rahera heard of the birth, took the first available plane and collected the baby from the hospital. This time Tilly's mother let her keep the child. In both cases Tilly refused to sign adoption papers.

Sometimes an atawhai relationship grows out of a temporary arrangement during which a bond is established of such strength that the birth parents decide to relinquish their rights for the sake of the child. Roimata Wiremu was very ill when she had her sixth child and her cousin looked after the baby while she was in hospital. During that time the cousin suffered a traumatic personal loss. The baby she was caring for was her comfort and lifeline: she clung to her and did not want to give her back. Out of aroha Roimata and her husband decided to leave the baby with her as an atawhai.

If the would-be mātua atawhai are only distantly related and/ or there are other complications, such as a surviving parent with clear legal rights or several siblings to be cared for, the discussion about who is to take care of the child may be conducted with considerable formality by the whānau involved.

When Hoera Robinson's wife died soon after giving birth to a daughter, her whānau invited Hoera and his family to a meeting at their marae to discuss the baby's future. Before they went Hoera's mother Waiora talked to him and her daughter Tira, who lived with her. Recognising that she was too old to look after the child alone, she suggested that she and Tira should do it together: 'E atawhaingia e tāua i tēnei pēpē' (Let this baby be cared for by you and I). At the meeting Hoera's wife's relatives 'came on very strong', pressing their claim to the child. Waiora had no man to speak for her, since Hoera was too young and too shy. She argued their case herself, and did it so effectively that the other whānau agreed to her proposal. She and Tira picked the baby up from the hospital as soon she was discharged.

Arahi Mahuru's mother died when he was eight years old, leaving a family of five children. Arahi's father had a good job in a freezing works town, too good to leave but a long way from the community where both his whānau and his wife's lived. Arahi reported:

> Some of our karani and mātua, they got together to talk about our situation. They had a meeting and decided as an interim measure that I would go to my uncle Renata, who was my father's first cousin, my brother Ware would go to our Karani Rangimarie (my father's aunt) and my two sisters and eldest brother would go to my mother's brother. We lived that way for at least twelve months before they held another meeting and decided we should be brought together as one whānau again, brothers and sisters, that we would do that at the home of Uncle Renata and his mother Karani Niwa, and that they would accept the responsibility of raising us until we left home. My father didn't play a major role in this meeting. It was mainly the karanis, Karani Niwa and Karani Rangimarie. They were the main players. They were widows and still had mokopuna at their places.

Once a decision is made, there is no specifically Māori ritual associated with the establishment of an atawhai relationship. However, the arrival of a baby in its new home is usually marked by karakia led by the appropriate person or persons among those present, and if the atawhai has not already been baptised the mātua atawhai arrange his or her baptism in the church of their choice. They may or may not take the opportunity to give the child forenames of their choosing, but normally the child takes their surname, whether or not this is required as part of a legal adoption.

The role of the kaumātua

Senior relatives often play a key role in the transfer of children within the whānau even when they do not atawhai them themselves. As Tamati Cairns explained:

> I was fourth of 14 natural born children. In my grand-parents' wisdom they already saw the other ten lined up because of the rapid process by which the four had come. So they made the decision at that time that number four had to move out—and subsequently another three of the 14 were relocated . . . the relocation and the decision for relocation were not carried out by my parents: they were done through the wisdom of the older people who saw a problem arising with childcare had my parents ended up with all 14. (Cairns 1991: 101)

This particular transfer took place among the Tūhoe in the 1940s, when young couples were expected to accept the authority of their kaumātua in all respects. Even then, some independently minded rangatahi tried to assert their rights over their children, but they usually gave in when the kaumātua argued that the transfer was best for the child. Wiki Thomas recalled that when her third daughter Wai was a baby in 1940 she often used to leave her with her childless sister Pare in a neighbouring settlement while she went shopping. Then she and Pare 'had words', partly over Pare's wish to atawhai the child; Wiki stopped leaving the baby with her sister—and the baby fretted. One day the sisters met at a tangihanga on a Kōtare marae. The baby was so pleased to see Pare and her husband that Wiki let them hold her. Next thing she knew, they had taken the baby on to their bus, which was about to depart. Wiki rushed over demanding her baby but her Uncle Charlie, who was the senior kaumātua in her maternal whānau, stepped in front of her. When Wai was grown up and herself a whaea atawhai, Wiki told her:

> It was at a tangi, and you were hanging on to your Daddy like dear life. I wasn't going to adopt you out, no way, but Uncle Charlie made me. He said, 'Give that girl to your

sister.' What he said then was law, so I did.

Today Māori parents are less likely to accept direction from senior relatives, but many are still strongly influenced by their views and accept their intervention as mediators. After Wiki Thomas was widowed her daughter Hera left her latest baby in her care while Hera struggled to overcome ill-health and a broken marriage. The baby was sickly and Wiki already had her hands full with three mokopuna in the house, so Wai called daily to help with the baby. When Wai suggested it would be easier if she took the baby home to look after, Wiki confessed that Hera had warned her not to let Wai take the baby home, lest she keep her. At this point Wiki's son Ned, now the senior male in the family, told Wai to take the baby home, as the most convenient arrangement. Wai recalled:

> The baby was fitting in well with us. We didn't want to give her back. I kept putting Mumma off when she asked for her. We had her three months. When I took her back, Hera met us at the door. She took the baby, but she had Max with her, he was about three years old; he got jealous and hit the baby, made her nose bleed. When he did that, our son sent him flying. Everybody was crying. When Ned saw Max hit Baby, he said to Hera, 'Is that what you are taking Baby back to?' Hera called my husband Ruka over and said, 'Here's your baby', and gave her to him.

Openness not secrecy

The atawhai relationship is characteristically an open one. The fact that children are atawhai is not kept secret, nor is the identity of their birth parents. For one thing, it is impossible: such information is usually common knowledge in both whānau and community. For another, the establishment of an atawhai relationship does *not* abrogate the child's relationship with his or her originating parents and ancestors but adds a new set of connections without replacing the old.

Māori strongly maintain the right of children to know their biological parentage, because it is the clue that gives them access, when they are old enough to value it, to knowledge about their ancestry. Such knowledge is needed in adulthood to enable them to move confidently into other Māori communities by establishing whakapapa links and to ensure that they do not inadvertently form a sexual relationship with a sibling or close cousin.

Because to them the atawhai relationship has positive value and is neither unusual nor shocking, mātua atawhai neither conceal their atawhai status from their children nor agonise about what and when to tell them. Some make a point of telling their atawhai at a young age, before they hear it from others. Some wait until it becomes a concern to the children themselves. Rahera Tipene said:

> As soon as Violet was old enough, I told her who she was, where I got her, who her mother was. At school people kept saying how different she was from us. That's when I told her—she was about eight.

Many leave the children to pick it up, as they pick up most knowledge, in the course of everyday living. Often this works: many atawhai cannot remember a time when they did not know and do not associate the knowledge with any kind of unpleasantness. As Wai Tahiwi recalled:

> I think it just came up in conversation, everyone talking, grandma, aunties, uncles. I think they were just talking and I caught on, just through conversation. No big deal.

But in some cases the tamariki atawhai fail to pick up the clues, so that the news comes as a shock, upsetting their confidence in their identity and their trust in their mātua atawhai. Naomi Mahuru had no suspicion of the truth until her supposed brother blurted it out one day when she was five or six. At the time she resented finding out that she 'didn't belong', that 'Mum and Dad' were really her grandmother (her mother's mother) and her grandmother's husband, and felt bitter towards her grandmother for not telling her. But by the time she had children of her own she had overcome such feelings: 'Now it doesn't worry me. I haven't any grizzles. I always had plenty of love and care.'

Members of whānau and community can be insensitive in the way they break the news, and even malicious. Rihi and Waaka Hamilton brought up Rihi's sister's daughter as their own. They were waiting to tell her when they thought she was ready when one day a passerby asked the girl what she was doing waiting at the roadside.

Netta told her she was waiting for her Mummy, and Mummy was Rihi Hamilton. This person said, 'That's not your Mummy, that's your auntie.' Netta said, 'I'll tell my Daddy on you for saying that.' And this woman said, 'He's not your Daddy, you have no Daddy.'

The shock of finding out from others requires sensitive handling. Wai and Ruka Tahiwi delayed telling Ben, the first of their three atawhai, about his parentage. Ben was seven when, unknown to them, children he played with did it for them. His teacher warned his parents that the quality of his school work had deteriorated, but when Wai tried to talk to him, he would not admit there was anything wrong. Then his birth-mother, whom he knew as Auntie Hera, came to stay. One day, when he kept jumping on the settee while she was cleaning the sitting-room, she scolded him and sent him outside, as most Māori aunts would have done. He complained to Wai about '*her* bossing me in *our* house'. Wai sat him down for a talk, and the real hurt emerged.

He said, 'She gave me away eh? She gave me to you. She didn't want me, so she's not coming here to boss me.' I said, 'You know why she gave you away?' 'She didn't want me, that's why.' I said, ' No. Mummy and Daddy couldn't have any kids and we were looking everywhere for someone for us. Then Auntie Hera came home with you, and I wanted you for my baby.' He said, 'Did you, Mummy? Did you really?' I said, 'Course I did, and Daddy wanted you too.' He went, 'Oooh!' I said, 'We had to ask Auntie Hera if she would give you to us. Auntie Hera was sick at the time and she didn't have a Daddy to help look after you. She didn't want to give you, but she was sorry for us and she thought you'd have a better chance being with us than being with her, because she was really sick, with no-one to look after you, and she had to go to work.' And he went, 'Oohh, that's neat. I'm glad you got me!'

Because they themselves view the relationship positively, mātua atawhai sometimes fail to appreciate that children need to know both the facts of their origin and the surrounding circumstances and motivations. Roimata Wiremu did not really know how her daughter Lucy felt about being atawhai'd by Roimata's cousin and her husband until she got into trouble in her teens and was placed in a Welfare Home. When her mātua atawhai admitted they could not manage her, the welfare officers suggested returning her to her birth parents. When Roimata arrived at the Home, Lucy refused to see her: Roimata overheard her shouting: 'She is not my mother, she gave me away!' Eventually she was persuaded to go home with Roimata. She did not stay long but she and Roimata had a long talk. Lucy confessed that she was angry and bitter at being given away, especially when her birth parents had legally adopted other children. Roimata explained that she and her husband Ned had not wanted to let her go but had agreed out of aroha for Roimata's cousin, who found comfort in caring for her in a time of grief and because of the bonding that had already taken place between her and her mātua atawhai.

Community attitudes

Because atawhai relationships are relatively common in Māori communities and whānau, they attract little attention. Occasionally, where there is particular reason, an atawhai is treated as 'special': for example, where he or she was taken to become the repository of tapu knowledge, to bear an ancestral name or to seal an alliance between hapū or iwi. But in most cases atawhai are not distinguished in any way from their mātua atawhai's other sons and daughters in the family, whānau or community. The word atawhai is never used in address, and in reference only in circumstances where clarification is necessary. Reflecting on the practice of atawhai, Nora Waaka noted:

Once the child has been adopted, nobody seems to talk about it. It's their child and that is all there is to it. They say, 'Te tamaiti a Mea.' 'Te tamaiti atawhai a rāua', never. [The child of So-and-so. The adopted child of those two, never.]

Her sister Maire Owens added:

That's it. You never hear them talking about it. You never hear somebody say to somebody, 'See that girl going round with Mere, that's not her child, that's So-and-So's child.' We all know but nobody passes any remark.

When 'we all know', there is no need for remark. Brought up in an iwi in a totally different part of the country from Nora and Maire, Will Nopera confirmed their observation:

The fact that I was adopted was never discussed, never spoken about. I was always regarded as the son of my foster parents and that was that, though of course close friends of the family knew. It never seemed to be a big issue to anybody. Foster parents and blood parents, these are terms I have picked up in order to clarify the situation. Because the subject was never discussed, the Māori words were never used. All I can remember, the word was mātua (that is, for both sets of parents).

In most cases tamariki atawhai not only know who their birth parents are but have personal contact with them, as residents in the same household, in the same or neighbouring communities, or as periodic visitors. Mereana Richards and her sister lived in the same house, but Mereana was brought up by their parents and her sister by their grandparents, who made all the decisions regarding her. Will Nopera lived with his mātua atawhai in a country settlement during the week but spent part of the weekend in town staying with his grandparents and while there usually visited his birth parents. Atakura Waru lived with her grandparents thirty-five miles by road from where her birth mother lived, but she 'came over from time to time to stay with us'. Wai

Tahiwi lived with her mātua atawhai in the next settlement to her birth parents.

> I'd see them. I'd go up to the farm for holidays, and I'd stay there one or two days. Then I'd say, 'I want to go home now.'

Tamariki atawhai may lose touch with their birth father and thus with their paternal relatives if their birth parents were never married or their relationship broke up. Rihi Hamilton's father went off to the city without knowing her mother was pregnant; when she was born her mother left her with her grandparents but later reclaimed her after marrying someone else. Years later, when she visited the city as an adult, an elderly relative gave her her father's name and address, but when she called on him she found that he had a wife and family and did not want to acknowledge her. Atakura Waru's parents parted and her mother re-married: she was an adult before she had much to do with her birth father.

Two sets of parents

Familiar with the concept and practice of shared child-raising, Māori have no difficulty accepting the idea that children can have more than two parents. Accordingly, they do not require tamariki atawhai to make an absolute choice between their birth parents and mātua atawhai, to cleave to one couple and disown the other. They frown alike on mātua atawhai who try to cut children off from their birth parents and on birth parents who try to alienate children's affections from their mātua atawhai.

Where the atawhai relationship is established at birth, Māori expect tamariki atawhai to give their primary love and allegiance to those who carry the main responsibility for bringing them up: the relationship with their birth parents is expected to be secondary and supplementary, very like and often assimilated to the relationship with aunts and uncles or older siblings. When the identity of their birth parents is not mystified by secrecy, atawhai are able to view it in perspective. Most come sooner rather than later to the conclusion that the parents who brought them up are the ones that matter most, provided that they were reasonably caring. As one atawhai said of her relationship with her three parents:

> She only born me; *they* cared for me. They are my real Mum and Dad. She's my Auntie.

Nora Waaka, who was separated at birth from her twin to be brought up as an only child by her birth mother's brother, was quite clear that:

> My real father and mother never forgot me, I was never discarded from the family. I liked my real parents, I never hated them. But in my own heart I never loved them as much as the ones who looked after me . . . When you are young, you are always with your adoptive parents. When they die, then you go searching, you look for your brothers and sisters.

Intentionally or not, atawhai express their attachment to their mātua atawhai in what they say and do. Erena was atawhai'd by Mere and Fred Rapine, who had several sons but no daughter. When her birth mother died, they all attended the tangihanga. Erena was standing with her mātua atawhai when her father suggested that she go up to stand beside the grave with 'your other family'. A witness reported that 'she just shook her head. She never walked away from Fred, she stayed with the one she called her father.' Wai Tahiwi reflected:

> I knew Wiki was my natural mother. From my point of view, she made me, that's it. But my foster mother was everything. She was the world to me. One day when I was little we went to town. She was yacking with some relative and I said, 'Come on, Mum, hurry up!' I wanted something. The other woman said, 'She's not your Mummy, Wiki Thomas is' and I said, 'I know she is, but I love *this* Mummy!' I looked at my mother and she was crying. My adopted parents were my parents as far as I was concerned. But I knew I had these other ones, that if anything

happened I could go back to them. My kids say to me,
'How did you feel?' and I say, 'I didn't feel anything, I
was happy, because I felt I had two sets of parents, and
they both wanted me.' When I went to the farm, sometimes
I felt like a visitor, an outsider, and yet sometimes I felt as
if they wanted me back with them.

As for the relationship between the two sets of parents, much
depends on the quality of the personal relationship between the
couples. Related to one another in so many cases as parents and
children, brothers and sisters, or cousins, they are expected to
and generally do regard each other as allies in caring for the child
they have in common rather than as rivals or competitors. When
Wai Tahiwi had any difficulty with her son Eru when he was
growing up, she rang up his birth mother, her husband's sister,
who 'was over like a shot'. However, she was called on and
responded in the same way when their other two atawhai played
up, though they came from Wai's 'side'.

Tensions can develop, however. If there is any discrepancy in
the circumstances of the two families, jealousy and misunder-
standing can sour interrelations. Kiwa Paki's mother promised
her baby to a childless cousin before she was born. When the
baby proved sickly she kept her till she was a year old, and the
mātua atawhai were fearful lest she reclaim her. Kiwa recalled:

There were seven of us and it was very hard not to go and
keep getting her back (for a visit). We remember quite
clearly our mother was told to keep away. We grew up
believing the best thing was to leave her to her adopted
parents.

In adulthood they found out that their sister resented what she
interpreted as their neglect.

The birth parents of atawhai get upset if they feel that the
atawhai are being treated in ways which either advantage or
disadvantage them vis-à-vis their birth siblings. This is particularly true where grandparents have chosen a mokopuna as a
repository for their knowledge. As Atakura Waru commented:

My natural mother, I'm sure that in many ways she did not approve of the way my grandparents brought me up. I was allowed anything I wanted. If I saw a handbag, an expensive handbag, in a shop, and I wanted it, my grandfather would buy it . . . [As for discipine], no one was allowed [by him] to touch me. My grandmother did tell me off but she never ever laid a hand on me.

Roimata Wiremu's experience was similar. As she recalled:

I lived with my grandfather until I was fourteen years old. I knew who my parents were but my whole world in those early years was my grandfather. He and the kaumātua who named me, they instilled the traditional teachings into me . . . When I used to go back to my mother's and she used to tell me to do this and do that, to do chores, my grandfather used to hold my hand and tell my Mum not to do that. He would say, 'Ehara ēna mahinga mō taku mokopuna.' (Those jobs are not for my mokopuna.) It created bad vibes.

Even when they are not closely related or personal friends, the behaviour of mātua atawhai towards their atawhai's birth parents is characteristically generous. Ngaire and Nika Eruera adopted Rose, the daughter of Nika's sister Lena. Nika died while Rose was quite young. When the time came to organise Rose's twenty-first birthday party, Ngaire arranged for Rose to be escorted by Lena's eldest son; taking the seat on her daughter's left at the top table for the celebratory dinner, she seated Lena on Rose's right, on the other side of her escort. Photographs of the occasion included one of Rose with her two mothers. Looking at it, Ngaire commented: 'I do not mind sharing Rose with Lena. It is me she calls Mum.'

Accessibility and separation

Like shared child-raising generally, atawhai adoption works best where the two sets of parents live in the same household or close enough for the atawhai to have ready and regular access to both. If they live or move farther apart, the relations of atawhai with their birth parents may be weakened. If the atawhai are young when separation occurs, a close attachment is less likely to develop. If affectionate relations have already been established, the atawhai may feel abandoned by their birth parents, with repercussions on their psychological development and their reaction if ever they have to return to their birth parents' care.

The scattering of family members, whether by marriage or in search of employment, also removes the safeguards built into atawhai adoption against neglect or abuse. When Hepa Larsen's widowed mother died leaving eight children under sixteen, there were not enough relatives in the same and neighbouring communities to care for them all and fourteen-year-old Hepa was taken in by an uncle he did not know, who had settled at a distance in his wife's community. Resented by cousins living in an already overcrowded house, Hepa was set to work on the farm and severely beaten for real and imagined faults. When none of his relatives cared enough to enquire after his welfare let alone intervene, Hepa ran away to the city where he found a caring family in a gang.

Adjusting kinship terms and behaviour

The kinship terms which the children use (or do not use) for birth parents and mātua atawhai reflect and also subtly shape the relationship they have with each.

When atawhai are taken as babies, their relationship with their birth parents is usually worked out in terms of a kinship relationship traced through one of the mātua atawhai. However, the practical and emotional aspects of each relationship also vary with personalities and with changing circumstances as the children grow up.

When their two sets of parents are of the same generation, tamariki atawhai generally call their mātua atawhai Mum and Dad or a Māori equivalent (such as Mama and Papa) and their birth parents Uncle and Aunt and behave in the ways associated with those terms. Wai Tahiwi did this as long as her mātua atawhai were alive and her own atawhai repeat the pattern. When one or both mātua atawhai die, an atawhai who is closely bonded to adopted siblings usually maintains the established pattern of relations with his or her birth parents, but an atawhai who is an only child or alienated from adopted siblings may seek a closer relationship with his or her birth parents. When her whaea atawhai died, Wai stopped calling her birth mother Auntie and adopted her siblings' variation of Mum, initiating a closer association with her family of birth.

When atawhai are brought up from birth by grandparents or relatives of the grandparental generation, the situation becomes more complicated and the choices more varied. If grandparents are relatively young and active when they take over the primary care of their grandchildren, the tamariki atawhai usually call them Mum and Dad and treat their birth parents as older brother and sister. Taken by her grandparents as the firstborn of their firstborn, Atakura Waru called them Mum and Dad and while they lived knew her mother as an occasional visitor:

> I always remembered her as the lady who brought me kewpie dolls. And she was Arapera to me, she wasn't my mother.

As the birth mother in the middle, Tui Netana explained:

> My son, who was brought up by my mother and father, calls my brothers by their Christian names. They are not uncles to him. All my other children call my brothers 'Uncle'. My brother's daughter, who was brought up by Mum and Dad, is 'sister' to him—actually she is his first cousin. His real sisters and brothers are still his sisters and brothers. He knows I am his mother but he calls me by my Christian name. My other kids call me Mum. Its sounds confusing but they work it out. He calls my Mum Mum. While my Dad was alive, I called him Dad and so did he.

If grandparents take over the care of grandchildren when well advanced in years, they may choose to retain their grandparental status, identifying the children they care for as mokopuna rather than atawhai and being called Tupu, Karani or whatever the family variation is. In such cases, the children in question may or may not use parental terms for their birth parents. Whatever they call the latter, however, they usually treat them as aunts and uncles.

Where the atawhai relationship is established when the children are older, they are likely to continue the kinship and behaviour patterns already developed, calling their birth parents Mum and Dad and their mātua atawhai Uncle and Aunt, Granny, Nanny or Tupu and treating them accordingly. The balance between the two parental relationships is likely to be more equal, but the atawhai relationship will still be more highly valued, especially if the change stemmed from neglect or abuse.

Sometimes atawhai in this position code-switch according to context. After her birth mother died, Ngaire Eruera spent several years in the care of her mother's sister Raiha Huriwai, whom she regards with great affection. She calls her Mum when talking to people who know the family history but introduces her to strangers as Auntie Raiha. Eru Paiaka, who was ten when his father's brother took him into his home, frequently quotes his sayings and obviously referred to him as a model. In talking about him, Eru shifts between calling him 'Pop', 'my foster-father' and 'my uncle' in English. In Māori there is no problem: he is 'tōku matua'.

Grandparents who care for grandchildren (whether from birth or not) find themselves in an ambiguous position, since they are at once parents and grandparents. They deal with the problem in a variety of ways. Some opt for one role or the other, while others combine the roles or alternate between them according to context. As already pointed out, some identify such grand-children as atawhai, while others address and describe them as mokopuna.

From the children's point of view, being brought up by grandparents has both advantages and disadvantages. They often receive much more personal attention than they would as one among many brothers and sisters, and they benefit from the knowledge, wisdom and patience their grandparents have had time to develop. Miriam Norton, who was brought up by her grandparents along with one other mokopuna, was clear that she received 'a far better education on the Māori as well as the Pākehā side' than she would have done in her parents' home. On the other hand, children brought up by grandparents may be lonely for companions of their own age, especially if they remain in remote rural areas after most of their relatives have emigrated. Sometimes they are so indulged that they become whakahīhī and the target of criticism in the whānau.

Ideally, when children are atawhai'd as babies, the relationship established is permanent and birth parents are expected to accept it as such and to act accordingly, whether or not it has been 'put through the Court'. However, as their circumstances change, some birth parents attempt to reclaim atawhai who have not been legally adopted. Until he was in his teens Will Nopera had a very warm relationship with his birth parents as uncle and aunt.

> Then it became evident that my father wanted me to return to his family and he kept on insisting that I call him Dad. I didn't want to hurt him and at the same time I didn't feel it was right to call him Dad because of the care and attention I had received and the love and respect I had for my foster parents, so I always avoided calling him Dad. This was a fairly difficult time for me.

Because the parties are already closely related, such attempts can usually be resolved (as this one was) by whānau consultation, but occasionally determined birth parents pressure ageing mātua atawhai to give up the children by threatening or actually taking legal action.

Because they are a generation older than the birth parents, though not necessarily old in absolute terms, mātua atawhai who bring up their mokopuna are more likely to die before their tamariki atawhai are fully independent. If this happens, the latter may be returned to their birth parents, but equally their care may be assumed by the couple who succeed to the mātua atawhai's place in the whānau.

The return of atawhai to the care of their birth parents requires adjustments on both sides. Even when close contact has been maintained, difficulties can arise, especially if the children are mourning the death or illness of their mātua atawhai and/or they have to cope with a marked change in material circumstances. While she lived with her grandparents, Atakura was the only child in a house full of adults; she was treated as a companion by

her grandfather, fed with knowledge, and in many ways indulged.
Then her grandfather died when she was seven and she went to
live with her natural mother, her mother's husband and other
children. In addition to her grief for her grandfather, she found
herself in a tussle of wills with her mother:

> When I went back to my natural mother, she didn't like
> my attitude. I remember her getting terribly upset at some
> of my comments . . . The first person to hit me physically
> was my natural mother, when I was eight years old . . . My
> grandmother used to get very upset about the way my
> natural mother disciplined me. You can guarantee that the
> times my grandmother and my mother had a row was
> through me . . . After a while I'd sit quiet and didn't say
> too much.

After living with her grandparents for twelve years, Rere Oliver
was sent back to her birth parents in preparation for her entry to
secondary school.

> It was a big family. I felt I wasn't important any more. I
> had been the only one before that. I couldn't comb my
> own hair—I must have been useless. Mum cut the whole
> lot off.

When the attachment between atawhai and their birth parents
is weakly developed, for whatever reason, the difficulties of
adjustment are compounded and may never be fully surmounted.
For his first eight years, Nika Cowan was loved and indulged,
along with a cousin of the same age, by grandparents living in a
remote rural community. When his grandmother died and his
grandfather became too ill to look after them, Nika was sent to
live in the city with his birth parents and nine siblings.

> The feeling I got was that they really didn't have bugger
> all time for me . . . My parents were so different from
> Grandma. Mum, she wasn't interested in the way I felt . . .
> I had to adapt to the way they were living, and I had to
> adapt pretty fast . . . I couldn't hack it, I felt bitter as hell.

Resenting having no money of his own, being ordered about, beaten and disregarded, Nika reacted by running away, stealing and behaving in ways that led to a Welfare Home and eventually Borstal. Looking back years later, he could see that 'the communication was all broken down between me and my mother, all wires were cut. It was as much my fault as hers.'

When atawhai are reclaimed by their birth parents or return to them after the death of mātua atawhai, often in their teens, the change in their circumstances is reflected in changes in the terms of address they use. Ned Wiremu was brought up by his eldest sister and her husband, whom he called Mum and Dad. When his birth father brought him home to help with the milking when he was fourteen, he had difficulty using these terms for his parents as they required. He succeeded eventually in addressing his mother as 'Mum' but mostly called his father 'Hey!' He expressed his continuing attachment to his sister and her husband by calling them 'Mummy Pani' and 'Daddy Jack'.

While most children atawhai'd within the whānau continue to have close contact with their birth siblings and other relations, physical separation and even the virtual severing of contact can occur as a result of quarrels, migration and re-marriage. As adults, however, separated siblings usually seek each other out, sooner or later. Tilly Teira had two daughters while still unmarried. Naomi was atawhai'd by Tilly's widowed mother, Violet by Tilly's mother's sister Rahera and her husband. Eventually Tilly went to Australia where she married and raised a family. Naomi's whaea atawhai moved away from her home settlement, so that Naomi and Violet grew up in isolation from each other, though they knew of each other's existence. In adulthood they sought each other out and became firm friends. Though they now live a thousand kilometres apart, they and their families keep in close touch. One day Tilly's Australian sons and daughters turned up at Rahera's place, obtained addresses for Naomi and Violet and established contact with both.

Inheritance

As with so many aspects of the atawhai relationship, there is no single, general, invariable rule governing the inheritance of property by atawhai. Rather, decisions are made, and judged right or wrong, in the light of particular circumstances. In this context, three questions are particularly relevant: what sort of property? what were the origins of the atawhai? and what was the duration and quality of the atawhai relationship?

In the case of property, Māori make an important distinction between ordinary property, acquired and owned by individuals during their own lifetime, and property tuku iho nō ngā tūpuna (handed down from the ancestors) and held in trust for other descendants. The former is available for the owner to dispose of as he or she will within the terms of New Zealand's succession law. The latter comprises land, specifically beneficial interests in Māori customary and freehold land, but also moral and emotional associations with ancestral land that has been alienated from legal ownership; heirlooms such as weapons, ornaments, cloaks and photographs of forebears; mātauranga (knowledge) comprising whakapapa, stories of the ancestors, waiata and sayings composed by or about them; and the intangible qualities of mana and wairua.

Succession to beneficial interests in Māori land is governed by special legislation which assigns the determination of title and succession to the Māori Land Court. The Māori Affairs Act 1953 directed that succession be determined by the Court in accordance with tikanga Māori, without mentioning atawhai. The Te Ture Whenua Māori/ Māori Land Act which replaced the earlier legislation in 1993 specifically provides for Māori holders of interests in Māori land to dispose of them by will to whāngai (sic), whom it defines as 'a person adopted in accordance with tikanga Māori'. Other kinds of ancestral property have no protection in law, except in so far as 'heirloom objects' may be exempted under S.10 from the provisions of the Matrimonial Property Act 1976 (Durie-Hall and Metge 1992: 67-68).

While accepting the right of mātua atawhai to divide the property they have accumulated themselves among all their children, including atawhai of whatever background, Māori feel strongly that ancestral property of all kinds should be reserved to those who have the right by descent through their birth parents as well as their mātua atawhai, that is, to blood relatives preferably taken from within the whānau of the mātua atawhai holding the property in question. Atawhai taken from the other parent's whānau should inherit from that side. This rule is, however, modified in practice by two other considerations, emotional attachment and lack of other heirs. Since the Te Ture Whenua Māori/ Māori Land Act 1993 was developed after exhaustive consultation with Māori, it may be assumed that the definition of whāngai was deliberately left as broad as possible in order to accommodate such contingencies.

Where an atawhai from outside the whānau is adopted from birth, brought up in close association with the land in question and establishes a strong emotional bond with adopted siblings as well as parents, the former are likely to approve their parents leaving the atawhai an equal share in ancestral as well as ordinary property. In such cases, as Atakura Waru put it:

> The mātua whāngai give them all the sustenance they would to their own children, including mana, wairua, mauri and land.

Instead of resenting it, she herself had been 'quite pleased' when her grand-aunt left ancestral land to her whāngai Eruera, 'because, though he was very different from her in terms of blood-line, he was her heart'. Relatives who have little or no emotional attachment to the atawhai concerned may be aggrieved at 'our land' going to 'outsiders' but rarely do more than grumble.

Where the mātua atawhai are childless, the atawhai relation is often established on the understanding that the atawhai will inherit all their property. When Kiwa Paki's sister was atawhai'd by a cousin of her birth mother, this issue was settled at the time of the adoption.

> My mother clearly understood that my sister was going to inherit from her mātua whāngai because they had no children and they had deliberately taken her to be their child. As far as they were concerned, she was going to inherit everything they had.

In such cases, an effort is made to take the atawhai from relatives on the appropriate side, but this is not always possible.

Where ancestral land is concerned, if atawhai inherit property from one set of parents, they cannot and should not expect also to inherit from the other. According to Nora Waaka:

> No use saying, my mother is over there, with the other family, I should have an interest in there as well as in this one. No, they were never like that in those days, when we were young.

Kiwa Paki's mother did not leave any land inheritance to the daughter atawhai'd by childless relatives. It was understood from the beginning of the relationship that all her inheritance would come from her mātua atawhai.

Particular difficulties regarding ancestral land arise in Māori families which comprise a mixture of atawhai from mother's and father's sides. On the one hand, the mātua atawhai are reluctant to make invidious distinctions between their children in the matter of inheritance, but on the other they have a responsibility to reserve land and taonga to the descendants of the ancestors who passed them on. Different generations often approach this problem differently. When a kaumātua announced his plans for passing on his inherited landholdings at a whānau party in 1994, his children (themselves of kaumātua status) protested vigorously against his exclusion of an atawhai from that part of estate because he was of Samoan extraction. In their view he was 'one of us'. The division of property on the death of the parents is the acid test of the quality of the relationship developed with both the mātua atawhai and their other children.

Where whakapapa is concerned, however, an atawhai does not have to make a choice: he or she inherits both. This is because whakapapa is social capital, used not only to distinguish a person from others by descent but also to make connections with as many kinsfolk as possible. In reciting whakapapa for social purposes, however, a speaker will identify an atawhai relationship as distinct from a birth relationship.

Māori attitudes to legal adoption

Legal adoption was developed by legislators as a means of safeguarding the status, identity and inheritance rights of children brought up by other than their birth parents. During the 19th century 'customary Native adoption' was recognised as valid by relevant New Zealand laws, but from 1901 New Zealand lawmakers limited this recognition in a series of legal steps, culminating in the Adoption Act 1955 and its 1962 Amendment. I cannot do more here than summarise this legislation, its implementation and consequences for Māori: a fuller account is available in Ann Else's book *A Question of Adoption* (1991: 172-96).

Pursuing the government policy of assimilation, the Adoption Act 1955 imposed the same requirements on all New Zealand residents with regard to legal adoption, except that cases in which the child and at least one applicant were Māori could be heard in the Māori Land Court and the required reports could be furnished by Welfare Officers from Māori Affairs as well as Child Welfare. The 1962 Amendment, however, removed Māori cases from the jurisdiction of the Māori Land Court to that of the Magistrates' Court.

From its draft stages, the Adoption Act attracted fierce opposition from Māori because it cuts across Māori values and practice on most key points (Durie-Hall and Metge 1992: 70-73).

Firstly, the Adoption Act establishes the adoptive parents as the legal parents of the adopted child in all respects, replacing the birth parents and severing the legal connection between the child and its birth parents and consequently between the child and its birth parents' ancestors and relatives. Māori deplore this on the grounds that connection by descent is an inalienable part of a child's inheritance, the source of an important part of their personal mana, and the basis of attachment to whānau, hapū and iwi and a wide network of kinsfolk. They reject the idea of the total replacement of one set of parents by another, arguing that the responsibility for caring for children can and should be shared by parents and other relatives. As kaumātua Moihe Eruera put it:

Parents can never be substituted, they can only be assisted. Though you are legally adopted, you are still the child of others by birth.

Secondly, the Act severely limits the right of relatives to be involved in the discussion and decision-making leading to adoption, apart from the birth mother. The consent of the birth father is required only if he is married to the birth mother, and other relatives can attend and speak during the Court hearing only after applying to and receiving permission from the judge.

Thirdly, the Act originally imposed strict secrecy on adoption records, effectively preventing adopted children from gaining access to information about their birth parents. This provision was modified by the Adult Adoption Information Act 1985, but access is still limited to adults and hedged with restrictions.

Finally, the Act allowed birth parents to stipulate the religion in which they wanted their child raised, but not the culture.

The Adoption Act did not achieve the legislators' aim of assimilation: the establishment of atawhai relations without legal approval continued, remaining the most significant form of adoption among Māori. When the hearing of cases was removed from the Māori Land Court in 1962, the number of Māori seeking legal adoptions fell markedly, because Māori felt out of place and uncomfortable attending the Magistrates' Court.

Where legal adoption was concerned, significant differences emerged in the way they were handled by welfare officers from Māori Affairs on the one hand and Child Welfare on the other. Until their responsibilities for social work were reduced and ultimately phased out in the 1970s and 1980s, Māori Welfare Officers mediated the conflict between tikanga Māori and the law by helping Māori to arrange and seek legal sanction for adoptions in accordance with traditional values. They were not always successful in doing this: some judges, for example, refused permission for grandparents to adopt grandchildren.

During the 1950s and 1960s increasing Māori urbanisation was associated with an increase in the number of Māori babies becoming available for adoption through Child Welfare. Approaching the issue from a Pākehā perspective in strict accordance with government policy, Child Welfare Officers recognised no responsibility to notify relatives of a birth, encouraged unmarried birth mothers to give up their babies secretly to strangers, and not infrequently disregarded relatives willing to adopt in favour of strangers. Since only a limited

number of Māori or Māori-Pākehā couples applied to Child
Welfare to adopt unrelated children, many of the adoptions
handled by Child Welfare involved the placement of Māori
children with non-Māori parents. While the Officers believed
that they were acting in the best interests of the children
concerned, official policy and its implementation left a legacy of
problems which are still coming to light (Else 1991: 191-96).

As the campaign against secret adoption gathered momentum
in the 1980s, Māori children legally adopted under that regime
revealed how the trauma of separation from birth parents was
compounded by alienation from Māori relatives and culture.
Under the law, Māori adopted by strangers were denied access
to the specific whānau knowledge needed to place themselves in
the Māori world and often also from general knowledge of tikanga
Māori. Not surprisingly, many of those adopted in this way have
exhibited disturbed behaviour, broken with their adoptive parents
and come to the notice of welfare agencies. Others, loyal to their
adoptive parents, endure a sense of incompleteness. Those taking
advantage of the Adult Adoption Information Act 1985 to seek
out Māori kin have had to overcome not only administrative
hurdles but also the wariness of relatives who may or may not
remember their birth parents.

After the Adoption Act 1955 was passed, mātua atawhai who
continued to establish atawhai relations without legal ratification
found themselves disadvantaged in relation to those who adopted
their atawhai according to the law. Without legal status as guardians, they were unable to prevent birth parents reclaiming their
atawhai against their wishes or Child Welfare Officers removing
them to foster homes. Though often in straitened circumstances,
they had difficulty obtaining access to State support for the child,
whether in the form of Family Benefit or Income Support.

Over the years, many Māori have come to see the advantages
of legal adoption and have learnt to use it for their own ends: to
prove to their atawhai that they 'really belong', to guarantee their
succession rights, to prevent birth parents reclaiming them, to
circumvent jealousies between siblings, and at times to keep birth
parents and other relatives at arm's length.

Coda

TAMARIKI ATAWHAI

Changing circumstances

Over the last twenty years major changes have occurred in the incidence of atawhai relationships, both legal and extra-legal, and in the attitudes and practice of government agencies relating to the placement of children in care.

While Māori have continued to establish atawhai relations of all kinds, two factors have brought about a decline in their frequency. Since the introduction of the Domestic Purposes Benefit in 1973, most single mothers now care for their children themselves in their own homes and do not place them for either atawhai or legal adoption. A decrease in the average number of children born to Māori couples has also reduced the number of children available to would-be mātua atawhai.

At the same time, those who do establish atawhai relations appear to be more willing to seek the protection of legal process. Especially when whānau members are scattered, come together infrequently or have lost touch with one another, adoptive parents find it advisable to establish the legal status of their atawhai and their own legal authority over them beyond challenge.

The last twenty years have also seen an escalation in the number of children coming to official notice as needing care and protection. The reasons underlying this development are complex, including but not limited to the effects of urban migration, economic difficulties, cultural alienation and the breakdown of many whānau. In response, Māori have been deeply involved in developing strategies for meeting the needs of these children, notably through the Mātua Whāngai programme, the work of the Māori Women's Welfare League and various regional, tribal and rehabilitative trusts. While these strategies are based on the principles of aroha and whanaungatanga, they usually involve the coming together of kaumātua and other adults on a basis considerably wider than that of the whānau. The resulting

254

committees and trusts may draw their membership from a hapū, an iwi, or in some cases from the members of different iwi living in a particular urban sector. Significantly, they continue to apply the traditional terms atawhai and whāngai even in these circumstances.

Both the problem and the remedies combine new elements with old. The children identified as in need of care are in most cases past the babyhood stage and often into their teenage years; they need help because of negative circumstances; and in many cases they come to notice because the support of their own close relatives and whānau has been lacking or ineffective. The relatives with whom they are placed are often relatively distant in genealogical terms and not well known before placement; they take the children into care out of aroha for the children's need and a sense of responsibility as Māori rather than their own positive desire for the relationship. When atawhai relations are established under crisis conditions in this way, they are tentative and rarely last very long. The mātua atawhai often have to cope with personality and behavioural problems, while the children have to adjust to a lifestyle and values different from what they have known. Under such conditions, success in terms of bonding and stabilised behaviour has been predictably limited but the Māori agencies and whānau involved have built up a store of experience on which to draw for further developments.

Over the last ten years, the Department of Social Welfare has also greatly modified its practice regarding adoption, influenced on the one hand by the recommendations of *Puao-Te-Ata-Tu* regarding tikanga Māori and on the other by the campaign for changed attitudes to adoption in New Zealand society in general. Accepting the importance of recognising social and cultural diversity and consulting more widely with relatives, the Department is currently making use of the Guardianship Act 1968 and the Children, Young Persons, and their Families Act 1989 to provide care for children which is reviewable and supplementary rather than invoking the irreversible and substitutionary provisions of the Adoption Act 1955. In the process, the Department is, ironically, moving closer to the Māori way of thinking and practice.

Conclusion

Like other aspects of Māori child-raising practice, atawhai
adoption was developed in and adapted to the needs of a network
of small-scale rural communities in which the whānau was the
dominant form. It provided for children who would otherwise
have been disadvantaged by circumstances of birth, bereavement
or economic hardship; it met the needs of adults for children in
the house to give meaning to their lives, to share the workload
and to inherit land, mana and intellectual property; and it helped
to integrate whānau internally and to strengthen ties between
whānau in the same and different communities. That is not to
say that it was trouble-free or invariably successful. It could not
prevent some children from feeling rejected by their birth parents
or deprived of the special love of a mother; it could not prevent
siblings being split up or atawhai being overworked or abused in
particular cases. But philosophically and in practice it had many
strengths and advantages.

For nearly a century and a half, the Māori have resisted
attempts by government law and policy-makers to destroy the
Māori way of adoption. Through changing circumstances, they
have continued to pursue their own way, adapting it to
accommodate (instead of being absorbed by) legal adoption and
developing new strategies, such as Mātua Whāngai and modified
forms of decision-making, to cope with cases where traditional
tikanga and safeguards have failed to operate as they should.

Very recently, official attitudes, policy and practice have also
begun to change in radical ways. Recognition of government
responsibilities under the Treaty of Waitangi has been combined
with a major reconsideration of the theory and practice of
adoption. The Adoption Practices Review Committee set up by
government in 1990 produced a report which included chapters
on 'The Relationship between the Adoption Act 1955 and the
Children, Young Persons, and their Families Act 1989', 'Māori
Adoptions' and 'Step-parent, Relative/Whānau and Special Needs
Adoptions', and asked whether development of the concept of
guardianship rather than adoption might not be more appropriate
to Māori needs. These issues are still under discussion.

From the background of their own philosophy and experience

of atawhai adoption, Māori have a major contribution to make to the discussion of all law relating to the care and protection of children, including adoption law.

Chapter 13

DEALING WITH PROBLEMS

Kua rite te wā, e whakapuru ai tātou
i ngā kowhao o te waka.[1]

The time has come when together we must
plug the holes in the canoe.

I
n the course of their careers, most families encounter
problems, whether of minor or major proportions. These
problems include individual crises, such as loss of occupation,
illness and death; conflicts arising from personal and structural
tensions; the shortcomings and wrong-doing of family members;
and the repercussions of external events, such as depression and
war. Māori who are members of a functioning whānau do not
have to cope with these problems alone. According to the value
system underpinning the whānau, whānau members have responsibilities to help each other in trouble, to protect the hurt and
vulnerable among them, and to discipline those who behave
badly, whether or not this means intervening in the parent-child
family. When the whānau canoe begins to let in water, disaster
can be averted if, and only if, whānau members work together to
find and deal with the sources of the trouble.

In this section I attempt to identify patterns in the way the
whānau of rural Māori communities dealt with problems of
various kinds in the middle decades of this century. It is based
on discussions with kai-whakaatu who grew up or raised children
in such communities and my own participant observation. I have
accordingly used the past tense. However, several of the incidents
described took place quite recently, indicating continuity amid
the changes of the last twenty-five years.

Comparing the stories told reveals three main processes.
Where the problem and/or the solution was relatively simple,
the older members of the whānau handled it, singly or jointly,
by decree or mediation. Where the problem was more complex,

involving more than one whānau and/or serious moral issues, they held a formal meeting (variously described as a kōrero or huihuinga) at which the matter was discussed and decisions made on what should be done and who should do it. Where the whānau failed to deal with a problem or the matter was of wider concern, the initiative for calling the meeting was taken over by the local hapū or community, as represented by a Marae Committee, Tribal Committee or Maori Committee (the Tribal Committee re-named). Governed by successive Acts of Parliament, the latter Committees were authorised to hear cases and impose limited penalties for specified offences, with the offender's consent.[2]

The handling of violence and abuse in family and community is a topic which warrants investigation as a problem in its own right. In this section I aim only to open up discussion on the subject by setting it in the context of whānau responsibility for, and discipline of, members.

Crises in child-care

In the 1940s, 1950s and 1960s, senior whānau members acted quickly when they saw a threat to the wellbeing of children, although it meant intervening in the parent-child family. Many circumstances could give rise to such a threat: immaturity and irresponsibility on the part of parents, large families which exhausted parental energies, severely limited incomes and job opportunities, marriage break-ups, re-marriage, illness or the death of one or both spouses.

Intervention often took the form of a relative coming or being sent, without waiting for a request, to stay in the home and help until the crisis was over. This was the particular role of unmarried and widowed aunts and grandmothers. Tui Netana's unmarried aunt regularly arrived when another baby was expected in the family and stayed for several months. Matiu Waimea recalled how the tensions which built up between his sibling-set and his step-mother were periodically relieved when his father's mother came to stay and took over the daily supervision of the younger children.

Relatives also helped children cope with real and imagined problems at home by providing a temporary refuge and care.

Epa Huritau had difficulty adjusting to his mother's re-marriage.

> Because of the in-fighting between my step-father and me,
> I ran away, to my uncles or my grandmother. No questions
> were asked when I arrived. Then two to three weeks later
> my mother or one of my brothers would arrive and say,
> 'You are wanted at home.' Three weeks later the hurt had
> disappeared. I went home. My step-father, he always acted
> as if I had just been down the road.

Moana Paiaka's brother Piripi was named after a tohunga, who
was well-known for arriving unexpectedly when there was need
in a family.

> He would turn up in the middle of the night when my
> brother was sick, and he'd say, 'Give me my namesake.'
> Our mother never argued, she knew she didn't have the
> power to heal him. So she meekly handed my brother over
> and he'd ride off into the night. When Piripi was older and
> got fed up with our house full of children, he would put
> his things in a kit, bid us farewell and go off to stay with
> the old man.

Especially in earlier generations, the kaumātua of the whānau
directed the transfer of whānau children from families under
pressure to homes where they would receive more individual
care. Sometimes this was a unilateral decision. In his account of
his adoption at birth Tamati Cairns related how his grandparents
took him at one week old to the home of his mātua whāngai
(Cairns 1991: 100-02). When two whānau both laid claim to a
shared grandchild, they worked it out in formal discussion in a
huihuinga. After Arahi Mahuru's mother died leaving five
children, his mother's and his father's whānau, which were based
in the same community, held a formal meeting at which they
decided to place two of the children with relatives on their father's
side and three with relatives on their mother's side, taking account
of the families' capacity to absorb them. A year later, when it
was clear the children were fretting for each other, another
meeting decided that they should all live together in the home of

their father's first cousin (see p 231, above).

On occasion, however, the whānau caring for the child decided that it was tika (right) to waive their rights and give the child a chance to get to know his or her other whānau. Niho Waata recalled:

> When my father died I spent about two years with my mother's parents. When my mother decided to marry again, it was contrary to tradition. My grandmother said it was wrong. She got in touch with my paternal grandparents and they came to get us.

Nuku Huatahi's parents gave him at birth to be brought up by his father's parents in the Bay of Plenty in order to absorb their deep knowledge of tikanga Māori, but when his grandfather died, they sent him to his mother's parents on the East Coast to become acquainted with his heritage on that side too.

Child offending

Along with the responsibility for ensuring that the whānau's children were properly cared for, the whānau accepted the responsibility for overseeing their behaviour and dealing with them if they offended against whānau or community norms. How whānau members handled offending on the part of whānau children depended upon its seriousness.

Ordinary, expected misdemeanours of the 'kids will be kids' kind were dealt with immediately by those kin who were present or got there first. When Nika Davidson was a boy in Kōtare, the children 'hung around together' in several groups. These were both neighbourhood and kinship groups, since whānau and neighbourhood were closely linked. Nika commented:

> I often think about the things we used to get up to. We used to clash at times with the other groups at the swimming hole in the creek. If our group from Te Kainga met the Hakea lot or the Puriri crowd, well! I recall my brother getting into a huge fight with one of the Puriri boys down at the pool—everyone used to swim there. The

old people came down from Te Kainga to stop it before it
got out of hand. Who? my Dad, my Uncle Hone and
someone else.

The 'old people' (parents in their thirties and forties) stopped
the fight but took no further action.

More serious offending, the kind that breached tikanga Māori
or broke the law, was dealt with in a whānau meeting. The group
Nika hung around with consisted mainly of cousins plus three
brothers from a family which had settled in Kōtare. At one stage,
while most were at intermediate school, leadership was assumed
by an older cousin of Nika's who was at secondary school. He
organised the group into stealing from the local storekeeper. The
group would troop into the small store and ask for something
they knew to be kept in the storeroom at the rear. While the
storekeeper was fetching it, they helped themselves to goods from
shelves and freezer. This had been going on for some weeks when
one of the cousins took too many ice-creams home and was
questioned by his father.

It came back to my Dad and we were all in trouble . . . I
knew that I had done wrong. My cousin who was the
ringleader was quite arrogant about it, he thought he could
get away with it. But then my Dad went to see his Dad and
his Dad went to see our neighbour Mani Harper and they
all got together and before we knew it we were having this
big meeting.

Nika's account of what followed is detailed and revealing.

When we were caught, they called this big hui, with all my
cousins, my uncles and my aunties and my grandmother
and Mani Harper, because his boys were involved. I'll never
forget that night. It was a night meeting, at Mani Harper's
home, two doors away from our house. I was terrified that
night, because I had never been to anything like this.
    The meeting started with karakia. As soon as they
finished that, they were into us. It was a good two to three
hour meeting. Every one of them that were in that house

that night questioned me, questioned my brother, questioned the others, in English and in Māori, a bit of both. I can't remember word for word what they said, but it was very much what I hear from elders in Family Group Conferences today, along the lines of respect and disappointment. They took turns in speaking. My grandmother didn't say much: to me her just being there was awesome. The person who really sticks in my mind as someone who spoke to me quite sternly was Mani Harper. My Dad, he'd give me a doing over anyway, it wouldn't worry me; but coming from other people, even from my uncles, it was quite different. Having the other guys telling me off, that terrified me.

We were given some hard labour. I don't know what anyone else's punishments were, but my brother and I, we had to cut some scrub on the back section behind our place. That went on for two weeks, and it was hard work. My grandmother Niwa, my father's mother, she used to pick lupin seeds on the sandhills, and I had to go and pick a bag a day for her. That went on all summer, in the heat.

As well as the chores we were given to do, we had to go the very next day, with the group of people who were there, to Mr Robinson's shop and apologise to Mr Robinson while everyone was standing around. I found that really hard to do, not because of the apology itself but because all the family was there and because of the extended family and neighbours who were watching us . . . Mr Robinson was good, he thanked us for apologising. Mr Robinson didn't come to the whānau meeting, I think he left it to the family to sort it out.

Nika did not know if any monetary recompense was made to the storekeeper. He did not recall the matter being discussed in the meeting, but when the boys had apologised they were sent out of the shop and the adults remained talking to Mr Robinson for another hour.

This experience made a deep impression on Nika who, after nearly twenty years in business, is now working as a field officer with Mātua Whāngai.

I am involved in a lot of Family Group Conferences. I often reflect back to that whānau hui. I can only say it was one of the most humiliating things that has happened to me, having to sit before a council like that. I was embarrassed. Because there were other people involved. It wasn't just my Dad or my Mum or my grandmother, it was the neighbours and my extended family too. The telling off I and my brother got was worse than anything I could have got even from my Dad.

He was grateful that the whānau dealt with the situation themselves and did not call in the police. Otherwise he would have had the beginnings of a criminal record. As it was, the hui was quite enough to put Nika off crime for life.

That experience taught me a lot. I can't speak for my cousins, but I can speak for myself and my brother. I have never intentionally gone out to steal anything since then.

Family disagreements

In the 1940s, 1950s and 1960s, closely knit whānau came together for a kōrero whenever disagreements between members threatened whānau unity. In this gathering they identified and worked through the cause of the problem until it was resolved.

One of nine children, Toro Karetai grew up in a rural community in the Far North in the 1950s in close proximity to his parents' brothers and sisters and their families. When the children squabbled on the way to school, or any of the adults 'got the huff' with one another:

they would call us together and the whole family would sit down and nut everything out: Was it them who failed or was it us who failed? . . . My Dad, his brother, Mum's brothers and sisters and their kids, it was a big get together and they used to iron everything out . . . We [the children] would sit there and listen, never say anything, they do the talking.

When Toro's parents and most of their family moved to the city they took the tradition of family get-togethers with them. When Toro proposed to marry Rewa, his parents disapproved, for reasons which are irrelevant here. They stayed away from the wedding and cut off communication with the young couple. One Saturday when Toro came home from work, Rewa told him that his brother Rob had called, invited them to his place for tea and was returning to pick them up. When Rob arrived, it was the first time the brothers had seen each other since the pre-wedding quarrel. They both cried and then stood in turn to make formal speeches of reconciliation. After a cup of tea, Rob took Toro and Rewa to his place.

> We were only there about ten minutes and the whole family walked in. They had arranged it for us to go there and they'd all come in. Dad came in. Well, we had our cry there. Dad stood up and mihi'd. Mum got up and she cried and she said, forget what she said before. Well, we had a big mihimihi there.

At the end, Toro's father asked if it was true that Rewa was pregnant. When that was confirmed, he announced that he was taking Toro and Rewa to live at his place. He would not take no for an answer and arrived next day with a truck to pick up their possessions.

Physical abuse

During the middle decades of the century, Māori (along with the rest of New Zealand) accepted the use of physical force as a normal and necessary option in the management of children, but the degree of force actually applied varied widely between the generations, between individual parents, between families and between communities.

Growing up before and during World War II in Tai Rawhiti, Eru Paiaka had not experienced violence in his own family but was aware that it occured in some families in their community. Reflecting on growing up in a Bay of Plenty community in the 1950s, Niho Waata said that:

I can't recollect any family at all which showed any signs
of violence. You know, they were the most placid of elders
back home, in the whole district. I can't remember any
one coming to school battered and bruised, like you have
today.

Arahi Mahuru, who grew up in Te Tai Tokerau about the same
time, was emphatic that children were well treated in his
community.

We all got a kick up the backside sometimes ... but brutality
towards children, I never saw any of that. That is not to
say it didn't happen but I never saw it. No brutality to us
from our uncles, our koroua. We respected them
tremendously. If we got a growling, we accepted it.

Many of the kai-whakaatu I talked to contrasted the gentle,
largely verbal disciplining of grandparents and older relations
with the literally heavy-handed approach of parents. Even so, in
their experience, parental chastisement was normally contained
within certain recognised limits. For minor everyday offences it
was limited to one or two buffets in the heat of the moment,
after which children were allowed to skip out of reach. More
serious offences attracted a 'hiding', often with a razor strop. In
many communities, however, there were some families in which
violence was the main means of communication within and
between the generations.
    Where whānau were strong and well-integrated, the involve-
ment of older relatives in child-raising provided an effective
safeguard against abuse. As Ruta Wakefield explained:

There was pressure on parents to treat children properly
because there was always someone watching, always
someone there to take children if they were ill-treated. The
child was not your child but everyone's, so there was no
baby-bashing.

As we have seen in the discussion of whānau values, traditional
teachings enjoined respect for women, but in most communities

there were some men who treated their wives with violence because they had had violent fathers or lost control of themselves when drunk. A certain amount of violent behaviour was tolerated, though *not* approved, by the women themselves as well as the elders, if the man was a good husband and provider when sober or if there was held to be provocation. Persistent and unrepentant offending, however, resulted in action being taken by the wife's whānau, especially her brothers, and, if that failed to effect improvement, by the local Marae or Tribal/Māori Committee.

Whatever the incidence of physical violence, particular whānau and communities always drew the line somewhere, marking off what was currently accepted as normal from what was excessive and acting to check those who overstepped the mark.

Whānau which were functioning effectively preferred to deal with excessive violence themselves. According to Eru Paiaka, one of the main ways it was handled was through the mediation of a third party. Kiwa Paki remembered:

> If a mother or father or both gave a teenage girl a hiding for some misdemeanour, she would run away to a grandmother or older cousin of the mother or father. They would tend to her and she would live with them for three or four days, maybe a week. It was a healing process that took place.

Sometimes a man who offended against community standards in this matter was punished and warned against repetition by giving him a taste of his own medicine. When Matiu Waimea went home on holiday during his training at teachers college, his father voiced his concern at the way his sister's husband mistreated her. Too old to do what he believed had to be done, he told Matiu as his eldest son to 'sort your uncle out, make sure it doesn't happen again'. Inhibited by his college education and his uncle's seniority, Matiu was relieved when the brother accompanying him assumed the responsibility. This brother was a farm labourer, physically as fit as their uncle.

> He beat our uncle up. My uncle did not resist to the level I expected . . . he knew he was overdoing it, he knew

retribution was to be expected. The best outcome he
wanted was to minimise the damage. He was cut about,
his eyes were blackened, a gash on his ear, his teeth
loosened. He lay bleeding on the floor and it was me who
said to my brother, 'Enough!' My aunt had retired from
the room. He made no intervention in his defence, he never
claimed it was unjust or verbally denied the charge . . .
After that he modified his behaviour. He had to be put in
the position where he learnt that he couldn't do that.

Matiu identified this punishment as muru, the traditional
method of combining punishment with compensation (Metge
1976: 26). In this case, however, there was no confiscation of
chattels, because the dispute was within the whānau, and taking
money or goods would have adversely affected the wife as well
as her husband. The aim was to make it clear to in-married spouses
that the whānau upheld certain standards of behaviour and would
act to enforce them. His father did not even contemplate calling
in the police. As Matiu said:

The local constable wasn't part of the deal. In a way I wasn't
sure about, there were prescribed behaviours people knew
about and prescribed ways of dealing with breaches of
them.

Wife-beating was also dealt with by calling a whānau
huihuinga. When he was growing up in Tai Tokerau in the fifties,
Arahi Mahuru was aware that three of his uncles offended in this
respect, always after a party when they had been drinking alcohol.
He remembered their children coming for help on one such
occasion and his Karani and uncle getting on their horses and
going to stop it. After such incidents, the whānau held a meeting.

I was present at one of these meetings. One of my uncles
started proceedings by karakia. Some of my aunties
comforted the auntie who had been beaten. The uncle who
did the beating up was told to 'Sit there and keep quiet!'
After karakia, my uncles had a mihi, they had a feed and
then they went home. My uncle who did the beating up

never said a thing, neither did my auntie who was beaten.

When whānau were unable or made no move to stop violence in their constituent families, it was usual for the wider community to step in, because the children of a whānau were also the children of the hapū which contained it. Growing up in Tai Tokerau in the 1930s, Wiki Thomas saw a neighbour use his stockwhip on a son who had bungled a farm task. She told her uncle, who served on the local Marae Committee. The Committee summoned the farmer to appear before it, stressed the unacceptability of such behaviour and drove the lesson home with a fine.

A leading member of the Tribal Committee in a remote Tai Rāwhiti community in the 1950s, Moana Paiaka's father was appointed an Honorary Welfare Officer attached to the Department of Māori Affairs.

> Our father was called frequently to deal with people being beaten, children being abused. He got all these frantic messages for help. Uncle Ned would arrive in his truck to collect our father and together they'd go and unmuddle all of these messes.

Where serious injury was involved, community representatives were bound by law to call in the police. Moana Paiaka recalled a case which occurred in her home community in the fifties. A local man beat his wife so badly that she and her unborn child both suffered permanent injury. The Tribal Committee directed an office-holder to call the police. The offender was sent to gaol and never returned to the community. The Tribal Committee arranged for the care of his wife and child.

None of my kai-whakaatu recalled their community dealing with a case of homicide.

During the 1970s and '80s, as the Māori population moved to urban areas and Māori rural communities became increasingly fragmented, Māori Committees (Tribal Committees re-named) pulled back from exercising the disciplinary functions they held under the Māori Welfare Act 1962. In some places, however, the idea of community involvement in the prevention and handling of offences including violence has been revived and developed

through the vision of advocates like Judge Mick Brown and Aroha
Terry. In West Auckland, Judge Brown encouraged the Police,
Social Welfare and Justice Departments to work with Māori
organisations in developing a scheme in which Māori community
councils hear cases and work out reparation and rehabilitation
programmes with the offenders, the victims and their families
(M.J. Brown 1994). In Hamilton abuse counsellor Aroha Terry
attracted national attention when she arranged for cases of sexual
abuse to be heard on marae, if the parties agreed (Consedine 1995:
81, 84-85).

In 1993, when innocent visitors to Kaitaia were injured by a
molotov cocktail and shotgun blasts from a gang headquarters,
the kaumātua of the five iwi represented in the town called a
huihuinga at a marae outside town, using word of mouth and the
local Māori radio station to notify members of the local Māori
community.[3] The meeting was closed to the news media and (most
unusually for hui in this area) to non-Māori other than those
married to Māori and a few long-standing friends who received
personal invitations.

After a formal welcome and cup of tea, speakers of both sexes
and ages varying from the twenties to the seventies, spent several
hours in a debate which crackled with strong emotions but never
got out of hand. Among the early speakers were those who could
supply firsthand accounts of the attack and the events preceding
and following it, close relatives of those involved, including the
hospitalised, and the gangleader, who courageously fronted up
on his own with a community worker as his sole support.
Speakers gave anguished expression to their aroha (grief and
sympathy) for the injured and their families and to the anger and
shame they felt for an act which had damaged the mana of the
whole Māori community and rent the hearts of family members
related to both injured and attackers. The gangleader tendered
his personal apology and regret for the hurts caused, accepted
responsibility as leader (though he was out of town at the time
and the attack was against his orders) and promised to do what
was required in the way of reparation. Though the police had
already made arrests, pleas were made for the guilty (known to
be in hiding) to come forward and confess.

After extensively canvassing explanations, causes and consequences of the outrage, speakers debated and eventually decided on several courses of action. These included, on the one hand, apologies and reparation delivered by local kaumātua to the victims' families, if and when they would receive them, and on the other, measures for mediating the inter-gang hostility which speakers identified as the root cause of the affair.

Sexual misdemeanours and abuse

Experts in tikanga Māori are adamant that, whatever their incidence, incest (kai-whiore, ngau-whiore) and rape (pawhera) are abhorrent to traditional Māori values. They are hara, offences against the spiritual as well as the social order. Like all societies, however, Māori society, past and present, has always included some who offend against its cultural values.

The *Concise Oxford Dictionary* defines incest as 'sexual intercourse between persons regarded as too closely related to marry each other' (1990: 597). The incest taboo handed down by pre-European Māori ancestors applies not only to sexual relations within the parent-child family (between parents and their children and between siblings) but also with relatives of the same, ascending and descending generations to the second and third degree (with some tribal variations in detail), that is, effectively within the whānau. Traditional wisdom stresses the importance of seeking mates outside the whānau, in order to ensure harmony within it and to forge links with other whānau by intermarriage.

Clear evidence that Māori have never condoned incest is contained in the words used to refer to it. Kai-whiore and ngau-whiore mean (literally) 'eat or bite tail', using the word reserved for the tail of an animal. To have sex with relatives within forbidden degrees is (it is implied) to behave like animals or to have sex (in effect) with oneself. Observance of an incest taboo distinguishes humans from animals on the one hand and gods on the other: to breach it is to cast doubt on one's humanity.

Incest being thus taboo, whānau members have a responsibility to protect children from abuse and corruption from within the group as well as from outside. According to Matiu Waimea:

In the structure I knew, it couldn't happen, it didn't happen, because there was a wider family that accepted responsibility, for mokopuna, for nieces and nephews, right across the pā.

The violation of women should likewise be a matter of deep concern to their whānau and hapū. Women belong equally with men to the category tangata (human being). In their own right and as te whare tangata (the house which shelters, has sheltered or will shelter the unborn child), they are tapu, to be treated with respect. For kaumātua Epa Huritau, rape is 'the worst crime of all. It makes me shudder, because it violates the deepest principles.' When Iritana Graham was young, 'you heard people say, He kurī! only a kurī [dog] will do that!'

In the 1940s, 1950s and 1960s, whānau which were functioning effectively provided protection for their children and young women by insisting that they always went about in twos, often under the protection of elder brothers or cousins, by warning them against being alone with certain men and by their relatives, especially the kuia, keeping a constant watch. Iritana remembered that at hui:

> the kuia, the old grandmothers, they were like X-raying machines. They watched everything that went on. They positioned themselves on the taumata tapu, they knew everybody that came in and they watched them like hawks.

They also passed comments which served to set guidelines for behaviour, for the girls in particular.

If the senior members of a whānau suspected or were informed of improper sexual conduct by or among whānau members, they called a whānau meeting to seek out the truth and decide what to do about it. Often it was the kuia who initiated such a step. Because they kept their eyes and ears open, they were often the first to pick up signs of something amiss. Children and young girls often preferred to confide in their grandmothers rather than in their parents.

Reflecting on his upbringing in a tightly knit community in Tai Tokerau, Arahi Mahuru recalled two cases of huihuinga called to deal with sexual offences. The first was called when a pregnant

teenager told the grandmother with whom she lived that one of
Arahi's uncles was the father of her child. The uncle concerned
was in the army. He was sent a notice informing him of the charge
and telling him to be at the home marae at such-and-such a date
and time.

> He arrived back; we had our meeting at the marae. First
> karakia, then mihimihi. Karani Rangimarie got up and she
> explained to the meeting what her granddaughter had told
> her. She spoke to my uncle and to the house. Several of my
> uncles got up to speak on the subject. It came to the time
> when my uncle had to reply. He got up, had a few words
> of mihi to the people. Then he said to Karani Rangimarie:
> 'E te whaea, tēna pēpē, ehara māku.' [Mother, that baby is
> not mine.] He had no sooner sat down than she jumped up
> and apologised to him; she immediately realised that he
> was telling the truth. She said: 'E te tamaiti e Ara, ka unu
> ahau i taku hē ki a koe. [I withdraw my wrong to you.] E
> tātou mā, e pai ana. Māku taku mokopuna e tiaki.' [To all
> of us I say, it is enough. I shall take care of my grandchild.]
> They did not cross-examine the girl.

Karani Rangimarie made no further attempt to identify the father.
When the baby was born, she took full responsibility for him.
The child's mother stayed with her and helped raise the child
until she married.

The second hui Arahi remembered involved an accusation of
incest against a man who was raising his children on his own
after his wife's death. It was a single offence. The girl, who was
about ten, confided in her grandmother, who took steps which
resulted in a hui at the marae which was attended by 'the whole
district', comprising several related whānau. The hearing was held
inside the meeting-house. It was an open hearing, from which
no one was barred. Most of the children stayed outside playing
or ran in and out, but Arahi, who was about ten at the time,
stayed inside throughout the proceedings.

> The old kaumātua did the karakia and the mihimihi and
> from there on it was the kuikuia, the grandmothers, who

had more to say than anyone else and who sorted the matter out. The girl was there right through the discussion. She wasn't asked to say anything. They did not doubt her word and her father admitted it.

The law was not called in, the father was not taken to court. He was put through the third degree on the marae. He faced the old people, he confessed, he accepted that he had done wrong. The kaumātua, when they got up to mihi, they had strong words to say to him, to make him feel whakamā.

... The decision was that the father was not to have any more contact with his daughter, she was not to live in the same house as her father. One of the karani took and raised her, the kuia who counselled her through her difficulty. She never left the district, she finished her schooling there. She forgave her father, she still loved him as her dad.

The father wasn't sent away, and he didn't run away to Auckland. They didn't take away his speaking rights—he wasn't a speaker anyway, he was a kitchenhand who worked in the whare kai, and he continued in that role. His punishment was whakamā, and his whakamā was extreme. He carried on living and being part of the community, and he received the support of the people.

In this case there was only a single breach and the whānau of the community, having made sure that the offence would not be repeated, did not push the penalty to the extreme. Because they knew the personalities and circumstances involved, whānau members attending hui of this kind were able to tailor procedures and penalties to fit the particular case.

When Iritana Graham was growing up in Tai Tokerau in the 1930s and '40s, sexual abuse cases were dealt with by the whānau concerned or by the Marae Committee, representing the hapū to which the local whānau belonged. Only adults attended such meetings: it was a tapu subject and children were excluded, apart from the victim. Iritana was an adult before she learnt the full details of cases which occurred when she was a child.

In one such case, a young girl was raped by her brother-in-law. It happened on a remote farm while her sister was in hospital.

One of the farm workers sent a message to the local rangatira, who was also chairman of the Marae Committee. He came at once, gathered the whānau together and held what Iritana described as a hui whakawā (judgement hui). The outcome was:

> All [the rapist's] rights were taken off him right there in the family gathering. His mana was taken off him, he wasn't allowed to stand up and speak [formally on the marae]. He went to his grave with that penalty. That man died a very unhappy man, because nobody would acknowledge him. Everybody got to hear of it, it went whizz! like that round the district and everybody became aware he is a rapist.

The girl's parents were dead, so the rangatira and his wife took her into their home and looked after her like one of their own. When it was known that she was pregnant, the whānau called another meeting at which it was decided to place the child with whānau members living in a distant community. This was done 'to take the hurt away from her' and to protect the child from whakamā as he grew up. There was no stigma attached to the girl. She later married a man who knew the full story and raised a family of ten children.

Generalising from the cases of which she eventually learned, Iritana asserted:

> The victim was always there, in case she was called upon to speak. The offender, the perpetrator, he had his right of reply, after all the mihimihi, whether to admit his offence or deny it. Most of the cases I heard of, they admitted it. They were put through the third degree and nine times out of ten the people would believe the victim, especially if it had happened before in that family . . . If the person admitted it, it made it easier for him, the punishment wasn't so great. His mana was taken off him and he was made to do all the manual work around the place, like plaiting muka ropes for the fishing nets.

When the offence was particularly serious and the offender

unrepentant, he was sent away out of the district and 'his name was never mentioned.' Offenders were not cut out of the whakapapa, for, as Iritana said, 'you can't do that' but 'his whānau was marked and talked about.' Sometimes he was cursed. The victim was 'awhi'd [comforted] by the Nannies'. If the man was not sent away, they moved her to another home.

In dealing with sexual abuse, whānau and community depended on strong leadership from koroua and kuia. When a leading kaumātua committed such offences, especially if he had high mana as a repository of esoteric knowledge, community members found it difficult to challenge him openly. Some communities took an indirect approach, warning their children against being alone in his company and keeping a close eye on his whereabouts. In other communities, however, the kaumātua acted collectively to deal with offenders regardless of status.

In the Tai Rāwhiti community where Eru Paiaka grew up, the Tribal Committee was particularly strong and handled all offences without fear or favour. One case Eru remembered involved a man respected for his descent, traditional knowledge and ability as an orator. When it came to light that he was responsible for his daughter's pregnancy, the Tribal Committee held a formal hearing. When he admitted his guilt the Committee decreed that he was never to sit on the paepae (speakers' bench) again but was to work in the kitchen, fetching and carrying for the women, and to clean the toilets. He was however to continue to pass on his knowledge to the young men privately.

In a similar case, the Tribal Committee went one step further and invoked the law. The offender was sent to gaol. The mother moved back to her own people, taking the children with her, helped her daughter raise her child there and never returned. When the offender was released from gaol, he came home but from then on 'kept a low profile'.

There was a kind of distancing after the law had taken its course. It was almost as if he didn't exist in the village. He has no status. There are unspoken messages there. He has ostracised himself in the community. I think it was personal choice rather than something imposed by the Tribal Committee. He leads a hermit's life. Every time I go back to the village he is never around but I know he is there.

In these cases, whakamā was a major element in the punishment. For the rest of their lives, the offenders bore the burden of knowing that they had smirched the mana of their whānau.

Whānau did not always have the skills or moral courage to deal with sexual problems, especially if the offender had high mana. Where whānau repeatedly failed to deal with incest and sexual abuse in their ranks, so that such behaviour became a pattern repeated from one generation to the next, the wider community gave up on intervention and resorted to ostracism. They warned their own children away from the children of such families, refused to approve marriage with their members, and generally pushed them to the fringes of community life.

Ostracism contained the problem but left the children born into such families unprotected from abuse. They also suffered from the whakamā of their family membership. Members of such families often migrated to escape an intolerable situation. Even then, they could not always free themselves from the patterning of generations and its consequences.

In dealing with offences by visiting kaumātua, communities were inhibited by the tikanga of respect for visitors and by fear of offenders using their mana to harm those who crossed them. It took somebody of comparable or greater mana to deal with kaumātua who offended in these ways. When Iritana Graham was about ten years old, a party of kaumātua came to her community on a visit and she was sent to escort one of them to a neighbour's house. On the way back he grabbed her in a way impossible to misinterpret. She broke free, ran for her life and told her father. Her father immediately confronted the offender, who claimed that he was 'only playing', but her father believed Iritana's account. A rangatira by descent and achievement, he ordered the offender to leave immediately and banned him from ever returning to the district. Iritana noted, 'he had a long way to go but he wasn't even given any kai!' The other members of his party apologised to Iritana's father; two went with the offender to make sure he left the district.

Drawing the threads together

Summaries based on recollections, my kai-whakaatu's accounts of whānau problem-solving relate to a variety of times and places, focus mainly on cases that were dealt with effectively and are mostly incomplete in coverage. They cannot and do not provide evidence on the incidence of various kinds of offending or the effectiveness of social control in Māori communities. Taken as a body, however, they affirm, reinforce and amplify each other clearly enough to confirm Māori claims that they are heirs to effective, rule-governed methods of handling problems in family and community, including disputes and misbehaviour. The existence and effectiveness of these methods have been and to a large extent still are doubted and overlooked by the rest of New Zealand society (Consedine 1995; Jackson 1988).[4]

The traditional methods thus revealed comprise a system of relatively formal tikanga associated with the conduct of hui on the marae and a set of relatively informal strategies, often but not exhaustively embodied in roles.

The tikanga of the marae and whānau huihuinga

Given the widespread interest among Māori in the 1990s in the reconstruction and development of whānau of both descent and non-descent based kinds, given the stress laid on Family Group Conferences in the implementation of the Children, Young Persons, and their Families Act 1989, it is imperative to identify the characteristic features of whānau huihuinga in as much detail as possible. What follows is a first attempt in this direction.

From my kai-whakaatu's accounts of huihuinga, it is clear that they shared a common format based on the tikanga more familiarly associated with the marae, ngā tikanga o te marae. These methods were not set out as a system of laws in a code or manual but were held in people's minds as a set of principles and values, weighed relative to each other, selected, organised and applied by senior members of the whānau drawing on experience and an array of precedents. In describing particular huihuinga, my kai-whakaatu typically slid over many procedural aspects of the hui process, taking them for granted as 'the way things are always done'. In the following summary I have drawn on my own experience to set the scene and to spell out details where they are necessary for full understanding of the process as a whole.

Right at the beginning it is necessary to clarify relations between the various activities governed by the tikanga of the marae. In the Māori world, every hui—every gathering of people—consists of three basic phases: welcome (pōwhiri or mihi), main business (kaupapa) and farewell (poroporoaki). These are logically distinct but may overlap somewhat in practice, when visiting groups arrive late or leave early.

When those gathering all belong to the same group, the welcome phase is reduced to the bare bones; if there are several parties of visitors, they are welcomed according to a set ritual, usually in successive ceremonies at a time set aside for the purpose at the beginning of the hui. At tangihanga (mourning gatherings), however, mourning parties arrive continuously throughout, and greeting and mourning are combined in one ritual for each party or group of parties. The welcome ceremony has five essential elements, which can be curtailed in length but not omitted: the karanga (calls of welcome and reply), remembrance of the dead (in words and with bowed heads), exchange of speeches, physical contact (handshake and hongi) and consumption of food by the visitors. Optional extras (challenge, action-song) are added as appropriate. During the main part of the hui, there may be one or more ceremonies (marriage, presentation, funeral, unveiling) but always there is speech-making, karakia (prayers) and the provision of food. The farewell phase is the mirror image of the welcome ceremony, initiated by those departing and relaxed in style.

Speech-making (whai-kōrero) is a key feature of all three phases but its character differs significantly in each. Speeches given during the welcome ceremony deal primarily with relations between the groups involved and refer to the kaupapa of the hui only in a general way. During the main part of the hui, speech-making may be the dominant activity, if the hui was called to discuss and make decisions about specific issues, or it may be carried on in the interstices of other ceremonies, whenever enough people gather in the meeting-house or on the marae. In both cases it is governed by tikanga designed to facilitate discussion and decision-making. While the kaupapa of the hui provides a central focus for speeches in this central phase, the tikanga allow for and indeed encourage the concurrent raising and exploration of other issues.

With this background in mind we can now concentrate on the application of the tikanga of the marae in whānau huihuinga.

The first point to note is that (according the accounts of my kai-whakaatu) whānau meeting to discuss whānau problems always chose to do so on familiar ground, where people were comfortable and knew what to expect, on a marae or in a home, as was most convenient or suitable. A marae was the preferred venue if the problem was particularly serious and if more than one whānau was involved. Otherwise the gathering was held in a home, chosen because it belonged to the senior couple of the whānau, was in a central location or had a suitably large room.

Unlike larger hui, where visitors were welcome, problem-solving huihuinga were completely private occasions, attendance being limited to members of the one or two whānau directly involved. While some communities allowed children to stay as observers, in most cases only adults were present, along with those children whose welfare was the central concern, provided that they were old enough to understand proceedings and to speak for themselves.

Huihuinga held to deal with problems were conducted with formality, according to the tikanga of the marae, scaled down and adapted to the size of the venue and the needs of the occasion. If a meeting was held in a home, it was said to become 'a little marae' for the duration, with all that that implied.

At whānau huihuinga, the welcome phase was kept firmly in its place as a prologue to the main business. If those present belonged to the same whānau, a kaumātua made a brief speech of welcome and went straight on to introduce the discussion. If two whānau were involved, especially if the visitors came from a distance, the hosts staged a more formal welcome, with an exchange of speeches and a cup of tea. This scaled down welcome ceremony lifted the tapu from the visitors and eased the tension caused by their joint problem sufficiently for them to begin talking.

Karakia were always said, usually just before beginning discussion. In Tai Tokerau, however, the hosts asked an appropriate person to say prayers right at the beginning, before the welcome. Moana Paiaka commented:

> People find it strange, the notion of having a karakia and then having a row. I explain, it's like putting a framework round the hui, and that holds the people in together.

Prayers and greetings over, those present proceeded to discuss the issue which had brought them together, adapting the tikanga which govern discussion and decision-making on the marae to suit the scale and purpose of the meeting. Discussion of the main issue was opened by one of the senior representatives of the host whānau. This opening speaker outlined the issue and the procedure to be followed. Following tribal practice, some whānau began by 'going round the circle', giving everyone present a chance to have their say, and then switched to the procedure called whaka-whitiwhiti (criss-cross), in which speakers speak when they choose from wherever they are sitting. In other areas, only whaka-whitiwhiti was used. Usually this meant that those of higher mana (kaumātua and those of tuakana lines) spoke first, followed by those with less mana (the middle-aged and young, members of teina lines, and in-married spouses). If the latter held back, the kaumātua encouraged them to participate, by 'opening it up' to particular categories of persons, inviting specific individuals or using a 'talking stick' which speakers held while speaking and passed on to someone of their choice. Ideally, the most senior representative of the home whānau spoke little and last. It was his or her responsibility to listen to the various views expressed, assess support for them and articulate the decisons reached at the end.

When those present belonged to the same whānau, all who wished to take part in the discussion were able and encouraged to do so. If more than one whānau was present, more of the proceedings was likely to be on a representative basis. Women took an active, often a dominant, part in discussion and decision-making, especially when their whānau met on its own and in cases affecting women and children. As well as contributing to the debate, they fulfilled important functions by protecting the vulnerable and mediating interpersonal clashes. It was usually the women, and especially the kuia, who intervened to defuse tensions with well-chosen songs, humorous comments or suggestions for compromise.

Participants announced their intention to speak by standing up, with or without a prior verbal signal such as 'Tihe mauri ora!' or 'Kia hiwa ra!', and continued to speak from a standing position. (For Māori, standing symbolises both vitality and formality; a speaker standing on the marae is in a state of tapu.) Once on their feet speakers held the floor and had the right to be heard without interruption, however unpalatable their remarks, provided they observed the tikanga of the marae. Those who disagreed with a speaker had to wait till they held the floor in their turn to voice their views. Low voiced comments from listeners were permissible and were used by kuia in particular to encourage or check their own whānau representatives when meeting with another whānau. Kuia also had certain strategies at their command to use if speakers breached the tikanga.

Under the tikanga governing discussion on the marae, speakers were not just permitted but actually enjoined to air grievances, anger and criticism. Expressed, such feelings could be dealt with; unexpressed, they festered and became dangerous. The same tikanga, however, identified the marae as tapu ground, placed limits on the use of intemperate language and physical violence, provided ritualised ways of expressing anger, and required disputants to listen to each other without interrupting or walking out. They were expected to accept mediation and if possible make peace with each other, leaving their angry words 'hanging on the walls' when they dispersed at the end of the meeting. To walk out of a huihuinga was to break off negotiations and risk the displeasure of one's own group.

Discussion in huihuinga had three main aspects which were pursued both successively and concurrently. Speakers pooled relevant information to build up a picture of the problem, determined causes and responsibility, and decided what to do. In each case, they worked to achieve consensus. This process needed ample time. Speakers set out different views and options and argued their respective merits, until eventually support crystallised around a particular option or a compromise between options. At this point those with minority views were expected to give in gracefully and add their weight to the majority view. As Arahi Mahuru said: 'Ki a koe, tuku ki raro. It is for you to put it down, to let go of your feelings.' Agreement had to be verbalised: in this context silence meant dissent, not assent. Securing members voiced commitment to the decisions taken was essential, because their continuing support was required for implementation.

Management of the discussion was vested not in a single chairperson but in the kaumātua (both koroua and kuia) collectively. Individual kaumātua spoke or refrained from speaking according to personality and experience, but they kept a close watch on all present and one or more intervened, when necessary, to bring discussion back on track, to mediate disputes and to open the way for the hesitant to speak. To these ends they used a variety of methods. Rising to speak, they might tackle the problem head-on or use oblique and humorous references to make their point. They made much use of non-verbal body language: a shake or sideways jerk of the head, raised eyebrows, a glare or, in serious cases, a bowed head, with gaze directed at their feet, the ultimate sign of disapproval and withdrawal. They made comments loud enough to reach but not override the speaker. When emotions ran high, kuia often started a waiata or action-song, releasing tension in physical action. Only as a last resort, after all else had failed, did the most senior among them take the drastic step of ordering someone to sit down or to leave the meeting.

When consensus was fully reached or when it became obvious that another meeting was needed to achieve it, the leading kaumātua carefully repeated the conclusions reached, making sure that everyone present knew exactly what had been decided and who was to do what. Then the kaumātua closed the meeting with appropriate prayers. Usually, unless there were cows to be milked or a tide to catch, those present ate a final meal together before dispersing and departing visitors left after a brief farewell.

Hui whakawā

When a huihuinga was called to consider an offence against the law and/or tikanga Māori, observance of the tikanga of the marae was particularly strict, enabling strong emotions to be both expressed and contained. In Tai Tokerau, meetings of this kind were called hui whakawā. (Whakawā means to accuse, investigate and judge.)

At huihuinga of this kind, the accused were required to be present and given the opportunity to speak to the accusation. Usually they said little, apart from denying or confessing guilt. If they were believed innocent, had a good record or could plead extenuating circumstances, other whānau members supported them by sitting with them and speaking in their defence.

Whether the injured parties attended depended upon whether they belonged to the group hosting the meeting. Those who belonged to the group were usually there. Relatives, especially the older women, sat close around them, providing physical and moral support, screening them from their abuser and speaking for them if they did not wish to speak themselves. If the injured parties came from outside the whānau, whānau members might investigate the case in their absence, but a visit and apology to injured parties was often included in the measures decided upon. This was likely to be carried out by a party representing the whānau, including or excluding the offender as appropriate.

In considering an offence, discussants sought to establish responsibility, to secure a confession accompanied by signs of whakamā and repentance, and to decide on appropriate methods of punishment and healing. In doing so, members of the offender's whānau recognised that they could not separate themselves from the offender but shared responsibility for his or her wrongdoings and for putting them right. Parents and grandparents especially often accepted blame for failing to discipline, guide or provide a good example to the offender. At the same time, they did not hesitate to scold the offender for lowering the mana of the group and its members.

In all but the most serious cases, punishment and healing went hand in hand, the main instruments being reinforcement of whakamā, confession, apology, reparation and behavioural change.

The whakamā felt by the guilty was recognised as part of their punishment, since it involved lowered self-esteem, depression and withdrawal from social interaction (Metge 1986: 25-33). Reference was frequently made to the proverbial saying 'Mā te whakamā e patu.' This is usually translated as meaning 'They will be punished by whakamā' but the word 'patu' (to strike or hit) implies a beating, in this case of a psychological kind. In so far as whakamā is a response to consciousness of fault, it is the necessary prerequisite and accompaniment of repentance and confession of wrongdoing. Speakers at huihuinga deliberately set out to deepen the offenders' whakamā by dwelling on the unacceptability of the offence and the harm done to the victim and to the mana of the whānau. When offenders admitted their guilt and appeared sufficiently chastened, members of their whānau re-established contact (both physical and social) and helped them work through and eventually emerge from whakamā, sensitively adjusting the time taken to the seriousness of the offence (Metge 1986: 94-98, 101-05).

Like whakamā, confession, apology, and reparation (utu) were at once part of the punishment of offenders and part of the process of healing the hurts inflicted on injured parties, on relationships within and between whānau and on the offenders themselves. Offenders were required to admit guilt and apologise for wrong-doing before their assembled whānau or its main representatives. This was hardly an easy option, especially after they had repeatedly been told by close relatives that their actions were unacceptable and had diminished the mana of the whānau. However, when it came to apologising to outsiders, the whānau members who imposed the penalty could be counted upon to support the offender through the ordeal. Often they added an apology on behalf of the whānau.

In my kai-whakaatu's accounts, reparation mostly took the form of cash or labour. If the offender was unable to raise the cash or if doing so would adversely affect innocent dependents, whānau members either helped with its assembling or paid the sum in full and retrieved some or all of it from the offender, perhaps in the form of service. The offender might be directed to provide labour service either to those who helped provide the reparation or to the community, usually at the marae. The oldest kai-whakaatu mentioned in passing cases where animals—horses, cows or sheep—were given or demanded as utu. This sounds more like the practice of muru, the formal taking of compensation for injury. However, a word which was mentioned only once. Instances of this form of reparation all pre-dated the Second World War.

Where appropriate, offenders were ordered to refrain from behaviour associated with their offending, on pain of more severe penalties next time. They might be told to moderate their drinking of alcohol, if that was a contributing factor, or to take out a prohibition order.

Many of the offences dealt with by whānau huihuinga were offences against New Zealand law as well as against tikanga Māori. From the stories told by my kai-whakaatu, it would seem clear that whānau and under certain conditions community committees felt no obligation to report all offences against the law to the police. Believing that the ties between descendants of a common ancestor had a spiritual as well as a physical dimension and caused spiritual as well as physical damage, they held that offences which disrupted ties between whānau members or threatened the whānau's future fell within the jurisdiction of the whānau, not the State. At the same time, their attitudes to the judicial process of the State were ambivalent, to say the least. While upholding due process of law in principle, they considered it alien in its basic premises, impersonal in principle and operation, and unattractively focused on punishment. In less serious cases, such as stealing by children, whānau acted to divert offenders from involvement with the judicial process, long before diversion became part of official practice. Only in particularly serious cases did whānau or community committees refer cases to the police, effectively using that course as one among several extreme penalties.

In dealing with offences, whānau continually strove to achieve a balance between aroha (love and support for kin) and upholding what they knew to be tika (morally and spiritually right). As well as repairing the damage resulting from particular offences, they were concerned to serve notice to their own members and to the rest of their community that they did not condone certain kinds of behaviour. Some offences, however, were considered so serious that aroha was completely overset, no reparation was accepted and the penalties imposed were both heavy and irreversible. They included the removal of mana and the right to play a leading part in whānau and community life, a lifetime of manual labour, ostracism and exile.

Strategies and roles of prevention and healing

In their stories, my kai-whakaatu highlight at least three strategies used within the whānau to prevent problems developing or escalating and to facilitate the healing process during and after huihuinga.

Prominent among these strategies was the provision of leadership by those of senior descent, age and wisdom, embodied in the roles of mātāmua and kaumātua (koroua and kuia). The danger of this strategy developing into petty tyranny was offset by emphasising the responsibilities which went with these roles, especially responsibility to act as trustee and guardian of whānau taonga (including knowledge) and to hand on that trust to suitable heirs. In the whānau even more than in hapū and iwi, mana had to be balanced and tempered with aroha, or divisions between the generations got out of hand.

Secondly, there was the strategy of constant observation and monitoring, a responsibility assumed mostly by older whānau members as they moved from more active, hands-on roles 'out the back' into those of front-people, especially at hui. These watching eyes and the associated gossiping tongues were often resented by younger whānau members and were sometimes cited as a reason for migration to the 'freedom' of the city. Nevertheless, they played a valuable role in whānau as a safeguard against abuse.

The dangers of intergenerational and interpersonal conflict were mitigated to a large extent (thirdly) by the recognised use of a third party as takawaenga (go-between, mediator). As Otene Reihana noted:

> No matter what the differences were between relatives, there was always somebody to serve as a link. Even when a whānau member became an outlaw, he was never wholly cast adrift. There was always someone who would talk to him.

This strategy provided a means of releasing the build-up of tension in relationships, especially between husband and wife, parent and child. It acted as a safety valve. This function might be assumed by different relatives under different circumstances, but sometimes individuals with a particular kind of personality or pivotal place in the whānau became repeatedly cast in the role.

Conclusion: dealing with problems in the 1990s

In this account of whānau problem-solving, I have used the past tense because most of the examples given occurred in the 1950s and 1960s. Over the twenty-five years since then, the capacity of kaumātua to take unilateral decisions has diminished, but the private huihuinga remains of primary importance as a means of dealing with problems among descent-based whānau, where they are well integrated and strong. It is increasingly used by Māori groups which look to the descent-based whānau as a model and was a major influence in the development of the concept of the Family Group Conference, as provided for in the Children, Young Persons, and their Families Act 1989 (Hassall 1996).

It must, however, be remembered that whānau methods of dealing with problems were worked out and function best in family groups where people bound by ties of kinship and shared experience associate closely in an ongoing corporate life and consequently have a strong sense of group identity and responsibility. To be effective in other situations, where people are held together by personal choice for limited terms or where group structure is loose or lacking, they have to be carefully considered, adapted and applied with understanding and consent. In particular deep thought needs to be given to applying methods associated with relatively small-scale groups to much larger ones (such as iwi).

In the decades when my kai-whakaatu were growing up, Māori acquired knowledge of whānau methods of problem-solving by constantly observing them in action, both in everyday life and at hui small and large. Today, the large majority of young Māori do not have such opportunities. Since the success of their application depends upon knowledge, experience and consent, these methods of dealing with problems have to be brought to consciousness, explained and taught in a way that has not been characteristic of Māori society.

Handed down from the ancestors, modified by successive generations to meet the needs of their time, whānau methods of dealing with problems (including but not limited to huihuinga) contain many insights and procedures which are psychologically sound and effective in practice. They are unquestionably deserving of close study, a valuable and undervalued resource for Māori and Pākehā alike.

Chapter 14

FLOWERING AND
NEW GROWTH

He puawaitanga nō te harakeke;
he rito whakakī i nga whāruarua.[1]

The flax flowers; new shoots fill the empty gaps.

The flowering of the flax is a spectacular sight, each bush
putting out towering flower stalks topped by red and
yellow flowers. Since the stalks displace the rito at the
centre of their fans, the eventual decay of the fans leaves empty
gaps but the flowering stimulates the bush as a whole to start
new fans. The whānau also has its times of flowering and makes
up its losses with new growth.

From the first time I heard the flax bush used as an image for
the whānau, I have been collecting whakataukī (proverbs) which
refer or can be applied to family relations (see p 315, below).
Using these to introduce the chapters of this book has served
several purposes. Taken together, they demonstrate the high value
Māori have always placed on relations at the family level, the
broad way in which they define such relations, and the priority
accorded connection by descent. Typically open to more than
one interpretation, they explore the ambiguities and ambivalences
of human relations, reject black-and-white judgments and remind
us that every form of social patterning has weaknesses as well as
strengths, the potential to limit as well as liberate, *and vice versa.*
Drawing lessons from the observation of nature, they highlight
the processes of growth, decay and regeneration, of continuity,
adaptation and change.

Continuity and change

Even in maturity, flax bush and whānau go on growing and
changing. As old growth dies, new growth takes its place. Like

290

the flax bush, the whānau survives changes in its environment and even transplantation to a new one by making appropriate adaptations. Provided it is cultivated with knowledge of its habits and needs, it grows as vigorously in the new environment as in the old.

If discussion of the place of the whānau in the 1990s is to be fruitful, it is necessary for those participating to grasp five key points:

- The word *whānau* has not one but many meanings.
- These include some meanings which have been handed down from pre-European ancestors and many of recent development.
- One meaning—'the whānau which comes first to mind' for most Māori—has primacy over the others.
- This whānau of primary reference is a corporate group defined in the first place by descent.
- The non-traditional meanings of whānau are extensions and metaphorical applications of this primary meaning; the whānau thus identified resemble and differ from the whānau of primary reference in significant ways.

The whānau which comes first to mind

The whānau which comes first to mind is recognised as a group by its members and others, distinguished by group symbols (notably a name) and involves members working together for common purposes on a continuing basis. Membership is defined in the first place by reference to an ancestor or ancestral couple as fixed starting point and in the second by participation on the part of descendants, their spouses and adopted children. Whānau members hold and endeavour to live by a set of common whānau values. The whānau outlasts the life of the foundation ancestor and the death or defection of other members, but eventually breaks up, usually into new groups of the same kind.

Adequately to characterise the whānau which comes first to mind it is necessary to hold two anthropological terms (descent-group and extended family) in tension, recognising that one or the other comes to the fore in different contexts.

This primary whānau, as it has operated for at least fifty years, is at once like and unlike the whānau household which was reported and described by European visitors to Aotearoa New Zealand in the late 18th and early 19th century. It maintains continuity with the pre-European whānau household in the prominence of descent as an organising principle, in adherence to traditional values, in the sharing of child-raising and in the way members work together for common goals. In the course of two hundred years, however, it has undergone significant changes, in spatial disposition (from concentration in a single household to distribution between several households, sometimes in different localities), in functions (from the management of all aspects of daily life, including production, consumption and child-raising, to co-operation and exchange between households on an 'occasional' basis), and in goals (from maximum social and economic self-sufficiency to the provision of support for largely self-sufficient individuals and parent-child families, the management of group property and the organisation of group gatherings). Finally, whānau membership, formerly essential for survival, is now optional. An unknown but relatively high proportion of Māori are *not* members of whānau, whether by choice or from lack of opportunity.

Non-traditional whānau

The late 20th century has seen an astonishing proliferation of new applications of the word whānau.

The non-traditional whānau thus identified differ from the whānau of primary reference in important ways. Only some are groups with an on-going corporate life; others are one-off groupings assembled for a short term only. The central principle of their recruitment and operation is *not* descent (whakapapa) but commitment to one or more common purposes (kaupapa).

By choosing to describe themselves as whānau, members of these non-traditional whānau signal that they look to the whānau of primary reference as model and reference group. Lacking descent to bind them together, they lay particular emphasis on adherence to whānau values and working together for common purposes values.

Different kinds of whānau

In view of its wide and widening range of meaning, it is advisable to indicate clearly how the word whānau is being used in particular contexts.

The many kinds of whānau can be classified in several ways. In Chapter 3 and the section immediately above I have distinguished between usages which are traditional, handed down (though not without change) from pre-European forebears, and those which are non-traditional, emerging in relatively recent times. It is important (secondly) to distinguish between whānau which are corporate groups, that is, whose members interact recurrently in a set of interconnected roles, and those which are social categories held in the mind or aggregations whose members interact in a limited and temporary way. Over the last twenty years, an important distinction has emerged (thirdly) between those whānau in which descent (whakapapa) is the chief basis of recruitment and organisation and those formed on other bases.

The whānau as remedy and resource

Since the 1970s, as the signs of stress and distress in sectors of the Māori population have become of increasing concern, Māori speakers and organisers have repeatedly and publicly highlighted the whānau as both remedy and resource, an instrument for intervening proactively to regain control over their own destiny. Writing of Kura Kaupapa Māori, educationalist Graham Hingangaroa Smith stresses that:

> there is an inextricable relationship between the social, cultural and economic emancipation of Māori on the one hand, and the revitalisation and maintenance of whānau structures on the other. . . . The whānau provides a culturally appropriate and nurturing context for Māori language, knowledge and culture. . . . the future of Māori is very much the future of the whānau and vice versa. (Smith 1995: 34)

Of the many programmes which have been established by

Māori for Māori, nearly all use the word whānau in their title or in describing the way they function. The whānau thus identified are all groups with an on-going corporate life but the practice common among Māori of shifting between meanings obscures the fact that two distinct kinds of whānau groups are being referred to: whānau groups for which kinship and descent (whakapapa) provide the fundamental basis of recruitment and connection, and whānau groups which are set up to fulfil a special purpose (kaupapa) with little or no reference to descent.[2] The distinction is, however, crucial for understanding and for social planning, because whānau of these two kinds have their own particular strengths and purposes, and their own particular problems. Throughout the following discussion I shall highlight this distinction by referring to these two kinds of whānau groups as *whakapapa-based whānau* and *kaupapa-based whānau*. The category whalapapa-based whānau includes the whānau of primary reference and groups of the kind I have called kin-clusters (see pp 42, 54-55, 126-27, above).

Whānau groups of these two kinds are sufficiently different to complement and reinforce each other instead of engaging in competition. Many Māori belong to kaupapa-based as well as whakapapa-based whānau, balancing their commitments to each as well as they can. Increasing numbers of Māori, however, are turning for support to whānau which are kaupapa-based when denied access to whānau which are whakapapa-based, especially in urban centres.

Both whakapapa-based and kaupapa-based whānau tackle social problems at the personal level, in direct interaction with people, but they do so in a wider socio-economic and political context. While the decline in the proportion of Māori who belong to whakapapa-based whānau is often cited as a cause of current social problems, it is a proximate cause, itself a consequence of the interplay of social, economic and political forces on a national and international scale. Māori programmes designed to tackle social problems by utilising the strengths of the whānau can have only limited success unless the State acts to support and empower them.

Whakapapa-based whānau

Programmes designed (like Mātua Whāngai) to use traditional, whakapapa-based whānau to remedy particular problems soon discover that where need is most acute whakapapa-based whānau are often missing, weakly integrated or dysfunctional, contributing to instead of resolving difficulties. As a result, organisations such as the churches and the Māori Women's Welfare League have developed programmes which concentrate in whole or in part on the building up of whānau of the whakapapa-based kind, encouraging Māori already belonging to whānau to improve their understanding of the concept and their care for each other and encouraging Māori who are not currently members to join or establish whānau.

In programmes aimed at supporting and strengthening what is still thought of as *the* whānau, the whānau with a descent-group core, it is vital to start with a realistic assessment of its strengths and weaknesses. In reaction against long years of official opposition, romanticising the whānau is understandable but unhelpful. Focusing only on its positive features leads to disillusion or defensiveness when real-life whānau fail to measure up to the ideal; denying problems in its functioning prevents whānau members from learning about the methods of conflict resolution at their disposal and allows minor problems to escalate into major ones.

Realistic assessment of the whakapapa-based whānau requires a degree of self-consciousness which was not traditionally characteristic of whānau members as a whole. Until at most a generation ago, only koroua and kuia who had retired from active leadership had the leisure to reflect on and articulate their understanding of its definition, values and functioning. Most other members were too immersed in living *in* the whānau to have the time or feel the need to do so. In the 1990s, however, when Māori are scattered widely through urban as well as concentrated in rural areas, when they face a wider range of competing pressures and opportunities, both existing and would-be whānau members would find it helpful to bring to consciousness all they take for granted and to seek out all the information available in the minds of older relatives and in books. Only then will they be able to discuss the usefulness of particular aspects of the whānau in relation to present needs and goals and to make informed decisions about what to hold fast, what to adapt and how. As has been shown, especially with regard to child-raising (pp 203-9, above), there are dangers in continuing to repeat inherited practices without under-standing their place in the wider pattern. Practices which made sense in one setting may become counter-productive when transferred to another where they cannot be fully realised.

On the basis of discussions with my kai-whakaatu, I suggest that the following points need to be spelled out for the sake of those organising or supporting whakapapa-based whānau.

Firstly, while descent and participation are both essential in establishing who belongs to a particular whānau, descent is of *primary* importance, the glue which holds the whānau together, the ultimate reason for participation. Whether or not they are personally remembered, the foundation ancestor or ancestral couple provide the whānau with its most important symbol and reference point. Ancestral land (if held) is an important asset and focal point for whānau life, but it is not essential and cannot oust the ancestor from this position of primacy. Descent is also the primary basis of leadership in the whānau and always a component of status, though it may be modified by competence in tasks valued by the whānau and willingness to use talents and outside qualifications in the service of the group. As a value, descent overrides social, economic and political differences. Whakapapa-based whānau hold together members whose occupational status ranges from long-term unemployed to highly qualified professional, cross-cutting class and income categories.

Secondly, because of the way it is structured and the complex interweaving of whānau values, the whakapapa-based whānau has certain inbuilt tensions, for example, between descend-ants and non-descendants of the foundation ancestor, between tuakana and teina, between the values of mana and aroha. Mani-festations of these tensions in interpersonal conflict are to be expected and should not necessarily be interpreted as indications of personal failure or imminent breakdown. Such tensions cannot be eliminated, for they are integral to the way the whānau functions. However, they can and must be managed, to prevent their undermining whānau solidarity.

Thirdly, as an institution the whakapapa-based whānau has access to remedies of its own for the problems generated by internal tensions, personal incompatabilities and unexpected misfortune. The most common of these remedies involves recourse to third parties. When a relationship becomes stressful, one or both of the parties involved (parent or child, husband or wife, older or younger siblings) are offered protection, time-out and nurturance by whānau members attached to them. These third parties often act as takawaenga (mediators), taking an active part in effecting reconciliation. Sometimes persons marked out by personality or status in the whānau become recognised takawaenga, who regularly take the initiative or are called upon as go-betweens when problems occur. Finally, there is the whānau huihuinga, a closed, formal gathering at which adult whānau members discuss and resolve problems using traditional tikanga. These remedies are both effective and adaptable. They deserve to be supported where they are in use and revived where they are not.

Fourthly, whānau members are frequently linked into complementary pairs, the parties to which carry out functions which are different from but necessary to complete those of the other. Such pairings include descendants and non-descendants of the whānau ancestor, men and women, tuakana and teina, kaumātua and rangatahi, tupuna and mokopuna, parents and other senior relatives. These relationships contain elements of both opposition and co-operation, which must be balanced. Each party has its own value; though one may be given greater prominence in some contexts, the balance is often redressed in others. Complementarity works well when both parties are present and willing to act in the prescribed way. But if one is missing, refuses to accept the limitations of their role or asserts dominance, the aims of the relationship cannot be properly fulfilled. If this is allowed to continue, the functioning of the whānau is upset, existing and potential members may be frightened off, and young people learn the wrong lessons.

Fifthly, it is important to recognise the dynamism which is characteristic of the whānau. Real-life whānau are always in process of change, passing through different stages of growth and decline. In the course of on-going operations and/or in times of crisis, whānau adapt traditional procedures to meet the challenge of their present circumstances, finding new ways of realising the aims and values bequeathed to them by their ancestors. Sooner or later, when their members become too numerous or too widely dispersed for effective communication and co-operation or the kaumatua responsible for holding them together dies, they disintegrate, to re-form, if conditions are favourable, into several new whānau. Trying to hold a whānau together past this point is either wasted energy or produces a group which operates more like a hapū than a whānau, whatever name it is given.

While new whānau usually grow out of the decay of the old, they can also be established by agreement at any time, with or without antecedents. When a kaumatua dies, relatives gathered for the tangihanga often start discussing the formation of a whānau under his name or that of a suitable ancestor. Called together by the convenor of a Family Group Conference, relatives who have never acted in concert may be motivated to do so when they become aware of the needs of young relatives searching for support and identity.

Key factors in the successful operation and adaptation of whānau are a high degree of commitment on the part of whānau members and strong, inspirational leadership, which may be individual or collective. These can only be generated within the whānau, but more general recognition of whānau and whānau activities as socially valuable would be helpful in preventing disillusion and burnout.

Belonging to a whakapapa-based whānau is rewarding. It provides a secure base, unconditional acceptance (except for serious offenders against whānau values), identity and a sense of belonging, financial and emotional support. But it is also demanding. It requires members to contribute to whānau activities in cash, labour and kind as and when needed, sacrificing aspects of individual and family comfort for the good of the wider group. And (ideally) it means accepting criticism as well as support and sharing responsibility for the wrong actions of other whānau members as well as pride in their achievements.

Whakapapa-based whānau and the State

However great their commitment, leadership and capacity for adaptation, whānau have a constant struggle to establish and maintain themselves, because the laws and administrative procedures of the New Zealand State place obstacles in the way and either deny or offer only limited support. If Māori efforts to strengthen the whakapapa-based whānau are to be successful, they need to be supported and empowered from without, by the State, as well as from within.

The first requirement is official recognition by legislators and policy makers of the existence, nature and potential of the modern whānau as a family form alongside and incorporating the parent-child family. Such recognition must take cognisance of the points set out above and of the optional nature of the whānau.

At present the whānau is explicitly referred to in only two Acts. Recognition of the whānau in the Children, Young Persons, and their Families Act 1989 has been of great symbolic importance but its practical effect is limited by the fact that whānau is left undefined and the Act relates only to children and young persons under 17 in special circumstances. The Te Ture Whenua Māori/ Māori Land Act 1993 provides for beneficial interests in Māori land or in general land owned by Māori to be constituted as a Whānau Trust, directing that 'the land, money and other assets of a whānau trust shall be held, and the income derived from those assets shall be applied, for the purposes of promoting the health, social, cultural and economic welfare, education and vocational training, and general advancement in life of descendants of any tipuna (whether living or dead) named in the order.' This meets the needs only of those who have land holdings and defines whānau as a descent category.

The second requirement is the review and revision of the laws which affect the operation of the whānau. Among the issues which need to be addressed are: assumptions about the nature of the parent-child family;[3] the rights and responsibilities of parents and senior relatives in relation to children;[4] the many issues surrounding adoption; the safeguarding of ancestral property other than land from alienation away from the descent-line; and the desirability or otherwise of providing the whānau with a legal

identity of its own.[5] The Adoption and Succession Acts are
currently under review, but they are being considered separately
by different agencies. Instead of a piecemeal approach, it would
make sense for all the issues to be considered in a general review
based on wide consultation between representatives of Māori iwi
and organisations on the one hand and representatives of
government departments, the Law Commission and family law
experts (many of whom are also Māori) on the other.

Before proceeding to consider particular laws, participants in
a general review would be well advised to debate the deeper issue
of the relation between ngā tikanga Māori and the laws of the
State (ngā ture). Is it enough to eliminate those legal provisions
which undermine tikanga Māori or should State laws be widened
to include measures which recognise and support Māori forms
and procedures, as in the Children, Young Persons, and their
Families Act? Or are the philosophical and procedural differences
between the two systems so different that ngā tikanga Māori
cannot be incorporated into State laws without distortion? If so,
what are the alternatives? I am strongly of the opinion that all
the issues should be debated openly, from both philosophical
and practical perspectives, so that decisions can be made on the
broadest possible base. In finding ways to reverse the legal
disadvantages under which Māori labour with regard to family
arrangements, the participants in such a debate are likely to
develop improvements to family law which will benefit both
Māori and non-Māori.

The third requirement is improved levels of knowledge and
understanding of the complexity of the Māori social situation on
the part of staff involved in forming and implementing Government policy with regard to family and related social welfare issues.
This should be an integral part of staff training and include
recognition of variations in cultural practice among Māori and
the need for sensitivity and flexibility when dealing with Māori
clients. Not all Māori belong or want to belong to whakapapa-
based whānau, speak Māori or are knowledgeable about tikanga
Māori. They should not be made to feel foolish or deprived as a
result. Some have chosen to belong to their spouse's whānau
rather than their parents'; some struggle to reconcile obligations
to whānau with obligations to non-Māori spouses. Whakapapa-

based whānau vary widely in effectiveness. Some constantly struggle to survive, others are strongly integrated and proactive, but most can be counted on to come together effectively in a crisis. Those Māori who choose the whānau option should be able to count on understanding and support in official quarters.

New growth from old

In developing programmes aimed at strengthening the traditional, whakapapa-based whānau, Māori social planners are building not on nostalgia for a vanished past but on firsthand experience of whānau operating now, in the 1990s, which provide effective and socially rewarding support systems for their members, deal proactively with problems and adapt imaginatively to change. As relief from abstract discussion, let me demonstrate this assertion through a particular example.

The Matangi Whānau is defined by reference to deceased tūpuna Rata and Whareroa Matangi and identified by the surname and land base inherited from the latter in the rural community of Awapikopiko on the East Coast. In 1995 it comprises some 300 persons, descendants of Rata and Whareroa, together with their spouses and adopted children.

Rata and Whareroa had nine children whom they raised in Awapikopiko between the two World Wars, making a subsistence living from inherited land to which Whareroa had established sole title through the Māori Land Court. Whareroa and his sons cleared their own land and earned extra income working on adjacent sheep stations. Most of the sons stayed on the land, exchanging help with farm-work and child-raising and working together at the marae. Of this generation only two members are still alive, both over 80. Most of the second generation also grew up in Awapikopiko, going to school together and sharing in the close interaction between their parents. In adulthood, some stayed on but many moved away in the late 1950s and 1960s in pursuit of education and employment. Eventually they settled all over New Zealand. In 1995 their children, the third generation, are nearly all married and some of the fourth generation are approaching maturity.

Of the total membership, only four families live in

Awapikopiko in 1995: the rest are distributed among nine urban areas, including one in Australia. Those living in Wellington, the largest single grouping, have elected three of their number as Chairman, Secretary and Treasurer and hold regular monthly meetings in different homes. Working to a prepared agenda, they listen to reports on hui held or attended, plan other projects, debate specific and general issues, catch up on whānau news and introduce potential spouses. In 1993 kapa haka sessions were introduced to enliven proceedings for the younger members. Business completed, those attending enjoy themselves singing and eating together. Special events like birthdays are celebrated with shared meals in home or restaurant. Those living in other urban centres are less formally organised but keep in touch informally, exchanging visits and telephone calls. These methods also tie together the households in different centres. They are supplemented by a newsletter produced in Wellington but including contributions from elsewhere.

Major whānau events are held on the marae in Awapikopiko, drawing a large proportion of whānau members back to their roots. As well as tangihanga and weddings, these include whānau reunions which have been held every three years since 1975 during the Christmas-New Year holidays.

In the 1980s whānau members with legal experience successfully applied to the Māori Land Court to have the land inherited from Whareroa incorporated, a large block of hill country as a Station Trust and a small block in Awapikopiko as a Whānau Trust. Both are managed by committees of elected trustees. The Station Trust employs one whānau member as farm manager and another to assist as needed. Struggling with poor land and high transport costs, the Trusts make barely enough to meet costs but they protect the land from alienation and subdivision, keeping it together under whānau control as a tūrangawaewae for whānau members.

The Whānau Trust deed guarantees whānau members the right to draw sustenance directly from the land. In 1995 four couples live on sections leased from the Trust at minimal rates, produce enough food for their own needs and carry on the whānau tradition of supplying marae, school and church with gifts in kind. Those who live at a distance make their contribution in cash, in labour on visits home, and by applying special knowledge in the service of whānau members, for example, in identifying sources of assistance, helping fill in forms, and computerising the mail-out of newsletters.

Whānau hui are organised informally. Once the family most closely involved announces the date, other whānau members pick up familiar roles without fuss. The responsibility for organising the triennial reunions however is assumed by the Whānau Trust Committee, which sets up a special subcommittee with a separate bank account for the purpose.

Instead of a whānau marae, the Matangi whānau has interests in two hapū marae in Awapikopiko, using them for hui and contributing to their upkeep and management. In death whānau members are buried in the Matangi section of the Awapikopiko cemetery, which is a hapū reserve.

Though they have withdrawn from active leadership, the two surviving offspring of Rata and Whareroa have a very special place in the whānau as 'ngā mōrehu' (the survivors). They are accorded the titles of Whaea and Matua of the whānau. Though other whānau members speak freely in whānau discussions, when the Matua Mōrehu is present he is always expected to speak last, articulating the emerging consensus in the traditional way. His eightieth birthday was celebrated by a hui in Awapikopiko.

While they do not interfere if families prefer to work out their problems on their own, whānau members of kaumātua status (mostly from the second generation) respond readily to calls for help, if need be travelling between urban centres at their own expense. They provide accommodation and listening ears to young people in trouble or recently arrived in town, support relatives in job interviews when asked, act as counsellors and mediators in marital disputes or take charge of children to give parents time to talk. Where cases of domestic violence or sexual abuse come to notice they take the initiative in calling a whānau hui. Having played leading roles in whānau affairs in the past, they have embarked upon a deliberate plan to encourage the next generation to take over, steering them towards special training courses, authorising financial assistance from whānau funds, providing accommodation while they are studying, and involving them in management of whānau activities. As a result, the whānau membership now includes four lawyers and two accountants, as well as several teachers and ministers. The organisation of the last whānau reunion was entrusted to a Sub-Committee made up entirely of young people, who set it up using e-mail and teleconference facilities.

Far from being destroyed by emigration from the home base, the Matangi whānau continues to flourish in spite of extensive scattering. The whānau is particularly fortunate in having a land base to serve as tūrangawaewae, gathering place and food source for the whānau. However, it would have been lost if key members with the necessary know-how had not used the instrument of the Māori land legislation to protect it. Located in a remote part of the country, the land would not be enough on its own to keep whānau members together.

A key factor in the whānau's continuing vigour is the strong bonding between members of the oldest generations and their commitment to each other, to the whānau and to whānau values, which has led them to spend themselves and their time, talents and income freely for whānau purposes. They have succeeded in communicating this commitment to the younger generations, mainly because they have been willing to use whānau resources to support them through education and vocational training and to give them plentiful opportunities for exercising their skills for the whānau. In each generation the whānau has been blessed with members who have set an example by striking a balance between whānau and personal concerns and been open to new ideas and technology.

The Matangi whānau has been so successful in holding its members together that it has grown well past the size at which most whānau segment. It is in fact comparable to the size of a small hapū. With the land protected against subdivision and modern technology making it easy to keep in touch over long distances, its leaders expect the Matangi whānau to continue in existence indefinitely. The question is, can it do so and remain a whānau? With the loss of the members of the first two generations and the birth of potential recruits five or six generations removed from Rata and Whareroa, can the whānau maintain the same level of commitment? Two things could happen. As the generations pass, a winnowing out process could take place, with some of

the descendants of Rata and Whareroa taking up their right to
membership while others let it lie, so that the whānau stabilises
around the optimum size at which it is possible to maintain
personal bonding. If the number who take up membership rights
continues to increase, groupings within the total membership may
set themselves up as whānau within the whānau, on the basis
perhaps of descent, perhaps of residence in the same city. Either
scenario would represent the development of further variants of
the whakapapa-based whānau.

Kaupapa-based whānau

Using the whakapapa-based whānau as their model, an increasing
number of Māori programmes and groups have been established
in recent years with a special purpose (kaupapa) as focus and
rallying cry. The kaupapa pursued cover a wide range, including
the placement of children with related families (Mātua Whāngai),
preservation of te reo Māori through the medium of language
nests (Kaupapa Kōhanga Reo), Māori directed schooling for
Māori children (Kura Kaupapa Māori), the care of urban or
institutional marae (for example, at educational institutions), or
the publication of Māori writing (for example, the Haeata
Whānau formed by and for Māori women writers).

These kaupapa-based whānau differ from their model in one
crucial respect: the main criterion for recruitment is not descent
but commitment to the kaupapa. Lacking descent to serve as a
unifying principle, kaupapa-based whānau place particular stress
on the other characteristic features of the whakapapa-based
whānau, whānau values and the ways of working derived from
them. Lacking an ancestor to serve as symbol, they elevate the
kaupapa or the whānau itself to that position. Typically, relationships between members are reinforced by the use of terms in use
in the whakapapa-based whānau. Consisting largely of kinship
terms, these are re-defined in terms of age: tama, tamāhine and
mokopuna for the youngest age levels, koroua, kuia and other
variations on grandparent for the oldest age levels, matua and
whaea, auntie and uncle for those in between.

Because of the greater element of choice in their formation,
face-to-face interaction is especially important for kaupapa-based

whānau. If it is lost even temporarily, bonding is more difficult to maintain. Without the glue afforded by descent, kaupapa-based whānau often have a higher turnover of members than whakapapa-based whānau. The length of their life, however, varies widely. They may be quite short-lived, winding up when the kaupapa is achieved or appears unlikely to be achieved, or they may last indefinitely, maintained at an optimum level by their high turnover.

Understandably members of kaupapa-based whānau tend to focus strongly on those values which promote togetherness: aroha, whanaungatanga, co-operation, loyalty. However, these values are only a selection from a wider range. They exist in a complex web of relationships of opposition and complementarity with mana in its many forms, and also with utu, which involves repayment for wrongs as well as good gifts.

With mana tupuna removed as the main determinant of relative status and especially of leadership (though it may affect relations between members who are also kin), kaupapa-based whānau offer considerably more scope than whakapapa-based ones for the exercise of mana tangata, mana based on personal qualities and performance. The other side of the coin, however, is greater scope for personal ambition and competitiveness between those whose mana has different origins: whether in status as tangata whenua in the local district, seniority in years, knowledge of tikanga Māori or expertise relating to the kaupapa. While kaupapa-based whānau are spared the tensions that arise out of the structure of the whakapapa-based whānau, they still have to deal with personal incompatabilities, individual ambition and unexpected crises.

In the course of time whānau set up to pursue one kaupapa typically acquire other functions as well, in particular the provision of emotional and practical support. This may be extended to include financial loans and gifts, shared child-care and the staging of life-crisis hui. However, difficulties can arise if the differences between whakapapa- and kaupapa-based whānau are forgotten. Isolated or alienated from their own kin, young people hungry for personal affirmation and access to Māori knowledge sometimes take literally the kinship terms in use in kaupapa-based whānau and seek more of older members than the latter are able to give. Much as they would like to respond, they already have commitments to their own whakapapa-based whānau and mokopuna. In some cases they are constrained by the tikanga that knowledge received from named ancestors should be reserved to their descendants. It takes time to form ties of personal affection strong enough to hold people of different ages, experience and outlook together in testing times.

As well as setting out their kaupapa and planning how to achieve it, kaupapa-based whānau are well advised to think through their differences from their whakapapa-based model and to work out how to minimise their problems and maximise their strengths. In particular, they need to decide at an early stage what qualities and qualifications, what forms of mana, should be given priority in what contexts, how and by whom conflict is to be managed, and what kinds of support members can and cannot expect of each other and the group. In doing this, they are greatly advantaged if they have access to advisers in and out of their membership who have had firsthand experience of whakapapa-based whānau and the opportunity to reflect upon and discuss it with experts in tikanga Māori. Kaupapa-based whānau are far more likely to achieve their aims if they model themselves on successful real-life exemplars rather than on a romantic, abstract image.

Because, rather than in spite of, the ways in which they differ from whakapapa-based whānau, those which are kaupapa-based serve valuable functions both in attacking particular problems directly and in providing alternative support systems for those cut off from access to their own kin. Their value is enhanced, not lessened, when they are identified as a new and distinctive kind of whānau, another stage in the whanau's history of adaptation.

Non-Māori and the whānau

This book has been focused on the whānau as a Māori family form. I noted in passing that many whānau include Pākehā and other non-Māori spouses and that tensions arise between Māori and non-Māori spouses because of different conceptions of family and family responsibilities, but I did not otherwise investigate the subject of intermarriage and its consequences for family and whānau. This is an area which requires detailed exploration.[6]

Whether married to Māori or not, non-Māori living in New Zealand have become much more aware in recent years of tikanga Māori in general and of the whānau in particular.

In less than ten years the word whānau has moved from being unknown to most non-Māori to being sufficiently familiar to be used in conversation and the news media without translation. It has joined the increasing number of Māori words which are an integral part of New Zealand English. This is an advance in so far as it indicates increased acceptance of Māori and Māori language in Aotearoa New Zealand. On the other hand, a little knowledge often interferes with the acquisition of more. When they adopt a word from another language, English speakers tend to fasten on part of its range of meanings, often a partial or secondary meaning which they find easier to understand than the primary one. Asked what whānau means, most non-Māori define it as 'extended family', which is only one of many Māori meanings, and invest that phrase with the meaning it has in their own lives, which almost certainly differs from the meaning it has for Māori. If, believing that they know what the word means, they cease to search for understanding at this point, they cut themselves off from the rich range of meanings the word has for Māori, fail to distinguish its principal referent from other kinds of whānau and are hopelessly confused by Māori discourse on the subject.

Recently, I have noted a tendency for non-Māori to use the word whānau outside Māori contexts, as a label for their own extended family or for an action group assembled to support them on a particular occasion. Some use the word in ways that conform to Māori usage but more often limited understanding leads to inappropriate applications. However well intentioned, such applications take the word out of its Māori context and alter its meaning. It would be better, I think, to reserve whānau for use in Māori settings and according to Māori usages.

As they learn more about the whānau of primary reference on which other whānau are modelled, non-Māori often discover ideas and practices which attract and impress them and which they would like to apply in their own lives and in the public life of the nation. Among those which come readily to mind are certain aspects of atawhai adoption (particularly its emphasis on adoption by relatives and its openness) and whānau methods of conflict resolution (including third party mediation and the whānau huihuinga).

Having worked for decades for the improvement of cross-cultural communication in Aotearoa New Zealand, I am greatly heartened by the increasing numbers of non-Māori striving to extend their knowledge of Māori language and tikanga through personal contact and formal study. On the other hand, as attitudes to Māori and Māori culture have become more accepting and especially as my own knowledge and understanding have deepened, I have become increasingly aware of how easily appreciation can pass over into appropriation.

Appreciation without appropriation

Appropriation is defined by the *Concise Oxford Dictionary* as 'to take possession of, especially without authority'. It is not all or always bad, provided it is done 'with authority'. Māori themselves have taken possession of many aspects of the social and cultural arrangements brought to Aotearoa New Zealand by English and European settlers, modifying them to fit into Māori contexts, re-orienting them to serve Māori goals, making them their own. But in the Māori case their borrowing was done not only with the approval but with positive encouragement from Pākehā law and policy makers.

A new factor enters the situation when borrowers occupy positions of power vis-à-vis those from whom they borrow. In Aotearoa New Zealand the appropriation we need to guard against occurs when non-Māori and more particularly Pākehā make use of Māori language and tikanga in ways which take control out of Māori hands. This results partly from the internalisation of our own cultural rules and the unthinking assumption that they are universal, partly from ignorance of the Māori rules and viewpoint, and partly from our failure as members of a cultural majority to understand the particular problems of minority groups. During my own growing years, I was nurtured by family and school on innumerable proverbs, songs and literature understood to be the common property of all speakers of English. When in adulthood I developed an interest in Māori stories, songs and whakataukī, I assumed that they too were generally available for study and only gradually came to recognise that this is often not the case, even for whakataukī.

Far from being common property, freely available to all comers, much of mātauranga Māori (Māori knowledge) is owned and collectively controlled by iwi, hapū and whānau, that is, by the descendants of the ancestors to whom it refers and by whom it was handed on. Māori who have internalised this understanding about the nature of knowledge (as I had internalised mine) refuse to generalise about mātauranga Māori and speak only of what they learnt and know as members of their own iwi, hapū and whānau. Those most expert in their group's knowledge are regarded not as free agents but as kai-tiaki, trustees and custodians, responsible for ensuring that it is conserved, handed on to appropriate inheritors and treated with respect. Apart from the most tapu core, the knowledge thus held is available for public presentation and discussion but those who do not belong to the owning group are expected to respect the proprietary rights of the group concerned by seeking permission to access it, reproducing it without distortion and acknowledging its provenance. It should not be too much to expect non-Māori to do the same. Very similar rules apply in the European tradition with regard to the published and unpublished work of other scholars.

To appropriate Māori knowledge without permission from its custodians not only breaks the Māori rules relating to the control of knowledge, it tramples on the mana and rangatiratanga of the groups concerned and of the Māori as a people. The concept of mana, already discussed at length (pp 87-98, above), should need no further explanation. Rangatiratanga has not been mentioned, because it is linked primarily with iwi and hapū, and with whānau only by extension. A complex concept, it derives from the root *rangatira*, the descriptive title for the leaders of iwi and hapū, who combine the functions of chief organisers, trustees of group property and representatives of their groups in external relations. Rangatiratanga refers most simply to the role and characteristic qualities of rangatira but, because of the symbolic relationship between leader and group, it is also and most often used to refer to the capacity of the group (iwi or hapū) to manage its own affairs, members and possessions. Especially when modified by the intensifier *tino*, rangatiratanga can also be extended from iwi and hapū to te iwi Māori (the Māori people) as a whole (M. Durie (ed) 1995).

In interacting with Māori as individuals and groups, non-Māori should never forget that the balance of power in Aotearoa New Zealand favours the non-Māori and especially the Pākehā majority over the Māori minority. Neither in national nor local government do Māori command the voting power to give effect to their decisions on matters that affect them. It is only in Māori settings such as marae and predominantly Māori homes and organisations that Māori are able to exercise rangatiratanga in a meaningful way. This is not the place to debate the propriety of this imbalance or whether or how it can be redressed. But as long as rangatiratanga Māori is limited in this way, non-Māori have (it seems to me) a moral responsibility to refrain from actions which reduce it further and to respect and support its exercise in Māori settings and with regard to Māori language, tikanga and taonga.

Once non-Māori recognise the danger of appropriation, we can guard against it by developing guidelines to govern our practice.

In exploring Māori language and tikanga, the first rule for non-Māori enquirers (especially researchers) is to establish an ongoing relationship with Māori mentors, preferably with a particular group, and continually to seek their advice, supervision and permission. Proceeding in this way conforms to Māori patterns of learning and teaching. It also elicits information and insights that would otherwise be blocked out by preconceptions on one side or the other.

Wherever and whenever tikanga Māori is being observed as such, whether in Māori or in other settings (such as an institutional welcome to an overseas visitor), non-Māori with access to Māori knowledge should leave the front (directive) roles to Māori and avoid undermining their rangatiratanga in any way. Instead they should fulfil supportive roles out of the public eye. They should *not* assume a front role on their own initiative nor accede to an invitation to do so, unless kaumātua of high mana insist. The more knowledgeable non-Māori are the more forcefully this rule applies, because the temptation to take over is also greater.[7]

In developing public programmes which affect Māori and/or incorporate Māori principles and practices, non-Māori knowledgeable about the latter should insist that Māori be appointed as equal partners with full decision-making powers from the beginning, not after most of the planning has been done, and should consistently support their right to serious consideration, even when disagreeing with their views. Māori operating in cross-cultural situations, especially when identified as Māori representatives, are subject to intense psychological and logistical pressures. Non-Māori who understand their values and operating methods and the pressures under which they labour can play a valuable role as interpreters, buffers and mediators between Māori and non-Māori parties. Like in-married spouses in whakapapa-based whānau, we are most valuable when we accept that we can never become full members of the Māori group but have our own special place in the national scheme of things.

The more familiar non-Māori become with Māori language, tikanga and taonga, the more likely it is that we will want not only to share in their practice in Māori settings but also to borrow aspects of Māori literature, art and social practice to apply in our own lives, in other words, to utilise Māori culture as a source of ideas and inspiration. Personally, I believe that cultural borrowing and cross-fertilisation is both legitimate and creatively exciting: I enjoy what Māori have done with many ideas borrowed from Pākehā, such as the flower ceremony associated with the cutting of the wedding cake at northern Māori weddings (see p 322, note 7, pp 128-29 above and the first photograph after p 160). But I also recognise that great sensitivity is called for when members of a dominant majority want to borrow from the culture of a minority group. Here I can only repeat the guidelines I have laid down for myself, for instance in my use of whakataukī in this work. Whenever possible, I seek instruction and approval from members of the owning group (preferably at iwi or hapū level), I avoid applications or changes that run counter to the thinking and purpose behind the original, I acknowledge the source and I accept sole responsibility for the end product.

Conclusion

This book has been focused mainly on the whānau which comes first to mind, the group Māori think of first when they hear the word. I have endeavoured to set it in context by referring to the problems facing Māori today, examining anthropologists' contributions to its study and charting the constantly expanding range of categories and groups to which the word is also applied.

Far from being comprehensive, the resulting work is a general introduction which aims to raise as well as answer questions and so to stimulate further research and discussion. There is need in particular for up-to-date field studies of both whakapapa- and kaupapa-based whānau in a range of different environments. Only on that basis can we find out accurately the proportions of Māori who are actively involved in, have occasional contact with or are isolated from whānau, how and to what extent parent-child families are affected by participation or non-participation in whānau, and what are the most common variations on the basic model of the whānau.

On the basis of my own experience and the knowledge with which I have been entrusted by my kai-whakaatu I confidently affirm that the whānau lives on in the 1990s, continually re-creating itself by putting forth new growth and adapting to changing environments. Whether in its traditional, whakapapa-based form or in newer kaupapa-based ones, the whānau is identified by Māori themselves as potentially the most effective form available to them for organising the provision of support and socialisation for children and adults, for nurturing new growth and for managing and achieving change.

The continued vitality of the whānau widens the range of models and options available to Māori and enriches our life together as a nation. Whatever our cultural background, we can all share in the sentiments expressed in perhaps the best loved and most quoted of all the whakataukī which use the image of the flax bush. This saying is attributed by Muriwhenua experts to a rangatira woman who accepted an arranged marriage to make peace for her people but was deprived of the capacity to have children by a curse. Her whakataukī is at once a lament for her personal loss and an affirmation of the value of continuity and growth.

Hūtia te rito o te harakeke,
kei whea te kōmako e kō?
Ka rere ki uta, ka rere ki tai.
Kī mai koe ki au, 'He aha te mea nui o te ao?'
Māku e kī atu,
'He tangata! He tangata! He tangata!'[8]

Using the image of the flax bush, the poet begins by asking and answering a rhetorical question:

If you pluck out the flax shoot,
where will the bellbird sing?
It will fly seawards, it will fly inland.

If you stop the flax bush growing, there will be no nectar-laden flowers to attract birds and no flower stalks for them to perch on. They will fly distractedly to and fro looking for food and a resting place. She concludes affirming in the strongest terms the value of children, the whānau which nurtures them, and the whole of humanity.

If you ask me, 'What is the most
important thing in the world?'
I will answer you:
'People! people! people!'

NOTES

General Note on Whakataukī

Though the word *whakataukī* is commonly translated as 'proverbs', whakataukī differ from English proverbs in significant ways (Metge and Jones 1995).

English proverbs are regarded as folklore, belonging to the public domain and available for general use without copyright. While some whakataukī are also common property in general use, many can be traced to particular sources and are claimed by particular iwi or hapū as ancestral taonga.

The metaphors and images used in whakataukī are highly condensed and cryptic. One symbol often has several referents and layers of meaning; necessary as well as unnecessary detail is omitted; and listeners are challenged to work out references and connections for themselves.

Whakataukī are not fixed in form. Iwi and hapū have their own variant forms and orators often vary the wording to suit the context.

While one interpretation may be generally favoured at any particular time, orators delight in finding new applications and interpretations.

In using whakataukī to illuminate understanding of the whānau, I have drawn whenever possible on the versions used among the iwi of Muriwhenua (the Far North), I have checked wording and translation with experts from the iwi concerned, and I have obtained their approval for my interpretation.

Chapter 1: The flax bush: family and whānau

1 This whakataukī came originally from the late Rev. Maori Marsden, a widely respected pūkenga (scholar) who traced his descent from all the iwi of Tai Tokerau (Northland). It was supplied by his tamaiti and ākonga (pupil) Shane Jones of the Muriwhenua iwi Ngāi Takoto and Te Aupōuri. Other versions begin 'Tungia te ururua' (Burn the overgrowth). See Brougham, Reed, Karetu 1987: 67.
2 *Harakeke* is the general name for New Zealand flax (Phormium tenax) of which there are many named varieties. *Pā* is the word for bush among the iwi of Tai Tokerau but some other iwi prefer *pū*. *Kōrari*, the word for the flower stalk of the flax, is also used in Muriwhenua as a synonym for *harakeke*.
3 For example, Tame Winitana of Tūhoe and Hone Kamariera of Te Rarawa.

4   Statistics 1981: 184, 1992: 59-60. A 'New Zealand Māori household' is
    defined as 'a dwelling where the occupier, or spouse of the occupier,
    specified that they belonged to the New Zealand Māori ethnic group'
    (Statistics 1992: 77).

5   The definition of a New Zealand Māori household given in the previous
    note allows for the presence of non-Māori as members.

6   The word *iwi* can be used (1) in a general sense to mean *a people*, as in
    te iwi Māori (the Māori people), or (2) more specifically to refer to the
    large socio-political groupings commonly described as *tribes*. Iwi also
    means (3) *bone*.

    Many Māori dislike the term *tribe* which is associated in their minds
    with colonial attitudes to (so-called) primitive societies. Over the last
    ten years it has become increasingly acceptable to use *iwi* without
    translation in both official and unofficial quarters, as (for example) in
    the Children, Young Persons, and Their Families Act 1989.

7   In the 1990s Aotearoa is widely accepted as the Māori name for New
    Zealand. Originally it applied only to the North Island, the South Island
    being Te Wai Pounamu. While New Zealand is recognised nationally
    and internationally as the official name of our nation state, Māori and
    many non-Māori New Zealanders use the Māori and state names in
    combination as an appropriate alternative, especially in contexts where
    emphasis is laid on the Māori people and their relationship with the
    land, as in this sentence.

8   For accounts of debates and changing practice regarding the definition
    of *Maori* see: Metge 1976: 39-42, Metge 1992: 54, Pool 1991: 3-25,
    Statistics 1992b: 68, 77, Gould 1993, Mason Durie 1994: 125-28.

9   Taken collectively, Māori can be described as an *ethnic group*. 'The
    term *ethnic group* was coined by social scientists to refer to groups
    whose distinctiveness involves more than biological connection. The
    adjective *ethnic* comes from the Greek *ethnos*, meaning *a people*. An
    ethnic group is a group of people who regard themselves and are
    regarded (how accurately does not matter) as sharing a common origin,
    culture and history. Typically, there is also a degree of social
    separateness, whether imposed or chosen.' (Metge 1990a: 12-13.)

10 Metge 1990a: 13-15. For example, *Pākehā* is said to derive from: (a) a
    transliteration of English *bugger*, a word in frequent use among the
    earliest English-speaking visitors to New Zealand; (b) the description
    pā kehakeha applied to the early settlement at Kororareka, which can
    be interpreted as meaning either *flea-ridden* (keha = flea) or *smelly*
    (kehakeha = offensive odour); (c) a Māori word meaning *foreign*; and
    (d) the word for limestone and white clay. The first two of these alleged
    explanations sound to me very like the stories Māori with a sense of
    humour invent when they do not know the true answer to a question,
    do not want to give it, or consider the question silly.

11 *Tangata* (pl. *tāngata*) *whenua* is literally *person (people) of the land*.
    The basic reference is to members of the descent group (hapū or
    whānau) associated with a particular territory by ancestral inheritance

and occupation. As such, they act as hosts to visiting strangers (manuwhiri, tauiwi) from other hapū or iwi and hold the right to determine the protocol governing the encounter. In recent years Māori wishing to assert their status as the original inhabitants of Aotearoa and signatories of the Treaty of Waitangi have identified Māori individually and collectively as tāngata whenua in opposition to all later comers, who are thus identified as visitors and strangers. This usage is analogical and derivative and should be clearly distinguished from the basic meaning of the phrase.

12 According to H.W. Williams (1971: 416-17), *tikanga* means: '1.n. *Rule, plan, method* . . . 2. *Custom, habit* . . . 3. *Anything normal or usual* . . . 4. *Reason* . . . 5. *Meaning, purport* . . . 6. *Authority, control.*'

13 For decades it has been customary to translate *iwi* into English as *tribe* and *hapū* as *sub-tribe*, implying that hapū are sub-divisions of and subordinate to iwi. This usage has wide currency among Māori themselves: for example, see Natural Resources Unit (Te Manatu Māori) 1991: 3.

Since the 1970s, however, this usage has increasingly come under attack from scholars, who suggest on the basis of historical and linguistic research that the hapū was the key organisational group in Māori society until the mid nineteenth century and that iwi did not become fixed groups of paramount importance until late in the nineteenth century in the course of dealings with the Crown (Orbell 1978: 115-16; Metge 1986: 36-37; Ballara 1995).

During the 1980s national Māori leaders initiated a drive to establish the iwi/tribe as paramount in the Māori social order, as a result of which this view was entrenched in the policies of government departments. In the 1990s, however, this interpretation is being challenged on the one hand by hapū and on the other by pan-Māori organisations such as the Ratana Church, the Māori Women's Welfare League and various Māori urban authorities.

14 Statistics 1994: 10-11; Mason Durie (ed.) 1995: 83-84, 88-90.

15 Statistics 1994: 16-18; Mason Durie (ed.) 1995: 76-77, 85.

16 Statistics 1994: 4-5; Mason Durie (ed.) 1995: 79-80.

17 Pool 1991: 209-11; Statistics 1994: 42-44; Mason Durie (ed.) 1995: 37.

18 Mason Durie 1994: 129-39; M.H. Durie, Black et al. 1994: 4-7; Mason Durie (ed.) 1995: 38-42, 90-92.

19 Duff 1990, 1993; Ministerial Advisory Committee 1986; Royal Commission on Social Policy 1988; Jackson 1988; Mason Durie 1994.

20 Mason Durie (ed.) 1995: 4-7. Several of these were sponsored by Government through government departments.

21 The works which come under this heading are too numerous to list in full here, but see especially short stories, novels and plays by Riwia Brown, Willie Davis, Alan Duff, Mihipeka Edwards, Patricia Grace, Witi Ihimaera and Apirana Taylor, and the following anthologies: Orbell 1970; Ihimaera and Long (eds.) 1982; Ihimaera (ed.) 1992, 1993a, 1993b, 1994.

22 When I use 'my' in this context I am indicating a relationship of affection and mutual respect, not in any sense one of possessiveness.

Chapter 2: Views from Anthropology

1 This is a Te Aupōuri whakataukī. It comes from the papers of Rev. Maori Marsden and its use was authorised by his tamaiti and ākonga Shane Jones of the Muriwhenua iwi Ngāi Takoto and Te Aupōuri. Rima Eruera of Ngāpuhi and Te Rarawa provided the following variant: Kia ū ki tōu kāwai tupuna, kia mātau ai koe, ko wai oti koe. (Trace out your ancestral stem, so that you know who created you.) For similar uses of the image of the kāwai (branching stem) of kumara or hue (gourd), see Brougham, Reed, Karetu 1987: 85; Riley 1990: 40-41, 44, 46; and Kaa 1995: 18-19.

2 Māori Affairs-Social Welfare-Justice 1986: 6-7, 10-11. (The pages of this publication are not numbered. To give these page references I have counted every page, including the blank ones.)

   As indicated on p 316, *iwi* means *bone* as well as *people* and *tribe*. Māori often use *bone* in English to mean *relative*. I have not been able to discover the origin of this usage but wonder whether Māori might have regarded bone rather than blood as the physical aspect of connection by descent. See Kaa 1995: 12-13.

3 In his book Hohepa indicates long vowels by doubling instead of the macron used in this work; thus he uses the spelling whaamere. To avoid confusion I have spelt this word whāmere in my text.

4 According to Raymond Williams, the word *family* acquired the dominant meaning of *parent-child family* between the seventeenth and nineteenth century and had already undergone several major changes in meaning before that.

5 Claude Lévi-Strauss suggested that, instead of the extended family being an extension of the parent-child family, it is rather the parent-child family which 'deserves the name of: *restricted family*' (Lévi-Strauss 1960: 272-73).

Chapter 3: The many meanings of whānau

1 This whakataukī was provided by Rima Eruera of Ngāpuhi and Te Rarawa. See also Macrae 1985: 5.

2 For example, Rev. Maori Marsden of Tai Tokerau, Hone Kamariera of Te Rarawa, and Tame Winitana of Tūhoe.

3 The word *adopted* here means adopted according to tikanga Māori, whether legalised or not: see pp 210-12. Some adopted children belong to the descent group through one or both of their natural parents.

4 In this usage the word *whānau* was borrowed into English and given a new and highly specific meaning. In writings about 'the whanau system' the word is used without italicisation and without marking the long vowel. I have preserved this usage in this paragraph. See Falkner,

McCormick and Mitchell 1979.

5 Personal communication by Keri Kaa, staff member at the Wellington College of Education, who was deeply involved in the discussion and decision making.

6 This booklet uses the double vowel instead of the macron to mark long vowels in Māori. In the title, however, the long ā in Whāngai was mistakenly left unmarked. I have reproduced the title as it appears on the booklet but marked both long vowels with macrons when the phrase appears in ordinary text.

7 See the discussion of the relation between iwi, hapū and whānau on p 37, above.

Chapter 4: The whānau which comes first to mind

1 This whakataukī comprises the final lines of a longer saying attributed to the rangatira Tūmatahina of Murimotu, North Cape. The full version was given by Haimona Snowden in his Foreword to Metge 1986. It runs as follows:

> Ruia, ruia, tahia, tahia! Kia hemo ake ai ko te hākoakoa kia herea mai ki te kawau korokī. Tātaki mai ra roto i tana pūkoro, whai karo. He kūaka marangaranga, kotahi te manu i tau ki te tāhuna, tau atu, tau atu, tau atu e!

For a full explanation see Metge and Jones 1995: 5 and Macrae 1985: 62-63. This saying is often used by orators to stress the importance of combining individual initiative and leadership with group solidarity.

2 *Tūrangawaewae* means literally *a standing place for (one's) feet*. Its basic application is to land holdings inherited from ancestors, which confer rights as tangata whenua in the vicinity and on the associated marae, then by extension to the marae on which a person is tangata whenua, and finally to any property used as a base.

3 Statistics 1994: 10-11; Mason Durie (ed.) 1995: 83-84, 88-90, 93-95.

4 Statistics 1994: 16-18, 42-44.

5 See discussion of the relation between iwi, hapū and whānau on p 317 (Ch. 1 Note 13), above.

Chapter 5: Whānau values

1 This whakataukī comes from the papers of Rev. Maori Marsden, pūkenga of Tai Tokerau. Its use was approved by his tamaiti and ākonga Shane Jones. Note the reference to one womb: in Muriwhenua the important ancestors who wove people together were often women. See Metge and Jones 1995: 4.

2 For a good introduction, see Patterson 1990 but read in conjunction with Metge 1993: 328-29.

3 See also Barlow 1991: 7-9 and Tauroa 1986: 121-22.

4 *Whanaunga* is given the meanings of both *relative* (general) and *blood relative* in H.W. Williams 1971: 487. Most Māori today use it with the

broader, general meaning.

5 *Mauri* is sometimes contrasted with, sometimes treated as a synonym of, *mana*. See Metge 1986: 74; Rangihau in King 1975: 11-14.

6 Kahukiwa and Grace 1984; Marsden 1975: 191-219; Patterson 1994.

7 For example, E moe i tangata ringa raupā. (Marry a man with calloused hands.) Aitia te wahine i roto i te pā harakeke. (Marry the woman who is frequently in the flax bushes.) Brougham, Reed, Karetu 1987: 50, 116.

8 Born in their parents' mature years, farthest removed from succession to their parents' status, pōtiki typically receive more nurturing and instruction from their parents than their older siblings do and often become leaders by achievement, through mana tangata. Famous pōtiki include Tūhoe-Pōtiki and Tahu-Pōtiki, foundation ancestors of Tūhoe and Ngāi Tahu respectively, and (of course) Māui-Pōtiki.

9 For example, Kahungunu, foundation ancestor of Ngāti Kahungunu, Poroa and Panakareao of Te Rarawa, Te Rauparaha of Ngāti Toa Rangatira, and Tā Apirana Ngata of Ngāti Porou.

10 See also A. Brown (ed.) 1994; Te Awekotuku 1991; Smith 1992; Irwin and Ramsden (eds.) 1995.

11 Māori Women's Welfare League 1993.

12 During my interview with Raniera Kingi I took handwritten notes. I typed up these notes and Raniera read, corrected and approved the typescript.

13 Metge 1976: 58-63, 232-35.

14 Women play a part in the lifting of tapu at the opening of a meeting-house, either as puhi (virgin) or as ruahine (woman ritual expert). It is sometimes claimed that women lift tapu because they are noa, but carrying out such a ritual act is itself a tapu activity.

15 In iwi where women engage in formal speech-making those who do so are usually past child-bearing age. However, male speech-makers also usually belong to the older age brackets.

16 As far as I am aware there is no whakataukī supporting male dominance. For every proverb which belittles women as a category there is another which belittles men.

17 This whakataukī was supplied by Hirini Tawhai of Te Whānau-a-Āpanui in the early 1970s and used in Metge 1976: 62-63.

18 One of the meanings of the verb *tui* is *lace, fasten by passing a cord through holes*, as in lashing the topstrakes to the hull of a canoe and lacing up shoes. It is an appropriate metaphor both for the exchange of goods and services and for the binding together of people which exchange expresses and achieves.

19 *Kotahitanga* is the name given to the movement for greater political autonomy for Māori which established the Māori Parliament of the 1890s (Metge 1976: 195). The word is also used in some iwi (for example, Te Arawa) to describe the committees which manage whānau and hapū affairs. In this case it can be translated as *union*.

20 This whakataukī was supplied by Keri Kaa of Ngāti Porou. The

Muriwhenua version, supplied by Shane Jones, runs: E kore te tūkau e kupukupu mōna anō me tana reka; mā tētahi atu tana pārekareka e kōrero. (Tūkau is an old variety of kumara.)

21 Matiu Te Hau of Whakatōhea. Unfortunately I did not record a Māori version of this saying nor have I found it in any of the books of Māori proverbs. However, the kaumātua of whom I have enquired assure me that the metaphor is in common use by orators.

Chapter 6: Structural tensions in the whānau

1 This whakataukī was supplied by Rima Eruera of Ngāpuhi and Te Rarawa. See Metge and Jones 1995: 5.
2 Personal communication from kai-whakaatu Arahi Mahuru.
3 This presents a difficulty. Because the placenta is tapu it cannot be stored in a freezer in association with food.
4 Barlow says that the word is an abbreviated form of *kaiwaiū i te poho*.
5 In the course of such arguments, contending parties can ruthlessly assert their rights, even going so far as to remove the tūpāpaku, or they can choose to recognise the higher imperative of 'arohanui ki te tangata' (loving concern for people). An example of this occurred when Ruby Haimona died a widow without issue. Raised as an atawhai by a Kōtare couple, she had married a Kōtare man and been an active worker in the Kōtare community. At her tangihanga, the whānau of her natural parents pressed their claim to take her to their home community for burial but graciously accepted the arguments advanced by her Kōtare whānau in favour of burying her with her husband in Kōtare. Symbolising both their claim and its relinquishment, six of the claimants lifted her coffin, held it in silence for a minute and gently laid it down again.

Particular difficulties arise when the deceased or his or her offspring have lost touch with their Māori relatives and heritage and when the spouse of the deceased is Pākehā. In such cases, spouse and offspring can become highly disturbed by what they see as disregard for their feelings and rights and unseemly wrangling over the coffin. The difficulties can be (and usually are) resolved when one or more of the kaumātua present assume the role of takawaenga (mediator). They explain to the bereaved family what is happening, advise them how to respond, speak for them if they wish, and make sure that all points of view are fairly heard.

Chapter 7: The Hamiora Whānau 1955-85

1 This whakataukī was supplied by Keri Ngapera Kaa of Ngāti Porou. The word pīpī describes a fledgling of any bird species. The one depicted in Toi Te Rito Maihi's drawing is a pīpīwharauroa (shining cuckoo), which is an insect-eater, whereas the kākā is a nectar drinker. The flax bush provides food for both. The fledgling cuckoo could also stand as a

metaphor for myself, who as a fledgling anthropologist was nurtured by the kaumātua of the Hamiora Whānau.

2   The following account is based on extensive interviews with whānau members, the minutes kept by the organising committee of the Hamiora Whānau Hui and my own personal involvement with the Hamiora Whānau since 1955. It has been checked by the Whānau members most closely involved and permission to publish granted both individually and by those attending a meeting of marae trustees on 8 January 1989. The name Hamiora is a pseudonym, as are all other names used in this case study. To protect the privacy of the Whānau, the original of the *Hamiora Whānau Hui* booklet has not been included in the Bibliography.

3   *Children* in this context are defined as *dependent children* and include some between the ages of 15 and 18 years attending secondary school.

4   Hamiora was identified in contemporary records by the use of his father's personal name as his second name but this name is not now used by the Whānau. Hamiora's children were all identified by having their father's personal name Hamiora added to their own. It was common practice among Māori in the nineteenth and well into the twentieth centuries for children to be identified in this way, by their father's personal name in the place of a surname. As a result, apparent surnames changed with each generation. (Compare early practice regarding Irish and Scottish names.) Gradually these second names were transmuted into surnames in response to the requirements of teachers and other administrators.

5   On the evidence of the *Hamiora Whānau Hui* booklet, there was a mistake in the information I was given in 1955 on the sibling order of the offspring of Hamiora and Atawhai. I have amended Figure 2, which otherwise is taken from Figure 5 in Metge 1964, to agree with this more recent information.

6   With a household belonging to the Rapine branch of the Samuels 'family', where there was more room.

7   This cake-cutting ceremony was an adaptation of the 'flower ceremony' which is a feature of Muriwhenua weddings. In this ceremony pieces of wedding cake are claimed by representatives of the hapū and iwi present, who are required to 'sing for their cake' before it is handed over. See Metge 1976: 141.

8   This was confirmed by an expert in Kōtare history from another Kōtare whānau.

Chapter 8: Sharing the caring

1   For details concerning this whakataukī see p 315 (Ch. 1 Note 1).

2   See p 317 (Ch. 1 Note 21).

3   *Tamariki* is used with the singular article *te* to mean *child* as opposed to *adult* (H.W. Williams 1971: 376). This usage is really a collective form, identifying the category *child*. *Tamariki* is also used as an

intransitive verb meaning *to be a child*, for example in the phrase 'ki au e tamariki ana' (to me when I was a child).

4   See H.W. Williams 1971: 106, 252. The northern and western iwi favour *kaumātua*, eastern and southern iwi prefer *pakeke*. Like *tamariki*, *kaumātua* can be used as an intransitive verb, with the meanings *to grow up*, *to become adult* or *to move from one developmental stage to another*.

5   *Taitamariki* has this form in both the singular and plural.

6   The word *rangatahi* is derived from the whakataukī 'Ka pū te ruha, ka hao te rangatahi.' 'The worn out net is cast aside, the new net goes fishing' (Kohere 1951: 36). Rangatahi is a particular kind of fishing net. Originally both the worn out net and the new net were assumed to be rangatahi nets, and the whakataukī was interpreted to mean 'when one leader dies, a new leader emerges to take over'. Late last century an orator used this whakataukī when suggesting that the old style of Māori leadership had had its day and should be replaced by the new style of the Young Māori Party. As a result, *rangatahi* came to mean *a young Māori leader*, as in the Young Māori Leaders Conferences (Metge 1976: 167-68). In recent years a further change has taken place and *rangatahi* is now used to mean *young person* (M.H. Durie, Black et al 1994).

7   One of my kai-whakaatu was told (by a kaumātua who witnessed it) of a hair-cutting ritual which may have served this function but I have been unable to find corroboration.

8   *Kai* is the Ngāti Porou dialect variant of *kei*.

9   In particular the laws governing adoption and succession to property other than Māori land.

Chapter 9: Parenting: emphases and avoidances

1   This whakataukī is given in Kohere 1951: 33, Brougham, Reed, Karetu 1987: 90 and Macrae 1985: 21. Kohere describes it as 'one of the most popular sayings of the Maoris: Lay by for a rainy day; have two strings to your bow; don't put all your eggs in one basket'. Kaumātua say that the word *kāinga* derived from *kā*, a (cooking) fire, the focus of domestic life. Strictly speaking, *kāinga* refers not to a house but to a settlement, which might contain one or several households.

Chapter 10: Grannies, aunts and uncles

1   This whakataukī is given in Brougham, Reed, Karetu 1987: 47. The interpretation given there fails to elicit the full potential of the metaphor of the cloak. In my opening paragraph I emphasise the complementarity of the two parts of the kaitaka, an interpretation endorsed by Toi Te Rito Maihi, an expert on cloaks and herself a skilled weaver.

2   Kohere 1951:43.

Chapter 11: Atawhai adoption: 'born of my heart'

1   This whakataukī is given in Brougham, Reed, Karetu 1987: 87. In my
    translation I have emphasised the intentionality implied by the use of
    hei.
2   For example, 2 Corinthians 12:9.
3   As a noun, *taurima* means *hospitality, attention to strangers* (H.W.
    Williams 1971: 402).
4   Steven Webster noted this tendency in Webster 1973: 8.
5   The increase in the number of sole-parent families which has been a
    feature of the last fifteen years has been particularly marked among
    Māori. In public discussion, the availability of the Domestic Purposes
    Benefit is often identified as playing a causative role in this increase
    and in the proportion of sole-parents establishing separate households,
    but these propositions remain to be tested by in-depth research. In
    1991, 36% of dependent children in sole-parent families lived in shared
    households and this proportion appears to be rising (Statistics 1994:
    17-20). Contrary to common belief, the Domestic Purposes Benefit
    can be paid to sole-parents living in shared households, for example,
    with parents or siblings, provided certain conditions are met.

Chapter 12: Atawhai adoption: process and consequences

1   These whakataukī were both provided by Rima Eruera of Ngāpuhi
    and Te Rarawa. The first spells out in full, as an imperative, the more
    common form 'Aroha mai, aroha atu' found in Brougham, Reed and
    Karetu 1987: 61. A variant version of the second whakataukī is found
    in Brougham, Reed, Karetu 1987: 47.

Chapter 13: Dealing with problems

1   This whakataukī was provided by Rima Eruera of Ngāpuhi and Te
    Rarawa.
2   Marae Committees may have grown out of the local Māori Councils
    set up by Act of Parliament in 1902. They are formed on the initiative
    of the hapū or community to whom the marae belongs, usually
    incorporated as Charitable Societies. Tribal Committees were set up
    under the Māori Social and Economic Advancement Act 1945 but
    renamed Māori Committees in the Māori Welfare Act 1962. See Metge
    1976: 207-29.
3   I attended at the invitation of the convenors. The bombing took place
    in the context of inter-gang hostility. Visitors from the city were
    mistaken for members of the other gang because of the colour of the
    jackets they wore.
4   This chapter was completed before the publication of Consedine's book
    with its chapter on 'The Maori Restorative Tradition', which contains
    material and conclusions similar to mine. I have not, however, referred

to it in detail, leaving the two chapters to stand independently in confirmation of each other.

Chapter 14: Flowering and new growth

1   This whakataukī was supplied by Keri Ngapera Kaa of Ngāti Porou. It has already been used to introduce the Hamiora Whānau in Chapter 7. See p 321 (Ch. 7 Note 1).

2   While the primary purpose of whakapapa is the tracing of descent, certain forms of whakapapa include spouses and are useful in tracing kinship connection through affinal links.

3   In particular, assumptions that two parents are normally present, that they always put their responsibilities to each other and their children ahead of those to other kin, and that the parent-child family is a separate and independent unit. See p 324 (Ch. 11 Note 5).

4   In particular, whether the Guardianship Act 1968 requires amendment to meet Māori needs.

5   The Te Ture Whenua Maori/Maori Land Act 1993 provides for the establishment of Whānau Trusts only where there are Māori land holdings to be managed. When whānau without such holdings wish to establish a legal identity, they have to make use of existing legal instruments such as incorporated and unincorporated societies and trusts, none of which are entirely appropriate. Lawmakers argue against defining the parent-child family as a legal entity on the grounds that doing so would inhibit recognition of variation and change. The whānau is larger than the parent-child family, exists independently of individual members, and therefore has a longer life. Do the same arguments apply?

6   The only published study of Māori-Pākehā intermarriage is Harre 1966, which concentrates mainly on the couples directly concerned and their parents. It would be most useful to have an up-to-date study which included exploration of intermarriage in the context of the whānau, with special reference to the effect on the marriage of the whānau membership of the Māori spouse and the effect of the Pākehā spouse on the practice of the Māori spouse and the whānau.

7   When a non-Māori has developed an in-depth appreciation of tikanga Māori through long association, it can be difficult to be content with a supporting role, especially when Māori who are young in years or knowledge make mistakes in tikanga which result in criticism of their groups. However, for a non-Māori to attempt publicly to correct such mistakes or to assume control only adds to the problem, besides breaching rangatiratanga Māori. In such circumstances it is best to consult and hand over damage control to a Māori third party or at least wait for an opportunity to comment in private.

8   *Tangata* (pl. *tāngata*) means *human being*, without in-built distinction of sex, hence person. The form used in the whakataukī is the collective singular, hence the translation *People!*

BIBLIOGRAPHY

Adoption Practices Review Committee, *Report to the Minister of Social Welfare*. Wellington: Department of Social Welfare, 1990.

Alpers, Antony, *Maori Myths and Tribal Legends*. Auckland: Blackwood & Janet Paul, 1964.

Ballara, Angela, Porangahau: The Formation of an Eighteenth Century Community in Southern Hawkes Bay. *New Zealand Journal of History* 22 (1) 1995: 3-18.

Barlow, Cleve, *Tikanga Whakaaro: Key Concepts in Maori Culture*. Auckland: Oxford University Press, 1991.

Beaglehole, Ernest and Pearl, *Some Modern Maoris*. Wellington: New Zealand Council for Educational Research, 1946.

Best, Elsdon, *The Maori*. Wellington: Polynesian Society, 1924.

Biggs, Bruce, *Maori Marriage*. Wellington: Polynesian Society, 1960.

Blank, Arapera, The Role and Status of Maori Women. In Phillida Bunkle and Beryl Hughes (eds.), *Women in New Zealand Society*. Auckland: Allen and Unwin, 1980: 34-51.

Brougham, A.E., A.W. Reed, Revised by T.S. Karetu, *Maori Proverbs*. Auckland: Reed Books, Revised Edition 1987.

Brown, Amy (ed.), *Mana Wahine: Women Who Show the Way*. Auckland: Reed Books, 1994.

Brown, Michael J., *Peaceful Families, Peaceful Society*. Auckland: Aotearoa New Zealand Foundation for Peace Studies, 1994.

Brown, M.J., L. Goddard and S. Jefferson (leaders), *The Children and Young Persons, and their Families Act*. New Zealand Law Society Seminar Papers. Wellington: New Zealand Law Society, 1989.

Cairns, Tamati, Whangai—Caring for a Child. In Gabrielle M. Maxwell, Ian B. Hassall and Jeremy P. Robertson (eds.), *Towards a Child and Family Policy for New Zealand*. Wellington: The Office for the Commissioner for Children, 1991: 100-2.

Craig, Elsdon, *Man of the Mist: A Biography of Elsdon Best*. Wellington: Reed, 1964.

Condliffe, J.B., *Te Rangi Hiroa: The Life of Sir Peter Buck*. Christchurch: Whitcombe and Tombs, 1971.

Consedine, Jim, *Restorative Justice: Healing the Effects of Crime*, Lyttelton, New Zealand: Ploughshares Publications, 1995: 81-87.

Davidson, Janet, *The Prehistory of New Zealand*. Auckland: Longman Paul, 1984.

Duff, Alan, *Once Were Warriors*. Auckland: Tandem Press, 1990.

Duff, Alan, *Maori: The Crisis and the Challenge*. Auckland: Harper Collins, 1993.

Durie-Hall, Donna and Joan Metge, Kua Tutū Te Puehu, Kia Mau: Maori Aspirations and Family Law. In Mark Henaghan and Bill Atkin (eds.), *Family Law Policy in New Zealand*. Auckland: Oxford University Press, 1992.

Durie, E.T., *Custom Law*. Unpublished Address to the New Zealand Society for Legal and Social Philosophy, 22 July 1994.

Durie, Mason, *Whaiora: Maori Health Development*. Auckland: Oxford University Press, 1994.

Durie, Mason (ed.), *Kia Pūmau Tonu: Proceedings of the Hui Whakapūmau Māori Development Conference*. Palmerston North: Department of Māori Studies, Massey University, 1995.

Durie, M.H., Tino Rangatiratanga: Maori Self Determination. *He Pukenga Korero: A Journal of Maori Studies* 1(1) 1995: 44-53.

Durie, M.H., T.E. Black et al., Maori Youth in Contemporary New Zealand. *Youth Policy Seminar Series October 1994*. Wellington: Ministry of Youth Affairs, 1994.

Else, Anne, *A Question of Adoption: Closed Stranger Adoption in New Zealand 1944-1974*. Wellington: Bridget Williams Books, 1991.

Falkner, Nancy, Godfrey McCormack and Ian Mitchell, The Whanau. *Education* 28 (8) 1979.

Firth, Raymond, *We the Tikopia*. London: George Allen and Unwin, 1936.

Firth, Raymond, Social Organization and Social Change. *Journal of the Royal Anthropological Institute* 84 1954: 1-20.

Firth, Raymond, A Note on Descent Groups in Polynesia. *Man* 57 1957: 4-8.

Firth, Raymond, *Economics of the New Zealand Maori*. 2nd Edition. Wellington: Government Printer, 1959.

Firth, Raymond, Bilateral Descent Groups: An Operational Viewpoint. In I. Schapera (ed.), *Studies in Kinship and Marriage*. London: Occasional Paper No. 16 of the Royal Anthropological Institute, 1963: 22-37.

Fyfe, Judith, *Matriarchs: A Generation of New Zealand Women Talk to Judith Fyfe*. Auckland: Penguin Books, 1990.

Gould, John, 'Maori' in the Population Census, 1971-1991. *Population Review* 18 (1 & 2) 1992: 35-67.

Government Review Team, *Report of the Review of Te Kohanga Reo*. Wellington: Government Printer, 1988.

Groves, Murray, Western Motu Descent Groups, *Ethnology* 2 1963: 15-30.

Harre, John, *Maori and Pakeha*. Wellington: Institute of Race Relations and Reed, 1966.

Hassall, Ian, Origin and Development of Family Group Conferences. In Joe Hudson, Allison Morrison, Gabrielle Maxwell and Burt Galloway (eds.), *Crime, Care and Conferencing: Promoting Partnership*. Australia: Federation Press, 1996.

Henare, Manuka, Nga Tikanga Me Nga Ritenga o Te Ao Maori: Standards and Foundations of Maori Society. In *Report of the Royal Commission on Social Policy.* Volume 111 *Part One: Future Directions.* Wellington: Royal Commission on Social Policy, 1988: 3-41.

Henare, Manuka, Development: Sovereignty or Dependency? In *Puna Wairere: Essays by Maori.* Wellington: New Zealand Planning Council, 1990.

Henare, Manuka, Te Tiriti, Te Tangata, Te Whanau: The Treaty, The Human Person, The Family. *Rights and Responsibilities,* Papers from the International Year of the Family Symposium on Rights and Responsibilities of the Family, Wellington 1994. Wellington: International Year of the Family Committee in association with the Office of the Commissioner for Children, 1994: 15-22.

Hiroa, Te Rangi (Peter Buck), *The Coming of the Maori.* Wellington: Maori Purposes Fund Board/Whitcombe and Tombs, 1949.

Hohepa, P.W., *A Maori Community in Northland.* Auckland: Anthropology Department, The University of Auckland, 1964.

Ihimaera, Witi and D.S. Long (eds.), *Into the World of Light: An Anthology of Maori Writing.* Auckland: Heinemann, 1982.

Ihimaera, Witi (ed.), *Te Ao Marama: Contemporary Maori Writing.* Vol. 1 *Te Whakahuatanga o Te Ao: Reflections of Reality.* Wellington: Reed, 1992. Vol. 2 *He Whakaatanga o Te Ao: The Reality.* Auckland: Reed, 1993a. Vol. 3 *Te Puawaitanga o Te Korero: The Flowering.* Auckland: Reed, 1993b. Vol. 4 *Contemporary Maori Writing for Children: Te Ara o Te Hau: The Path of the Wind.* Auckland: Reed, 1994.

Irwin, Kathie and Irihapeti Ramsden (eds.), *Toi Wahine: The Worlds of Maori Women.* Auckland: Penguin, 1995.

Jackson, Moana, *The Maori and the Criminal Justice System, A New Perspective: He Whaipaanga Hou.* Part 2. Wellington: Policy and Research Division, Department of Justice, 1988.

Kaa, Arapera Hineira, *Nga Kokako Huataratara: The Plumes of the Kokako.* Auckland: Waiata Koa, 1995.

Kawharu, I.H., *Orakei: A Ngati Whatua Community.* Wellington: New Zealand Council For Educational Research, 1975.

Kahukiwa, Robyn and Patricia Grace, *Wahine Toa: Women of Maori Myth.* Auckland: William Collins, 1984.

Keesing, Roger M., *Cultural Anthropology: A Contemporary Perspective.* New York: Holt, Rinehart and Winston, 1976.

King, Michael (ed.), *Te Ao Hurihuri: The World Moves On.* Wellington: Hicks Smith and Sons, 1975.

Kohere, Reweti T., *He Konae Aronui: Maori Proverbs and Sayings.* Wellington: A.H. & A.W. Reed, 1951.

Lévi-Strauss, Claude, The Family. In Harry L. Shapiro (ed.), *Man, Culture and Society.* New York: Oxford University Press, 1960: 261-85.

Mahuika, Api, Leadership: Inherited and Achieved. In Michael King (ed.), *Te Ao Hurihuri: The World Moves On.* Wellington: Hicks Smith and Sons, 1975: 86-113.

Macrae, Jane, *He Pepeha, He Whakataukī Nō Tai Tokerau.* Whangarei: Department of Maori Affairs, 1985.

Makereti, *The Old-Time Maori*. Auckland: New Women's Press, 1986.
First published London: Victor Gollancz, 1938.

Maori Affairs-Social Welfare-Justice, Departments of, *Maatua Whangai*.
Wellington: Government Printer, 1986.

Māori Women's Welfare League, *Te Timatanga: Tātau, Tātau*. Wellington:
Māori Women's Welfare League, 1993.

Marsden, Maori, God, Man and Universe. In Michael King (ed.), *Te Ao
Hurihuri*. Wellington: Hicks Smith, 1975: 191-219.

Metge, Joan, Marriage in Modern Maori Society. *Man* 57 No. 212 1957:
166-70.

Metge, Joan, *A New Maori Migration: Rural and Urban Relations in
Northern New Zealand*. London: Athlone Press, 1964.

Metge, Joan, *The Maoris of New Zealand*. London: Routledge and Kegan
Paul, 1967.

Metge, Joan, *The Maoris of New Zealand: Rautahi*. Revised Edition.
London: Routledge and Kegan Paul, 1976.

Metge, Joan, *In and Out of Touch: Whakamaa in Cross Cultural Context*.
Wellington: Victoria University Press, 1986.

Metge, Joan, *Te Kohao o Te Ngira: Culture and Learning*. Wellington:
Learning Media (Ministry of Education), 1990a.

Metge, Joan, Te Rito o Te Harakeke: Conceptions of the Whānau. *Journal
of the Polynesian Society* 99 (1) 1990b: 55-92.

Metge, Joan, Ko Te Wero Maori—The Maori Challenge. In *Family Law
Conference: The Family Court Ten Years On*. Wellington: New Zealand
Law Society, 1991.

Metge, Joan, Review of John Patterson's *Exploring Maori Values. Journal
of the Polynesian Society* 102 (3) 1993: 328-29.

Metge, Joan and Shane Jones, He Taonga Tuku Iho Nō Ngā Tūpuna: Maori
proverbial sayings—a literary treasure. *New Zealand Studies* (Stout
Research Centre, Victoria University of Wellington) 5 (2) July 1995:
3-7.

Ministerial Advisory Committee on a Maori Perspective for The Department of Social Welfare, *Puao-Te-Ata-Tu (Daybreak)*. Wellington:
Government Printer, 1986a. *Appendix to Puao-Te-Ata-Tu*, 1986b.

Natural Resources Unit, Manatu Maori, *Maori Values and Environmental
Management*. Wellington: Manatu Maori (Ministry of Maori Development), 1991.

Ngata, H.M., *English-Maori Dictionary*. Wellington: Learning Media
(Ministry of Education), 1993.

Olsen, Teresea, Gabrielle Maxwell and Allison Morris, *Maori and Youth
Justice in New Zealand*. In Kayleen Hazlehurst (ed.), *Popular Justice
and Community Regeneration: Pathways of Indigenous Reform*.
London: Praeger, 1995: 45-66.

Orbell, Margaret, The Traditional Maori Family, in Peggy Koopman-
Boyden (ed.), *Families in New Zealand Society*, Wellington, Methuen
(N.Z.) 1978: 104-19.

Orbell, Margaret, *Contemporary Maori Writing*. Wellington: Reed, 1970.

Orsman, Harry (ed.), *Heinemann New Zealand Dictionary*. Auckland: Heinemann Educational Books, 1979.

Patterson, John, *Exploring Maori Values*. Palmerston North: The Dunmore Press, 1992.

Patterson, John, Maori Environmental Virtues. *Environmental Ethics* 16 1994: 397-409.

Pere, Rangimarie (Rose), Tangata Whenua. In *Puna Wairere: Essays by Maori*. Wellington: New Zealand Planning Council, 1990.

Pere, Rangimarie Turuki, *Te Wheke: A Celebration of Infinite Wisdom*. Gisborne, New Zealand: Ao Ako Global Learning New Zealand Ltd, 1991.

Pool, Ian, *Te Iwi Maori: A New Zealand Population Past, Present & Projected*. Auckland: Auckland University Press, 1991.

Puketapu, Kara, *Reform From Within*. Wellington: Department of Maori Affairs, 1982.

Reed, A.W., *Treasury of Maori Folklore*. Wellington: A.H. & A.W. Reed, 1963.

Riley, Murdoch, *Maori Sayings and Proverbs*. Paraparaumu: Viking Sevenseas N.Z. Ltd, 1990.

Ritchie, James, *The Making of a Maori*. Wellington: A.H. and A.W.Reed, 1963.

Ritchie, James and Jane, Children. In Erik Schwimmer (ed.), *The Maori People in the Nineteen Sixties*. Auckland: Blackwood & Janet Paul, 1968.

Ritchie, Jane and James Ritchie, *Child Rearing Patterns in New Zealand*. Wellington: A.H.and A.W.Reed, 1970.

Ritchie, Jane and James Ritchie, *Growing Up in New Zealand*. Sydney: George Allen and Unwin, 1978.

Ritchie, Jane and James Ritchie, *Growing Up in Polynesia*. Sydney: George Allen and Unwin, 1979.

Ritchie, Jane and James Ritchie, Socialization and Character Development. In Alan Howard and Robert Borofsky (eds.), *Developments in Polynesian Ethnology*. Honolulu: University of Hawaii Press, 1989.

Royal Commission on Social Policy, Nga Kohikohinga Mai No Nga Putea i Whakairia ki Nga Tahuhu o Nga Whare Tupuna: An Analysis of Views Expressed on Marae. In *Report Of the Royal Commission on Social Policy*. Volume 1 *New Zealand Today*. Wellington: The Royal Commission on Social Policy, 1988: 253-98.

Salmond, Anne, *Hui: A Study of Maori Ceremonial Gatherings*. Wellington: A.H. & A.W. Reed, 1975.

Salmond, Anne, Tipuna—Ancestors: Aspects of Maori Cognatic Descent. In Andrew Pawley (ed.) *A Man and a Half*. 1991: 334-47.

Scheffler, H.W., Descent Concepts and Descent Groups: The Maori Case. *Journal of the Polynesian Society* 73 (2), 1964: 126-33.

School Publications Branch of the Department of Education, *Māori Children and the Teacher*. Wellington: Government Printer, 1971.

Schwimmer, Erik, Guardian Animals of the Maori. *Journal of the*

Polynesian Society 72 (4) 1963: 397-410.

Schwimmer, Eric, *The World of the Maori*. Wellington: A.H. & A. W.Reed, 1966.

Schwimmer, Erik (ed.), *The Maori People in the Nineteen Sixties*. Auckland: Blackwood & Janet Paul, 1968.

Schwimmer, Eric, The Maori *Hapū*: A Generative Model. *Journal of the Polynesian Society* 99 (3) 1990: 297-317.

Smith, Graham Hingangaroa, Whakaoho Whānau: New Formations of Whānau as an Innovative Intervention into Maori Cultural and Educational Crises. *He Pukenga Korero: A Journal of Maori Studies* 1 (1) 1995: 18-43.

Smith, Linda Tuhiwai, Maori Women: Discourses, Projects and Mana Wahine. In S. Middleton and A. Jones (eds.), *Women and Education in Aotearoa 2*. Wellington: Bridget Williams Books, 1992.

Statistics, Department of, Increase and Location of Population, *New Zealand Census of Population and Dwellings 1976*, Vol. 1, Wellington: Government Printer, 1977.

Statistics, Department of, Maori Population and Dwellings, *New Zealand Census of Population and Dwellings 1976*, Vol. 8, Wellington: Government Printer, 1981.

Statistics, Department of, National Summary, *Census of Populations and Dwellings 1991*, Wellington: Department of Statistics, 1992a.

Statistics, Department of, New Zealand Maori Population and Dwellings. *1991 Census of Population and Dwellings*. Wellington: Department of Statistics, 1992b.

Statistics, Department of, *New Zealand Now: Maori*. Wellington: Department of Statistics, 1994.

Taiapa, Julia Te Urikore Turupa, *Tā Te Whānau Ohangā: The Economics of the Whānau*. Palmerston North: Massey University, 1994.

Tauroa, Hiwi and Pat, *Te Marae: A Guide to Customs & Protocol*. Auckland: Reed Methuen, 1986.

Te Awekotuku, Ngahuia, *Mana Wahine: Selected Writings on Maori Women's Art, Culture and Politics*. Auckland: New Women's Press, 1991.

Te Puni Kokiri (Ministry of Maori Development), *Oranga Whānau: The Whānau Well-Being Projects*. Wellington: Te Puni Kokiri, 1994.

Webster, Steven, *Maori Adoption*. Working Paper No. 21. Auckland: Department of Anthropology, University of Auckland, 1973.

Webster, Steven, Cognatic Descent Groups and the Contemporary Maori: A Preliminary Assessment. *Journal of the Polynesian Society* 84 (2) 1975: 121-52.

Williams, Herbert W., *A Dictionary of the Maori Language*. Seventh Edition. Wellington: Government Printer, 1971.

Williams, Raymond, *Keywords: A Vocabulary of Culture and Society*. London: Fontana, Flamingo Edition, 1983.

Winiata, Maharaia, *The Changing Role of the Leader in Maori Society*. Auckland: Blackwood & Janet Paul, 1967.

GLOSSARY

aituā *n.* misfortune, calamity; applied especially to death.

aroha *n.* the usual translation *love* is not an exact equivalent for aroha. Its primary reference is caring, compassionate love for others, especially love for relatives. It is also used to convey: sympathy for those in sorrow or trouble; gratitude; and approval. It is *not* properly used for sexual love. See pp 80-81.

arohanui ki te tangata *n.* caring love towards (all) people; see tangata, p 335, below.

atawhai *v.t.* show kindness to, be liberal, foster; *a.* kind, liberal; *n.* liberality, grace (especially of God). Used by iwi of Tai Tokerau as an adjective to describe adoptive relationships and as a noun to describe adopted children; see pp 211-12.

atua *n.* spirit, god; with capital A, God.

awhina *v.t.* assist; *n.* assistance, contribution, donation.

hākari *n.* feast, especially the climactic meal at a hui.

hapū *n.* a middle-range socio-political grouping defined by descent from a named ancestor through both male and female links, generally associated with a local district and community, commonly regarded as a subdivision of an iwi; see p 316 (Ch. 1 Note 13).

hara *v.i.* violate tapu; *n.* sin, offence.

hē *a.* wrong, erring, mistaken; *n.* error, mistake, fault; opposite of tika.

hui *n.* generic term for a Māori gathering, typically held on a marae and organised according to ngā tikanga o te marae.

huihuinga *n.* reduplicative form of hui, used by kai-whakaatu to refer to whānau gatherings called to discuss and deal with internal problems.

hui whakawā *n.* a hui called in order to investigate and adjudicate on an offence; see pp 283-87.

iwi *n.* a people, as in te iwi Māori (the Māori people); a large-scale socio-political grouping defined by descent from a named ancestor and usually translated as tribe; bone; see p 316 (Ch. 1 Note 13).

kai- *prefix* one who performs the action indicated.

kai-karanga *n.* woman who does the karanga on behalf of her group.

kai-kōrero *n.* person who acts as representative, formal speech-maker on behalf of his or her group; in the case of the welcome ceremony, a man in most iwi.

kaitaka *n.* highly prized flax cloak consisting of a finely woven, plain body and tāniko borders; see pp 9 and 175.

kai-tiaki *n.* one who guards or takes care of someone or something; may be human (a legal guardian, trustee or custodian) or non-human (a

332

guardian animal or spirit associated with a particular place or whānau, which protects whānau members but repels intruders).

kai-whakaatu *n.* literally, one who makes (something) come out; an informant who is actively involved in the development of understanding; see pp 28-31.

karakia *n.* ritual chants; prayers.

karanga *v.t.* call, summon; *n.* stylised, chanted calling reserved to women, used to call visitors to enter the marae, to reply to such calling, and to acknowledge presentation of a koha.

kaumātua *n.* a person of senior social status, of either sex, who is knowledgeable in tikanga Māori; a person of grandparental or equivalent age of either sex; adult, grown-up; see pp 135-37.

kaupapa *n.* basic idea, topic, plan, principle.

kaupapa-based whānau *n.* whānau formed to address particular issues, principles or purposes.

kawa *n.* rules of marae protocol; ritual dedication of a new meeting-house or waka.

kin-cluster *n.* a group of kinsfolk, related in a variety of ways, who lack a descent group core, but who interact for common ends; see pp 42, 54-55, 126-27.

koha *n.* gift, donation, especially that given by visitors to their hosts during a hui.

kohanga reo *n.* language nest; centres for pre-school children run on Māori lines and using Māori as the language of communication; now organised on a national basis and partially funded by the State.

kōmiti *n.* Māori transformation of English committee, comprising all members with relevant qualifications, who elect representatives to a smaller executive.

kōrero *v.t.* tell, say; make a formal speech; *n.* story; conversation; formal debate.

koroua *n.* male kaumātua.

kotahitanga *n.* oneness, unity, solidarity; see pp 102 and 320 (Ch. 5 Note 19).

kuia *n.* female kaumātua.

kūmara, kumara, *n.* Ipomoea batatas, sweet potato; completely absorbed into New Zealand English. For that reason, the macron marking the long vowel ū is omitted when used in an English text.

Kura Kaupapa Māori *n.* movement and schools devoted to Māori methods of teaching and the use of the Māori language as the medium of instruction.

mana *n.* spiritual power; authority stemming from the indwelling of spiritual power; prestige; the ability to do and get things done; see pp 87-98.

manaaki *v.t.* show respect or kindness to; care for, look after, especially guests; *n.* caring in the fullest sense of the word, the expression of aroha; see p 99.

manuwhiri (manuhiri) *n.* visitor, guest; the opposite of 'host' at a hui.

'Māori land' land inherited from Māori ancestors and held on special Māori freehold title which is determined by the Māori Land Court in accordance with the Te Ture Whenua Māori/Māori Land Law 1993; see Metge 1976: 109-11.

marae *n.* open space in front of a meeting-house; the combination of this open space with meeting-house, dining-hall and other buildings, comprising a marae complex on land which may or may not be scheduled as a marae reserve; used for communal gatherings.

mātāmua *n.* the first-born (in some iwi the firstborn male) in a set of siblings.

mātauranga *n.* knowledge, especially knowledge of cultural importance to Māori; from mātau, to know.

mate *a.* dead; sick, ill, in declining health.

matua (*pl.* mātua) *n.* parent of either sex (but in some iwi father); siblings and cousins of parents' generation.

mauri *n.* life principle of both human beings and other aspects of nature; material object representing the life principle of someone or something; see p 320 (Ch. 5 Note 5).

mihi *v.t.* greet; *n.* greeting; speech of greeting; welcome ceremony on marae or similar location, synonym for powhiri.

mihimihi frequentative form of mihi, hence sometimes used to indicate repeated greeting speeches = welcome ceremony.

mokopuna *n.* grandchild of either sex, together with all relatives of the same generation; see p 137.

muru *v.t.* to take compensation from an offender according to tikanga Māori; *n.* the ritualised process of taking such compensation.

noa *a.* free of religious restriction; ordinary; relaxed; the complement and antidote of tapu; see pp 85-86, 95-96.

ora *a.* alive and well in body, mind and spirit; *n.* life and health in fullest measure; see p 86.

pono *a.* true, genuine (not hypocritical); see p 87.

poroporoaki *n.* speech of farewell addressed a) to hosts by departing visitors, b) to the living by a dying person and c) by a mourner at tangihanga; the farewell ceremony at the end of a hui when departing visitors exchange speeches with hosts, and hosts wish departing visitors a safe journey home.

pōwhiri *n.* chant or action-song of welcome; welcome ceremony on the marae.

pūkenga *n.* person of either sex with advanced training in mātauranga and tikanga Māori.

rangatahi *n.* young leader; young person; see p 323 (Ch. 8 Note 6).

rangatira *n.* person of senior descent and high rank; chief of a hapū and in many cases of iwi (the remaining iwi use the term ariki); also applied metaphorically to the director of an enterprise and in the expression *hoa rangatira* used by husbands to refer to their wives.

rangatiratanga *n.* the role and characteristic attributes of rangatira; the capacity and right of a group to manage its own affairs; see pp 310-11.

taha *n.* side, dimension; *taha tinana, taha wairua*, the physical, this worldy dimension and the spiritual, other-worldly dimension; see pp 82-86.

taitamariki *n.* young person between puberty and full social adulthood; see pp. 135-36. Taitamariki has this form in both the singular and the plural (cf. tamaiti, *pl.* tamariki).

tamaiti (*pl.* tamariki) *n.* child, children; see pp 135-36.

tangata (*pl.* tāngata) *n.* human being of either sex, person.

tangata whenua *n.* person connected with a marae or locality through a line of occupying ancestors and (ideally) owning 'Māori land' in the vicinity; host(s) at a hui; see pp. 316-37 (Ch. 1 Note 11).

tangi *v.t.* weep, lament; *n.* a stylised form of lamentation in which women express grief after a death and when meeting after a long separation (during which friends and relatives have died).

tangihanga *n.* funeral wake lasting several days from the time of death, including the successive arrival of parties of mourners, mourning (expressed in tears, tangi and speeches), funeral, a funeral feast, and the lifting of tapu from the bereaved home.

tāniko *n.* technique of weaving by single pair twining which produces a very close weave and geometric patterns in two or more colours.

taonga *n.* treasure, something highly prized, tangible and intangible, animate and inanimate, passed down the generations; see pp 68-70.

tapu *a.* in a state of religious restriction, which may be translated as sacred or polluting according to context; *n.* the rule prohibiting access to something tapu; see pp 85-86.

taura moko *n.* a grandchild closely attached to and constantly in the company of grandparent(s).

taura whiri *n.* a rope woven (technically plaited) of many twisted strands; see p 79.

taurima *v.t.* entertain (visitors); treat with care, tend; *n.* hospitality, attention to strangers. Used by iwi of Taranaki as an adjective to describe adoptive relationships and as a noun to describe adopted children; see pp 211-12.

Te-Ao-Tū-Roa *n.* literally, the World Standing Long, this world of space, time and mortality as contrasted with the spiritual world of Te Ao-Marama, the World of Light; see pp 82-83.

teina (*pl.* tēina) *n.* younger sibling of the same sex; cousin of the same sex and generation in a junior line.

tika *a.* straight, direct; just, fair; right, correct; see pp 86-87.

tikanga *n.* the right way, a rule or custom embodying accepted understandings of what is tika; see pp 86-87.

tikanga Māori *n.* the right Māori ways, rules or guidelines for living generally accepted as tika; see pp 20-21.

tinana *n.* body, the main part of anything; the real person (as opposed to an apparition); a symbol of the material, tangible aspects of Te-Ao-Tū-Roa; see pp 82-86.

tomo, tono *n.* formal meeting of kin to discuss a marriage and arrange the wedding; the form *tomo* is favoured in Tai Tokerau, *tono* in Tai Rāwhiti.

traditional *adj.* indicating that something has been handed down from previous generations, not without change but adapted as necessary in the process; see pp 49-50.

tuakana (*pl.* tuākana) *n.* older sibling of the same sex; cousin of the same sex and generation in a senior line.

tūpāpaku *n.* deceased person in the period between death and burial.

tupuna/tipuna (*pl.* tūpuna/tīpuna) *n.* ancestor; grandparent of either sex, together with all the relatives of the same generation; see p 137.

tūrangawaewae *n.* standing-place for one's feet, the base where one stands firm and secure; often applied but not limited to the marae; see p 319 (Ch. 4 Note 2).

ture *n.* system of law introduced to New Zealand by the colonial government; see p 21.

ū-kai-pō *n.* mother; the land of one's ancestors; Papatuanuku; see pp 110-13.

utu *n.* return for something received, whether good or bad; reciprocity, compensation, price; see pp 100-1.

waiata *n.* song-poem, sung or chanted in unison.

wairua *n.* spirit; the incorporeal aspect of the person; see pp 82-86.

wānanga *n.* the specialised knowledge of the tohunga; commonly used today to describe hui called to discuss particular teachings or issues.

whaea *n.* mother; siblings and cousins of mother's generation.

whakaaro *n.* thought, intention; understanding; plan; *whakaaro nui* (great thoughts) values; see pp 79-105.

whakahīhī *a.* lofty; vain, conceited, arrogant.

whakaiti *a.* humble, modest.

whakamā *a.* used to describe a range of feelings from shyness through embarrassment to shame and behaviour involving varying degrees of withdrawal and unresponsiveness; see Metge 1986: 25-36.

whakapapa *n.* descent line(s) tracing the connection between ancestors and their descendants; the recital and study of descent lines and associated kinship linkages; see pp 48 and 90-91.

whakataukī *n.* proverbs, proverbial sayings; see p 315 (General Note on Whakataukī).

whāmere *n.* transliteration of English family, used as synonym for whānau.

whānau pani the immediate family of a deceased person during the tangihanga.

whanaunga *n.* relative, blood relation, usually used today with the broader meaning, that is, including spouses and affines (in-laws); from whanau, *v.i.* meaning to incline towards.

whāngai *v.t.* feed; nourish, bring up. Used by eastern and southern iwi as an adjective to describe adoptive relationships and as a noun to describe adopted children; see pp 211-12.

whenua *n.* land; ground; placenta.

INDEX

Bold numerals indicate main references

abuse: physical, 265-71; safe-guards against, 266, 287; sexual, 271-77
action-group, **47-48**, 55-56, 126-27
adopted children, 41, 62-63, 107-8, 210-57
adoption, 130, **210-57**; see atawhai adoption, legal adoption
Adoption Act 1955 & Amendment 1962, 141, 210, 250-53
Adoption Practices Review Committee, 256
Adult Adoption Information Act 1985, 252, 253
affiliation (to descent groups), 38, 113
age structure, Māori, 22-23
ahi kā, 77
aituā, 86
ancestor, foundation, 48, 63-64, 130-32
ancestors/ancestry, 21, 48, 52-53, 62-65, 84, 88, 145; burial with, 111; see tupuna, mana tupuna and whakapapa
ancestor-oriented groups, 39-42, 114-33, 301-5; see descent group and whakapapa-based groups
anthropological terms, 47-50, 52-53
anthropologists, 33-50
Aotearoa, 16, 18, 308, 316 (Ch. 1 Note 7)
appropriation, 309-12

aroha, **80-81**, 98, 219, 286
arohanui ki te tangata, 87, 321 (Ch. 6 Note 5)
assimilation (resistance to), 17, 256
atawhai, 211
atawhai adoption, **212-57**; Māori attitudes to, 212-14; openness, 233-36; community attitudes, 236-38; two sets of parents, 238-41; adjusting kinship terms and behaviour, 242-47; inheritance, 247-50; Coda, 254-57
atawhai relationships: duration of, 218-19; reasons for, 219-27; process of establishing, 228-31
aunts, 190-99
avoidances, parental, 159-62, 166-74
awhina, 99, 127; see support

Beaglehole, Ernest and Pearl, 27, 135
Best, Elsdon, 34-37
Brown, Judge Mick, 270
burial: of placenta, 110-11; of dead, 111-13, 321 (Ch. 6 Note 5)

cake ceremony, 128-29, 322 (Ch. 7 Note 7)
care-giving, shared, 138-209, esp. **148-49**
child(ren), terms for, 135-37, 322 (Ch. 8 Note 3)
child-care, crises in, 259-61
child offending, 261-64
child-raising, 134-209; see

337

identity, 24
incest, 95, 271-74, 276-77
inheritance, in adoption, 247-50
iwi, 21, 37, 53, 76, **316** (Ch. 1
  Note 6), **317** (Ch. 1 Note 13)
iwi Māori, te, 18, 316 (Ch. 1
  Note 6)

jealousy, 104

kai-karanga, 72, 73, 96, 108
kai-kōrero, 72, 96, 106-7, 108
kaitaka, 9, 175
kai-tiaki: human, 68-69, 226, 287,
  310; non-human, 70, 84
kai-whakaatu, 9, 28-31
karakia, 83, 279, 280-81
kaumātua, 16, 72-74, **135-37**, 147,
  186, 228, 276, **283**, 287; role in
  adoption, 232-33
kaupapa, 279
kaupapa-based whānau, 294,
  305-7
Kawharu, Hugh, 38-43
kin-cluster, **42**, 54-55, 126-27
Kingi, Raniera, 93-94
kinship, 40, 81-82
kinship terms, **137**, 145;
  adjustment in context of
  adoption, 242-47; affines,
  107-8
koha: see awhina, support
kōhanga reo, 25, 56-57, 153-54,
  305
kōhungahunga, 136
kōmiti: marae, 118; whānau, 72;
  see Marae Committees
kōrero, 69-70, **182-84**; see stories
koroua, **72-73**, 276, **283**, 287
kotahitanga, 72, 102, **320** (Ch. 5
  Note 19)
kumara vine, 10-11, 33, 48, 318
  (Ch. 2 Note 1)
kuia, **72-73**, 272-74, 276, 282, **283**,
  287
Kura Kaupapa Māori, 305

law, 21; attitudes to, 286
leadership, **72-73**, 88-89, 106-7,
  130-32, 272-74, 276, **283**

mahi, 84
mahinga, 21
mahinga-a-ngākau, 98-100
mahi tahi, 99
Makereti, 27
mana, 85, **87-98**, 188-89, 220, 275,
  276, 277; mana tane, 91-98;
  mana tāngata, 88, 306; mana
  tupuna, 88-90; mana wahine,
  91-98; mana whānau, 89-90,
  102, 277, 284
manaaki, 87, 99
manuwhiri, 21, 87, 316-17 (Ch. 1
  Note 11)
Māori Committees, **259**, 269, 276,
  324 (Ch. 13 Note 2)
Māori, definition of, 19, 316
  (Ch. 1 Note 8)
'Māori land', 68, 248, 299
Māori population, 19
Māori Women's Welfare League,
  86, 92, 295
marae, 66, **68**, 96-97; tikanga of
  the, 278-83
mātāmua, **72-73**, 88-89, 145
mātauranga Māori, **69-70**, 82-98;
  transmission of, 94, 182-88,
  224-26
Matangi Whānau, 301-5
mātua, 211; mātau atawhai, 210-
  57, **211**
Mātua Whāngai, 25, 58-60
mauri, 83, 320 (Ch. 5 Note 5)
mediation, mediators, 259-60, 267,
  287-88, 297; see third parties
men, role and status of, 72-73, 91-
  98, 130-2
methodology, 28-31
migration, 22, 75, 202-3
mihi, mihimihi, 273-74, 280
models, 29, 50, 77-78
mōkai, 27
muru, 268, 286

names, group, 65-66, 115, 322
(Ch. 7 Note 4)
naming, personal, 142-46
namesakes, 129, 145, 260
noa, 85-86, 95-96
non-Māori, 20; and the whānau,
307-12

Orbell, Margaret, 45
ora, 86
organisation, whānau, 72-74, 126-
30
ostracism, 277, 287

pā harakeke, 16, 114, 134, 290, 314
Pākehā, 18, **20**, 109, **316** (Ch. 1
Note 10), 321 (Ch. 6 Note 5);
see non-Māori
Papatuanuku, 83, 95, 111
parents, **158-74**; two sets of, in
atawhai adoption, 238-41
parenting, multiple/shared, 138-
209, esp. **148-49**, **158**
placenta, 110-11, 321 (Ch. 6
Note 3)
pono, 87
poroporoaki, 279
pōtiki, 89, 170, 320 (Ch. 5 Note 8)
pōwhiri, 279, 280
praise, parental avoidance of, 159-
62, 166-68
principles of child-raising, Māori,
140-41
problems, dealing with, 258-89
property, whānau, 68-70, 248
proverbs, see whakataukī
Puao-Te-Ata-Tu, 25, 26-27

quarrels, 11, 264-65, 321 (Ch. 6
Note 5)

rangatahi, 136, 323 (Ch. 8 Note 6)
rangatira, 277
rangatiratanga, 310-11
rape, 95, 271, 272, 274-76
reciprocity, 66-68, 73-74, 100-1,
141, 156

reparation, 285-86
reunions, 71, 125-30; fourth
photograph
ringa wera, 84
Ritchie, Jane and James, 27, 137-
39, 158
rito, 15-16, 134, 314
rope, 79

Salmond, Anne, 10, 46, 131
Schwimmer, Eric, 45-46
segmentation, whānau, 74, 119,
121, 124, 133
self-esteem, children's, 161, 162,
168, 181-82
sex, parental avoidance of talk
about, 171-74
siblings, 52, 88-89, 106-7, 113,
164-65, 231, 247
sole parenthood, 22, 220-23
speech-making, formal, **96-97**,
107, 132, **279-80**, 281-83, 320
(Ch. 5, Note 15)
spiritual beings/dimension/realm,
82-86
spouses, 62-64, 73, 76, 90, **108**,
112, 124, 129-30
stories, storytelling, **69-70**, 183-85;
sacred, 83
support, 66-68, 99, 127
symbols, group, 65-66

taitamariki, 135-36, 323 (Ch. 8
Note 5)
takawaenga, 259-60, 267, 287, 297
tamaiti, tamariki, 16, 135-37, 322-
23 (Ch. 8 Note 3)
Tāne, 95, 110
tāniko, 9, 175
tangata, 314, 325 (Ch. 14 Note 8)
tangata whenua, 21, 42, 316-17
(Ch. 1 Note 11)
tangihanga, 70, 111-12, 119, 279,
321 (Ch. 6 Note 5)
taonga, **68-70**, 100, 140, 248-50
tauiwi, 20, 316-17 (Ch. 1 Note 11)
tapu, **85-86**, 94, 95-96, 184, 185,